Shipwrecks
of the
Channel Islands

by

John Ovenden and David Shayer
in association with Paul Haslam

Dedicated to David Shayer

Seeker
Publishing & Distribution
in the Channel Islands

Originally published in hardback in 2002
This reset and redesigned edition published in 2014 by
SEEKER PUBLISHING
Units 1 & 2 Elms Farm
La Route de la Hougue Mauger
St Mary
Jersey   JE3 3BA

www.seekerpublishing.com

Origination by
SEAFLOWER BOOKS
www.ex-librisbooks.co.uk

Printed by
CPI Anthony Rowe
Chippenham, Wiltshire

ISBN 978-0-9927159-2-2

© 2014 John Ovenden and David Shayer

Ordinarily the sea conceals her crimes. She delights in privacy. Her unfathomable deeps keep silence. She wraps herself in a mystery which rarely consents to give up its secrets. We know her savage nature, but who can tell the extent of her dark deeds? She is at once open and secret; she hides away carefully, and cares not to divulge her actions; wrecks a vessel, and covering it with the waves, engulfs it deep as if conscious of her guilt. Among her crimes is hypocrisy. She slays and steals, conceals her booty, puts on an air of innocent unconcern, and smiles.

Victor Hugo: *Toilers of the Sea*

CONTENTS

Foreword		6
Acknowledgements		7
Introduction		9
Two Discoveries of International Importance		
The Guernsey Roman ship	A	11
The Alderney Elizabethan ship	B	14
Two Mysteries		
The *Vierge de Bon Port* (1666)	C	19
The Casquets and HMS *Victory* (1744)	D	21
HMS *Boreas* (1807)	E	27
The *Normandy* (1870)	F	33
The *Waverley* (1873)	G	42
The *Havre* (1875)	H	46
The *Caledonia* (1881)	I	51
The *Brighton* (1887)	J	55
The *Ibex* (1897, 1900)	K	62
TBD *Viper* (1901)	L	76
The *Liverpool* (1902)	M	92
The *Hilda* (1905)	N	98
The *Roebuck* (1911)	O	111
The *Caesarea* (1923)	P	118
The *Princess Ena* (1935)	Q	127
The SS *Schokland* (1943)	R	136
HMS *Charybdis* and HMS *Limbourne* (1943)	S	146
USS PT 509 (1944)	T	182
MV *Heron* (1961)	U	207
MV *Radiant Med* (1984)	V	214
Sources		225
Index		229
About the authors		232

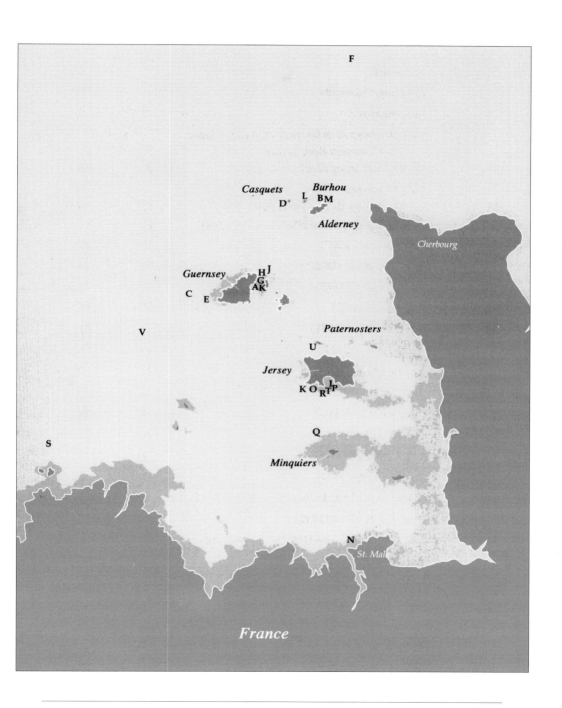

F

Casquets   Burhou
D   L   B M

Alderney

Cherbourg

Guernsey   H J
       G
C   A K
  E

Paternosters

V

U

Jersey

K O R T P
      I

Q

S

Minquiers

N

St. Malo

France

Foreword

Potential readers examining the list of ships covered will at once see that some major shipwrecks known to them are not included. We decided at the outset to cover a limited number of losses in detail, some in considerable detail, and this has meant unavoidable omissions.

In selecting the ships for this book we have applied what are hopefully consistent and productive criteria. We have tried to strike a balance between vessels used for trade and for passenger conveyance, and have given parity to the neglected topic of warships, covering the three types in a broad chronological spread. Wrecks off all three of the larger islands have been included and we have for the most part selected ships where we have first-hand diving experience of the wreck site, or were able to call on the expertise of those who discovered them. Two ships of international maritime archaeological importance are included, both discovered in the 1980s.

In addition to consulting newspapers, official reports, logbooks, diving logs and other primary print sources, we have interviewed a number of individuals in the islands, the UK, Germany and the USA who were participants in some of the events described after 1940.

The number of major wrecks recorded in the two bailiwicks since 1800 alone runs into many hundreds; we hope to rectify some of our omissions in a future second series.

Acknowledgements

We are especially grateful to Richard Keen, Tony Titterington and Fred Shaw, who generously shared their diving knowledge with us and provided detailed information about the wrecks they have discovered, researched, or purchased, allowing us to quote from their records and diving logs. In particular we wish to acknowledge help with the Guernsey Roman ship, the *Vierge de Bon Port*, the *Boreas*, and the *Brighton* from Richard; help with the *Princess Ena, Caesarea, Schokland* and PT 509 from Tony; and help with the Alderney Elizabethan ship and *Viper* from Fred. We would also like to thank Martin Woodward for his contribution to the section on HMS *Victory*, and Alain Launay and Leigh Bishop for details on HMS *Charybdis*. The account of PT 509 was only possible with access to Shelton Bosley's large personal collection of papers, and we thank him for allowing us to use these and for giving invaluable assistance in tracking down documents in the United States. We would also like to thank the members of the Charybdis and Limbourne Association for their encouragement, and for making key documents on the two ships available to us.

We also wish to thank: Adrian Walker; Audrey Hodges; Dr Jason Monaghan; Mrs Cara Voelcker; Mrs Doris de Carteret; Royston Raymond; Peter Arnold; Bill Hustler; John Eskdale; Eric Brookes; Gerald Evans; Neil Wood; Roger Roberts; Jim Duckworth; Reg Moyes; Ernie Mosley; Steve Keeling; Sydney Leleux; Michael Edwards; Donald Fisher; Russell Schuster; Norman Hoyt; Al Duquette; Bob Hatmaker; James O'Leary; Vincent Ricci; Dean Wilkinson; Hans Constabel; Christian Cremer; Peter Bisson MBE; Rudolph Reuter; Sam Clapp; Captain John Wallbridge; Brigitte Meheust; Manonmani Filliozat; the staff of Southampton, Weymouth, Cardiff and Newport Reference Libraries; the staff of the Guildhall Library, City of London; the staff of the Public Record Office; the Guille-Alles and Priaulx Libraries in Guernsey; Jersey Reference Library; the National Maritime Museum; Raad Voor De Scheepvaart, Amsterdam; Directoraat-Generaal Goederenvervoer, Rotterdam; the Archives Municipale, St Malo; the Marine Accident Investigation Branch, Southampton; the RNLI, Guernsey; the PT Boat Association.

We wish to extend special thanks to our translators, Carolein Colbeck-Welch (Dutch), Helen Peel (French) and Angela Trigg (German), and to thank Brian Byron for his superb artistic reconstructions which contribute so much to the book.

We are grateful to the following for photographs: Mrs Cara Voelcker (photo of Captain George Voelcker of *Charybdis*), Michael Hannigan, Dave Hocquard, and Mr H.R. Toms.

Picture Acknowledgements

Cover painting and illustrations (pages 16, 22, 105, 153, 159, 163 and 190) Brian Byron; David Jory for *Radiant Med* painting.

Special thanks for underwater photographs to Graham Holly for *Victory, Viper* and PT 509; Leigh Bishop of Deep Image for *Charybdis* and *Limbourne*; Paul Jeandron for *Schokland*.

Special thanks due to Rena, Tracy and Jane for all their forebearance during the writing of the book.

JO, DS

An nineteenth-century engraving showing the main light of the Casquets reef, seven miles to the west of Alderney

Introduction

Despite their historical English ties, the Channel Islands lie in the French Bay of St Malo. This great inlet, with 180 miles of coastline running south from Cap de la Hague round to Les Sept Iles west of Perros-Guirec, was dry land as recently as 18,000 years ago. As the post-Ice Age water levels rose to flood the plain, the islands were formed, but the inundation was so shallow that numerous ridges, peaks and plateaus scoured down to their base rock have remained at or just below the surface. Within the bay the deepest water, west of the islands, is 80 metres (260 feet), and for the most part it is no more than 20 to 50 metres (66 to 164 feet). At lowest spring tides, the channels between south-east Jersey and the French coast, or between Guernsey and Herm, appear to be continuous shoal and rock. If the newly-built Titanic had been laid level on the sea bottom anywhere in the bay, her masts and funnels would have projected well above the water. Drop the sea level in the bay 50 feet and the visible land mass would treble in extent; drop it 150 feet, and roads could be constructed between the islands.

This shallow sea with its numerous projecting rock hazards is subject to some of the fastest currents in Europe, and it can also boast one of the highest tidal ranges in the world. The mass of water pouring out of the narrow eastern English Channel twice a day gathers dramatic speed as it is released into the bay, and currents can run at up to ten knots accompanied by a tidal rise and fall of over 10 metres, or 32 feet. All this makes for interesting navigational challenges, and ship disasters have always been a prominent feature of life for Channel Islanders. Cobalt blue water, white beaches and cliffs covered with wild flowers are only some of the aspects which the islands present; when fog rolls in or a Force Nine is blowing you have all the ingredients for maritime nightmare in some of the most dangerous waters in the northern hemisphere. Given the life-threatening nature of the hazards, it is surprising that none of the Channel Islands' lighthouses, with the exception of the eighteenth-century Casquets light, were built before 1860, and three only after 1909 (Hanois 1862, Corbière 1874, Platte Fougere 1909, Alderney 1912, Sark 1913). As late as 1922 we find a debate going on in Jersey as to whether a light should be erected at Grosnez to cover the north-west corner of the island and the Paternosters, and in the following year the States of Guernsey is considering whether there are sufficient funds to build a beacon on the Roustel (the rock lies in the middle of the main approach to St Peter Port harbour). In 1887 a London newspaper, *The Echo*, stated that the voyage from Southampton or Weymouth to the Channel Islands was more dangerous than that from Liverpool to New York, and these dangers have been reduced but not eliminated by modern navigation aids.

In 1962 John David, a maritime historian, listed 392 known wrecks that had occurred around Alderney, Guernsey and Sark between 1278 and 1962 (a list extended by Eric Sharp in 1968). Had wrecks around Jersey been included, that total would easily have doubled. Almost every substantial rock, David suggested, has been the scene of some mishap at some time. Many of these disasters were the result of human error, but the errors often occur in situations where sea and weather have exerted complex, enigmatic or immensely powerful pressures on human beings. Sometimes accidents occur because human agents are complacent or careless, but mostly problems come from the frightening power which wind, waves and currents can exert in rock-bound waters. As Victor Hugo recognised, the forces involved sometimes seem to come from outside the natural world as we know it, combining to tear steel plates like tissue paper, or lift and drop substantial vessels down cliff-height wave slopes like twigs.

Those unfamiliar with the sea sometimes forget that passing from Point A to Point B in a boat is quite different from a land journey; at sea the road one travels on is in constant, rapid movement as the whole mass of water shifts around the tidal clock. It is also easy to forget how heavy cold sea water is. A vessel taking a large wave over her deck and superstructure is being submitted to a blow measuring hundreds of tons.

Accounts of shipwrecks provide 'good' stories, but they are grim events and can subject people to extremes of terror and violence. They can devastate families and communities, and obliterate loved ones without trace. They can also show men and women at their most selfless and courageous, both on the part of those caught on stricken vessels and by those who rescue them. Over centuries this cumulative impact of losses and unceasing contest with the sea has become an integral strand in the social fabric of the islands, and the generations have devised rituals to deal with it. To tell the story of Channel Island wrecks is to describe a key constituent of island history.

Two Discoveries of International Importance

The last twenty years of the twentieth century saw the discovery of two wrecks in the waters of the Channel Islands, unique (to date) and of international significance to maritime archaeologists and historians. Given the unchanging nature of sea hazards and of the dangers around the islands – dangers significantly greater before the lights, buoys and marks of the nineteenth and twentieth centuries – it is not surprising that vessels have been coming to grief since at least Roman times. What is surprising is the fact that any such wrecks should remain partly preserved over the centuries for the modern diver to find. In the case of the Guernsey Roman and Alderney Tudor ships, the capacity of timber and metal to resist rot, rust, worm, the never-ending friction of rapid tides and seabed upheaval is astonishing. In both cases the ships were found by chance in the course of other activities, and in the case of the Roman ship were found just in time. A few more years would have seen the dispersal and complete destruction of the surviving remains of one of the most important historical wrecks to be recovered in Europe in modern times.

The Guernsey Roman ship

A complete account of the finding and excavation of substantial sections of this vessel will be found in the fully illustrated *A Gallo-Roman Trading Vessel from Guernsey* by Margaret Rule and Jason Monaghan, published by the Guernsey Museum in 1993. There is an excellent permanent exhibition at the Guernsey Maritime Museum at Castle Cornet which includes artefacts recovered from the wreck, together with a small model of the ship and short videos describing the background to its discovery and excavation. Details of the ship can also be found on the European Commission's NAVIS website. What follows is a brief summary to whet the reader's interest.

On the one day in the year when no large ships are entering or leaving St Peter Port harbour – Christmas Day – Guernsey diver Richard Keen went looking for scallops between the pierheads. It was 1982. As he moved over the seabed he saw wooden ribs sticking up out of the sand and made out the vague outline of part of a buried hull. The timbers did not strike him as being particularly old, and he thought the vessel might have been a nineteenth-century stone barge lost just outside the harbour.

One year later, on Christmas Day 1983, he returned to the site. More of the silt cover had gone, exposing larger sections of the timbers, and he saw some pieces of tile lying nearby which his trained eye told him might be Roman. When a piece of timber was removed and submitted for radiocarbon testing, its age was put at AD 110 plus or minus eighty years.

Richard had begun diving professionally after leaving school in 1967, founding his own diving and salvage company. He had undertaken the underwater surveys of the giant ore carrier *Elwood Mead* which was wrecked off Guernsey's west coast in 1973, and of the oil rig Orion which came ashore at Grandes Rocques in 1978. Along with his expertise in salvage he had developed a knowledge

Guernsey harbour entrance

of marine archaeology, and the long list of his finds includes the *Boreas*, the *Brighton*, and (with Fred Shaw) the *Stella*, along with the Guernsey Roman ship.

The eddies and currents which were exposing the ship were also about to destroy it. The larger cross-Channel ferries introduced in the early 1980s had deeper draughts, and were churning up the bottom every time they entered or left the harbour. Once the extraordinary date of the wreck was clear, it became a matter of urgency to survey and salvage it as quickly as possible. Further pressure was added by the proposed plan of the Harbour Board to dredge the harbour entrance in 1986.

The Guernsey Maritime Trust was accordingly established in 1984 to rescue the ship, and over £80,000 was raised. Margaret Rule of *Mary Rose* fame agreed to lead the survey and Dr Monaghan took responsibility for the post-excavation research. Excavation was carried out between 1984 and 1986 in very difficult conditions. Work had to be interrupted every time a ferry or cargo ship passed in or out of the harbour, and the effect of this constant traffic was to muddy the water, reducing visibility for the divers and putting down new layers of deposits every day. After a meticulous seabed survey and the retrieval of many artefacts, the timbers which comprised most of the keel, the floor and some strakes of the oak-built vessel were cradled and lifted ashore in April 1985. Some timbers were seven metres long and weighed a ton once in the air. They were put in large fresh-water tanks in St Peter Port prior to despatch to the Mary Rose Trust at Portsmouth for treatment with polyethylene glycol and freeze drying.

'Asterix', as the ship was nicknamed, had caught fire and gone to the bottom in shallow water some time around 280 AD. She was a merchant vessel, twenty-five metres long, flat-bottomed, with a single mast and sail. She had been carrying a quantity of pine resin blocks, possibly as cargo, and these had melted, flowing over the timbers and into the crevices, preserving them. At that date there were no extended harbour works at St Peter Port, and ships would have made their way between the White Rock and Castle Rocks to the shoreline. The ship went down not far from what is estimated to have been the lowest tidal line at that time, possibly in no more than four to five metres of water.

Her structure was sturdy and the building techniques used to make her were functional rather than decorative. She was carvel-built, the strakes butted edge to edge and nailed onto a frame with caulking along the seams. Marks of axe, adze and saw were clearly visible on her timbers, and the iron nails, some as long as 790mm (31 inches) had been driven through pre-drilled holes and bent over (all the nails had rusted away, but their ghost impressions were clearly defined). Charring was visible on some of the wood.

The vessel was built for trade around the west coast of France and in the English Channel, and exhibited all the characteristics of Gallic ship design during the Roman period. The most striking feature was the way she corresponded closely to the description of a typical vessel from north-west Gaul (Brittany) given by Julius Caesar in his *De Bello Gallico* over three hundred years prior to her loss. She is unique in being the largest, most intact sea-going vessel of her time found outside the Mediterranean.

The artefacts recovered included eighty coins, over 800 fragments of pottery (from cups, bowls, beakers and amphorae), fish hooks, pieces of a wooden bowl and spoon, a pewter spoon, a small stone quern for grinding corn (bread was apparently made on board), barrel staves and a bronze bearing, probably from a bilge pump. An unusual feature was the presence of some kind of oven on board, possibly standing on a tiled base. The pieces of distinctive brown/orange Roman tile or tegulae may have originated there. The coins and pottery confirmed a date of around 280. The 3.7-metre stern post was recovered but the bow section of the vessel was missing and there were no traces of a sail, although small strands forming part of a rope were identified.

Excavations carried out in St Peter Port near La Plaiderie, which in Roman times was closer to the shoreline, have shown evidence of store and warehouses in use between the late first and fourth centuries AD, confirming that St Peter Port was used as a transit port between Brittany and the south coast of England. 'Asterix' would have been only one of many trading vessels calling at the island. The survival and successful recovery of a large section of the ship has been possible through happy paradox. The fire that sank her preserved her; the propeller eddies that were about to break her up for good, one thousand seven hundred years later, revealed her.

The Alderney Elizabethan Ship

One spring evening in 1974, Alderney fisherman Bertie Cosheril was pulling up his lobster pots just west of the Ledge, a large submerged reef half a mile north of Corblets Bay on the north coast of the island. As he pulled in the line a long, thin, encrusted object came up with it, looking like an ancient firearm with a very long barrel. Back in Braye he showed the object to local divers Fred Shaw and Dave Rendell and they asked if he would take them out to the site. Using his shore marks (a cow and a clothes-line according to Fred Shaw) Bertie found the spot again, and Fred went down. The last words he heard Bertie shout as he went over the side were, 'Bring us up a cannon, Fred.' The water was thirty metres deep but very clear. As Fred reached the bottom, he saw a substantial tubular object coated with marine growth lying on rock a few metres from him. Closer examination showed that it was indeed a cannon. He marked the site with a rope, and a few days later he and Dave dived there again. This revealed a second cannon, an anchor and some pieces of timber. The weather then closed down, they had other projects to pursue, and they did not dive there again for sixteen years.

In August 1990 Fred decided to return to the site, accompanied by several members of the Alderney Sub-Aqua Club. At first their attempts to relocate Bertie's cannons were unsuccessful, but in the spring of the following year, 1991, accompanied by Martin Woodward, a diving and salvage expert from the Isle of Wight, they found not only the original two cannons but two more lying in sand thirty-five metres away. Close inspection showed that the cannons were very early, possibly as early as 1600, and suddenly the finds were beginning to look extremely important. A team of Alderney divers now began a survey of the area, and laid a grid prior to recording the positions of any artefacts found. This early survey recovered more muskets – Bertie's object had been a musket – some clumped together in a mass, together with animal bones, pottery shards, pieces of timber, a disc-shaped piece of lead that was later identified as a pan weight, and a 'brass cone' that turned out to be an apostle, or gunpowder holder, that would have hung on the belt of a

The musket from the Elizabethan wreck, recovered by Bertie Cosheril

musketeer. Some of the pottery shards were shown to Bob Burns, archaeological officer at the Guernsey Museum and he dated them approximately to the late sixteenth or very early seventeenth century. He was also able to say that the pottery came from France, Germany and the Low Countries.

The diving team was now concerned that the wreck should be protected, and they informed David Jenkins, Alderney's Receiver of Wreck. The States of Alderney then issued a protection order under the Wreck and Salvage (Vessels and Aircraft) (Bailiwick of Guernsey) Act 1986, setting up an exclusion zone of 200 metres radius around the site. Licences were then issued to the divers, allowing them to continue their survey. During the summers of 1991 and 1992 an astonishing array of objects was recovered. These included one flintlock and twelve matchlock muskets, fifty cannonballs, star shot, thirteen peascod breastplates, helmets, a pair of brass stirrups, a pewter porringer, the sole of a leather shoe, another lead pan weight, a wooden bilge pump handle, and a Bellarmine (a pottery jug with a bearded face moulded into the neck). Most items, with the exception of the pottery, were put into small fresh-water tanks, and the Guernsey Museum then donated a large tank for the express use of the project which was set up in the Old Stables near Braye harbour.

It was clear that a site of major importance had been found, possibly unique in Europe, all the indications pointing to the wreck being a lost Elizabethan ship from the last part of the sixteenth century. The States of Alderney decided to seek archaeological help, and in 1992 appointed Michael Bowyer, from Bangor, as director of the project. He immediately turned his attention to the artefacts recovered so far, sending some off the island for professional conservation treatment and freeze drying at York and Oxford University. He also called on Oxford University's MARE unit (Marine Archaeology Research and Excavation) under Mensun Bound to help with a pre-disturbance survey. The combined Bangor/Oxford survey was undertaken in the summer of 1993. This brought up more artefacts, and early estimates suggested that the wrecked ship had been about sixty feet long (this was later revised downwards). The mainland diving teams were now having to come to terms with the huge tidal rise and fall and the seven-knot current off the north of Alderney. Time spent on the wreck was limited on some days to a few minutes, and at other times no diving at all was possible. Matters were complicated by the constant movement of the sand cover over the remains, revealing or covering large areas between the tides. Fred Shaw recounts a number of dangerous moments diving on the wreck. One inexperienced diver was swept away from his partner, swallowed water, and nearly drowned. On another occasion Fred became entangled in a seabed line, and only escaped by taking his wetsuit off, and on a third occasion he suffered a bend on the wreck and had to be rushed to the decompression chamber on Guernsey.

The challenges were to date the vessel, and establish whether or not it was English. If it did come from Elizabeth I's fleet then this was the first ship from her reign to be discovered (Henry VIII's *Mary Rose* sank earlier, in 1545). The lead pan weight bore the

Queen's mark, and allowed a dating after 1587–88 when the mark was first introduced, and armour and weapons were later confirmed as being of a type in use between c.1585 and 1595. It was known that the pinnace *Makeshift* had been lost in the Channel around 1590 and there was speculation that the Alderney wreck might be her.

Ilustration showing a possible fate for the Elizabethan wreck

Another line of speculation was opened up by the historian R.B.Wernham, author of a number of books on Elizabeth's reign, whose suggestion was taken up by David Keys, archaeology correspondent of *The Independent*, and developed by Dr John Nolan of the University of Maryland. This concerned a letter in the Public Record Office written in November 1592 by Sir John Norreys or Norris, one of Queen Elizabeth's military commanders in France. In 1590 France was under extreme threat from Spain, and a large Spanish army had invaded Normandy and west Brittany. If northern France were to be taken by the Spanish, an invasion of Britain was likely, and Norris was one of the commanders despatched to Normandy with British troops to help Henry IV of France resist the Spanish advance. On 29 November Norris wrote to Lord Burleigh and the Privy Council in London referring to 'a shyyp that was cast away about Alderney' which had been carrying despatches to him that month. Was the Alderney wreck this ship, crossing to Granville with despatches, arms and troops for Norris's army?

In the summer of 1994 one of the cannons was raised, together with part of a gun carriage. The cannon was found to be loaded, the muzzle sealed with a tampion and the touch hole with a lead plug. After restoration on the mainland it was returned to the island. A second important lift was made in 1996 when the ship's rudder, still attached to part of the stern post by its pintles, was brought up. A tar ball from the rudder still retained its smell. The rudder was wrapped up on the seabed and lifted carefully on a cradle. The first attempt to raise it in very foggy weather on 20 June failed when the underwater lines became entangled, but the following day it was brought to the surface with the help of lifting bags. There was a dangerous moment getting the swinging cradle on board the recovery vessel in the swell, but it was shipped safely, and brought back into harbour to be placed in the recovery tank.

Subsequent measurement and appraisal of the rudder by Ian Painter and Jason Monaghan – the latter appointed wreck project director in August 1996 – showed that it must have belonged to a bigger ship than the *Makeshift*, the dimensions of which were known. This conclusion was also arrived at by Owain Roberts of Bangor in 1997, using a computer reconstruction and working from rough sketches of the rudder back to a hypothetical hull. It now seemed likely that the vessel had been a military supply ship, possibly English, possibly servicing the army in Normandy or Brittany.

Lack of answers to key questions meant the need for more work to be done, but there was the constant problem of finances. Up to 1994 funding for the project had come from the States of Alderney and from the efforts of islanders, who had organised jumble sales and other small fundraising activities. All the professionals were generous with their time, many sponsors had come forward, and transport services were provided free of charge by Aurigny Airways and the Alderney Shipping Company. However, the costs of diving, recovery and conservation were considerable, and the project was desperate for a large injection of funds. In 1994 the Alderney Maritime Trust was set up, principally to raise money for the Elizabethan ship project, but also to oversee management of all the historic ships around Alderney, ensuring their protection. In 1996 the States of Alderney transferred management responsibility for the wreck to the Trust, when Dr Monaghan, who had played a key role in the work on the Guernsey Roman ship, was appointed.

The rudder was then sent to the York Archaeological Trust for conservation treatment, and a thin cross-section was removed and sent to Cathy Groves of the University of Sheffield for dendrochronological analysis. Dendrochronology uses the rings in wood not only to give the age of the timber, but to show the region in which it grew. The hope was that the timber would be revealed as English in origin. Unfortunately the profile of the rudder did not present a sufficient number of rings to allow a reliable analysis. Another piece of timber was then tested and was declared to be of oak originating in south-east England, and cut in 1575. Although it is possible that the ship was merely refitted at some point in an English yard, this evidence strengthened the argument for an English-built vessel.

The first research phase on the ship and the raising of the rudder were the subject of a video, made in 1996, and shown on the BBC *Horizon* programme in 1997. Some of the information in that video has now been superseded by further research. At the time of writing (January 2002) speculation on the wreck is moving along the following lines (we are grateful to Dr Monaghan for information): the rudder dimensions suggest a vessel between 78 and 110 feet in length, probably a merchant ship. The timber sample, cannons, muskets and armour are English, and the pan weights indicate a vessel that either traded with England or was English in origin. The ship was lost after 1587 and probably before the end of the 1590s. The evidence to date allows her to be the ship Norris refers to in his letter, but other possibilities cannot be ruled out – for example she might have been an English or Channel Island privateer, or a supply ship sailing to the islands to reinforce the defences there rather than to France. The fact that Norris does not name the lost ship in his letter suggests that it was not one of the Queen's ships, but a civilian merchantman chartered for the occasion. The abundance of pottery from the Low Countries on board may indicate that she was bringing English troops from Flanders to fight in France – such troop movements by water took place at that time. If she is Norris's ship she sank between 27 October, when the fleet sailed, and 29 November 1592, the date of his letter, but if she was carrying despatches to him, it is likely that she sailed after the main fleet had left on the 27th.

It is not possible to say how the ship foundered, although Norris refers to very bad weather in the November of 1592. The course for Granville would have been down the Race to the east of Alderney. Perhaps the vessel, armed and carrying military equipment, was driven by tide and weather too close to Alderney's northern rocks while trying to go down the Race; perhaps she was trying to make Alderney harbour. The fact that the guns were lashed down at the time of the sinking suggests that she was not under attack. The Ledge has four metres of water over it at lowest tide, but no trail of debris has been found on the seabed between the wreck site and the reef consistent with a destructive strike on the rocks. This may be because no such debris was left, or because of the fact that the bottom here is a thick layer of constantly moving sand.

The range of artefacts recovered makes the wreck one of world-class significance. To date nine cannons have been located (one raised), together with a unique gun carriage, twenty brass apostles (the largest number to be found in one place), a basket-hilt sword with gilt finials, a pewter tobacco pipe (the only recorded example found), over two dozen ceramic hand grenades, the carved bone ends of a fan and parts of leather scabbards. Undoubtedly many items still lie just under the seabed. At present, work on the wreck has stopped. The site is under twenty-four hour surveillance, and members of Alderney's Sub-Aqua Club go down at regular intervals to check the area, but it is the view of the Trust that work should not be resumed until proper funding is available to cover the costs of further exploration, recovery and conservation. Unfortunately this will require substantial sums of money. A book about the ship was published by Dr Monaghan and Mensun Bound in 2001.

Two Mysteries

1. The *Vierge de Bon Port* (1666)

Somewhere to the north-west of Guernsey and within four miles of the island, a cargo conservatively estimated as being worth in excess of a million pounds lies on or just under the seabed. The perishables – tobacco, leather, pepper, aloes – have long since dissolved into oblivion, little of the ebony will have survived in recognisable form, but the gold is certainly still there. Some accounts maintain that there were also rubies, opals and amethysts in substantial quantities, and these may also be awaiting discovery over three hundred years after the French ship carrying them went to the bottom. If the British frigate that sank her noted her position, the details have not been handed down, and the records of the French East India Company, the lost ship's owners, were long ago destroyed by fire.

The *Vierge de Bon Port* was a 300-ton, twenty-two-gun merchantman under the command of Captain Trouchet or Truchot de la Chesnay. She was one of four foundation vessels purchased by the French East India Company, set up with the approval of Louis XIV in 1664, and her home port was St Malo. The company held the sole rights to trade and colonise in the Indian Ocean, and investors were eager to lay out money for what promised to be spectacular returns. In March 1665 the *Vierge de Bon Port* and her sister ships *Le Taurau* and *Saint Paul* sailed for Madagascar. After loading a substantial cargo, valued at the time as being worth somewhere between half a million and one million gold louis, the *Vierge* began the return journey in February 1666, and on 8 July entered the English Channel. There is some disagreement in the accounts as to what happened next. It has been claimed that the ship was heading for her home port of St Malo, but this makes no sense given her arrival off the north-west of Guernsey on the 9th. In fact she was aiming for Havre-du-Grace (modern Le Havre) to discharge her cargo closer to Paris. She took too southerly a line, and when land was seen to the south-east it was assumed to be the French coast at or past Cherbourg, but was actually Guernsey.

This would not have presented major problems but for the fact that France had declared war against England on 9 January 1666, and the crew of the *Vierge* was blissfully unaware of this. The captain had even spruced the ship up for her triumphal entry into port, and she was 'fardee comme une coquette, ajustee de banderolles, les galeries peintes a neuf et tous ses vieux dehors revetus de belles apparences' ('made up like a coquette, covered in ribbons, woodwork newly painted and all dolled up beautifully') – Charles La Roncière *Histoire de la Marine Française* 1899. This confidence and happy anticipation of fortunes made was rudely checked when a Royal Navy frigate out of St Peter Port came alongside and put a broadside into her.

The *London Gazette* for 9 July 1666 printed an account of events as seen from the Guernsey naval squadron's point of view. The frigate *Orange* under Captain Christopher Gunman had been west of the island with a privateer the *Have-At-All* investigating a convoy, and were returning to the island when they came upon the *Vierge* and another French ship.

'The lesser of them was pursued by the *Have-At-All*, but the greater was undertaken by Captain Gunman, who coming up with her, hailed her, and found her to be a French ship of 300 tons and twenty-two guns belonging to the French Royal Company, and bound homeward from Madagascar; after which he gave her a gun, she in answer striking her top sail, but having been, as the captain afterwards said, twenty-two months [sic] at sea, knew not of any war, till it was presently proclaimed by a broadside given by the frigate; upon which they fell to it and fought for five hours with much resolution, but the night coming on, the English pressed them more vigorously, and made ready to board them, but the French unable to make further resistance, called for quarter, which the captain granted them and commanded the French out of their ship, sending his carpenter on board with many soldiers to stop their leaks, which it seems were many, and to bring her in, being not a league [three miles] from the shore...'

The marines who clambered eagerly on board the smoking *Vierge* then either failed to get at the holes in her hull because of the tightly packed and substantial cargo, or went on a looting spree, ignoring the condition of the ship, with the result that in a very short time she went under, taking over thirty of the *Orange* crew with her. No doubt Gunman had had sufficient time to realise the value of what he had captured, and its likely beneficial impact on his personal finances, before seeing it disappear below the surface.

The *Vierge* suffered severe damage in the fighting. Masts were brought down and she was holed in at least four places at or below the waterline, taking in so much water that the pumps could not cope with it. According to the account given by Souchu de Rennefort (*Histoire des Indes Orientales,* 1688) there was a fatal misunderstanding which cost additional lives. With their deck covered with dead or wounded, and the

An intriguing find recovered by a trawler in the general area where the Vierge de Bon Port was presumed lost

surgeon unable to get around to everyone, the French called out that they were ready to surrender. The English replied, 'Bon, quartier' ('quarter given') and this was apparently misheard on the *Vierge* as 'non quartier', and fighting went on for another hour. It also appears that there was a conflict on board the *Vierge* between the captain, who wanted to fight to the bitter end, and some of the crew and passengers (it seems there were travellers on board) who had endured enough and wanted to surrender. Another officer was begged to take command, and a young cabin boy was sent to lower the flag, but a cannon ball took his leg off. Eventually with at least forty French dead or wounded, part of the ship on fire, and most of her guns dismounted, the *Vierge* made her surrender clear and the English promptly came alongside and boarded, Gunman watching from the poop deck with his sword in his hand. Seven of his crew had been killed, several by musket fire. According to Rennefort the boarding force might have been spurred on by talk of jewels hidden in some of the officers' cabins. When the vessel went down, 'en un clin d'oeuil' – 'in the twinkling of an eye' – he maintains that there were 120 men on board and that they were calling for help, climbing the mizzen mast or jumping into the sea, although many were still trapped below decks. The *Orange* put out a boat which picked up some of those in the water.

The captured French crewmen were taken in to Guernsey, and then transferred to prison on the Isle of Wight. Here Truchot de la Chesnay died before having a chance to explain to his masters the reasons for the disaster. Attempts to locate the wreck have been made by French and British divers, but so far without any success.

2 The Casquets and HMS *Victory* (1744)

It is no exaggeration to say that hundreds of ships have been lost on the Casquets. The extent and height of the reef and its position west of Alderney and Cap de la Hague make it a terrible threat not only to ships passing south into the Bay of St Malo, but to traffic moving along the main east-west routes of the English Channel. The heart of the reef, five miles due west of Alderney, is a mile and a half long. Here a sequence of large rocky islets, ranging between 4 and 20 metres above water, is strung out like a mountain range. Around the main rocks lie extensive ledges and small isolated peaks, with dangerous banks and shoals to the north-east and south. At this spot the great tidal sweep around the Bay of St Malo narrows into the funnel of the eastern Channel, and the tides run in complex patterns at up to 10 knots – faster than most human beings can run. Between the rocks and over the shoals there are even faster tide rips and violent overfalls. The reef exerts an inward pull on ships, and in addition is a notoriously foggy place.

The newspaper letter writer who proposed that the reef should be blown up after the *Stella* disaster in 1899 may have had only a tenuous hold on reality, but certainly would have stirred sympathy in the hearts of many seamen and Channel Islanders. Even with today's charts, radar, radio beacons and satellite navigation systems, the section on the Casquets in the Channel Pilot makes unnerving reading; 'breakers', 'hazardous', 'no vessel should attempt to pass between', 'use only with local knowledge', 'violent eddies', 'tremendous overfalls'. Divers working near the rocks with magnetometers today are hampered by the numerous readings of sunken metal that they obtain, and for miles around the light rock the bottom is littered with maritime debris. If the English Channel has a graveyard, it is here. Until 1724 there was no light on the reef, and most bad storms brought a wreck. In 1722 a group of ship owners asked Thomas Le Cocq, proprietor of the rocks, to erect a light, offering him a halfpenny per ton levy on all passing vessels. Le Cocq obtained permission from King George I to proceed, and he then came to an arrangement with Trinity House, as a result of which a triangular pattern of lights on three towers was erected on the highest

Admiral Sir John Balchen's flagship Victory being overwhelmed by a fierce storm in 1744

rock, first lit October 1724. This distinctive formation was to distinguish the hazard from anything already in place on the English and French coasts. The three coal braziers inside glazed lanterns had to be kept going by the keeper, and their varying intensity and modest height (only 30 feet) meant that they were easily obscured by spray in bad weather. Coal was replaced by oil in 1770, and in 1818 a revolving mechanism for the lights was introduced, which had to be wound up by hand. The towers were increased in height in 1854 to 120 feet above sea level, and by 1877 only one light, on the St Peter tower, was considered necessary. The lights did not prevent at least ten major wrecks on the reef during the nineteenth century. Exactly twenty years to the month after the first lights were erected and lit, the worst wreck ever on the Casquets occurred. On the night of 4–5 October 1744, in a tremendous storm, the Royal Navy's flagship *Victory* went onto the rocks with the loss of 1100 men. This *Victory*, which predated Nelson's flagship, was utterly destroyed, and with one possible exception not a single body was recovered. A small quantity of timber was washed up, but the bulk of the ship disappeared below the water taking all hands, her captain Samuel Faulkner, and Admiral Sir John Balchen with her.

An early engraving showing the Casquets reef with three lights

Victory was a 100-gun first rate ship of the line, possibly carrying 110 guns, and at the time of her loss was not just the largest but also considered to be the finest ship in the Royal Navy. She was relatively new, having been built in 1737. She had been constructed from the frames of the ex-HMS *Royal James* of 1675, and she had superb lines, although some considered her ornate stern galleries to be too high. She was reputed to have the best set of guns in the navy. With a length along the gun deck of 174.5 feet and a beam of 50 feet, she was only slightly smaller than Nelson's *Victory* at 186 and 51 feet respectively.

War had been declared against France at the end of March 1744, and *Victory* and a squadron of fourteen ships under Admiral Balchen had left England for the Mediterranean in July. On the way they went to the assistance of Admiral Sir Charles Hardy, blockaded into the River Tagus by the French. Hardy was escorting a convoy of British supply ships. On 6 July twenty Dutch warships went to Hardy's aid, and on the 15th Balchen and his group arrived. The French then retreated to Cadiz, and the combined British fleet proceeded to Gibraltar.

On the return voyage in November, Balchen's squadron was caught in a terrible storm in the Bay of Biscay and the western Channel. Although the group was scattered in the hurricane-force southwesterly winds and huge waves, all the ships managed to make Portsmouth successfully with the exception of the flagship, which was last seen near the Scilly Isles. Some of the ships suffered severe damage; HMS *Exeter* lost masts, and had to throw guns overboard to survive, and *Duke* had over ten feet of water in her hold. It was assumed at first that *Victory* might have been driven back down the Channel and that she would arrive once the storm moderated, but days passed and there was no sign of her. Vessels were sent down Channel to look for her, but nothing was seen.

A fishing boat then reported finding timber debris just off Alderney, obviously from a large vessel. The Admiralty despatched two sloops, *Falkland* and *Fly*, to the island, and these reported quantities of timber washed up, on the beaches, including pieces of mast, spars, parts of gun carriages stamped 'Victory' and some gilded woodwork. In the succeeding days several seamen's trunks were washed up, together with a portmanteau of clothes bearing the name of Captain Cotterell who was captain of marines on board *Victory*. Timbers were also washed up on Guernsey. The keeper of the

Aerial view of the Constantia aground on the eastern end of the Casquets reef in 1967

Casquets lights reported hearing guns being fired during the night of the 4th–5th, but the storm had been too fierce to see anything. It appeared that the navy's finest ship had been driven onto the reef, broken up overnight, and gone to the bottom with the Admiral and all hands. One body, possibly from the ship, was washed up weeks later in Cornwall, but apart from this there was no sign of the main part of the vessel or any of her crew. Her loss stunned the nation, and was one of the worst disasters to befall the Royal Navy.

In 1758 the Admiralty ordered twelve new ships of the line, including one 100-gun first rate, and when it was proposed that she should be named 'Victory' there was strong opposition on the grounds that the name was unlucky. The new ship's keel was laid in 1759, and the supporters of the name won the argument. This new Victory was to become the best known ship of the line in the world.

Martin Woodward searching with sidescan sonar

Admiral Balchen's *Victory* has been the great elusive Channel Island wreck. No one knows exactly where she struck on the reef, and to date despite many attempts no one has found her. Her substantial ballast and guns lie somewhere on the seabed, probably with some timbers still preserved and with potentially many artefacts from the period. Guernsey diver Richard Keen and Fred Shaw from Alderney have carried out extensive searches for the wreck, and Comex UK has funded a major project to locate her, so far without success. Martin Woodward has spent hundreds of hours searching for her, and he reports as follows:

In 1983 I researched the wreck, and found the circumstances of her loss a gripping story. After much deliberation as to the likely place where she struck, I went to Alderney in June 1984 to commence a magnetometer survey of the area around the Casquets. This survey ended up covering a total of fifteen square miles of seabed with staggering amounts of resultant magnetic anomalies. It was immediately obvious that the whole area was saturated with magnetic rock, which gave constant readings on the proton magnetometer, and consequently made life extremely difficult when selecting contacts to dive on. In an attempt to calculate the localities of the rock seams, I recovered several samples of rock from the seabed for analysis, and it was discovered that they were multiple seams or dykes of lamprophyre. Samples of this rock caused a maximum deflection of 40 degrees on a pocket compass, and was rich in iron oxide, thus causing problems with the magnetometer. Despite this, I calculated the approximate direction of the seams by comparison with magnetometer results, and used this information to be more selective with the contacts we subsequently dived on.

Over the following years I have returned to Alderney whenever time allows, and continued with the search for the wreck of the elusive *Victory*. A large number of the surveyed areas have now been dived on, without success, but the search continues. It is a very difficult area to work due to the vicious tides, minimal slack water times, and deep water. However the 'process of elimination' factor has now effectively been used to cover much of the search area, although there are numerous contacts still to be investigated by diving. The majority of the shallower areas have now been dived, and it seems increasingly likely that she lies in deep water, having struck the rocks and then drifted on before sinking. There are still many theories from other researchers that she may lie elsewhere in the Channel Islands, but that is for them to speculate on.

The wreck remains firmly at the top of my priority list, not because of any commercial aspect, but because I have researched and visualised the wreck site so many times that I am determined to be the one to see it first. Added to that, it is probably one of the most difficult sites to find because of the environment, but that naturally makes it more of a challenge. It would undoubtedly be an incredible sight to behold on the seabed, and an extremely important wreck to our national heritage. Archaeologically, a great deal could be learnt from the wreck site, and there is the potential for a major exhibition of the recovered material.

(We are grateful to Martin for this account and for details of *Victory*'s design and history.)

Diver searching the seabed off the Casquets

In 2008 one of the world's greatest maritime mysteries was solved when Odyssey Marine Exploration discovered the shipwreck of HMS *Victory*.
For more details visit: http://www.shipwreck.net/hmsvictory.php

HMS *Boreas* (1807)

After October 1805 and Trafalgar, the Royal Navy controlled the seas of Europe, but Britain was increasingly isolated in the land war and things were not going well for her in 1807. Napoleon was seeking to close all the continental ports to British trading vessels, and he had forced Russia into an alliance, threatening Britain's Baltic interests.

Although the threat of a French invasion of England and the Channel Islands had retreated, the islands remained in the front line as an important secondary naval base. Sir James Saumarez was admiral in command of the station, and the squadron under him was responsible for watching the French ports, escorting cargo vessels and troop carriers crossing to the islands, and attacking any French ships, merchant or navy, that put to sea. Warships based at Guernsey endured a comparatively safe but fatiguing existence.

The destruction of HMS *Boreas*, a 533-ton Royal Navy frigate on the Guernsey station, in November 1807 was caused not by the enemy but by a savage storm which drove her onto the Hanois rocks in the night, where she broke up with heavy loss of life. The *Boreas* was a new ship, built in 1805. She was 138 feet long overall, with a 32-foot beam, and she carried thirty-two guns – twenty-two nine-pounders, four six-pounders, and six eighteen-pound carronades or 'smashers' (short, wide-muzzled guns with devastating power at short range). She was commanded by Captain Robert Scott.

Throughout the short daylight of Saturday 28 November the wind increased steadily to gale force over the island, and in the afternoon a signal was passed to the British squadron anchored in the Little Russel that a pilot cutter with two pilots was in trouble out to the west of Lihou Island. The *Boreas* was despatched to give aid, and she proceeded around the south coast of Guernsey in very heavy seas. She managed to locate the cutter out to the west of the island, and coming up with it took the pilots on board and secured the vessel for towing. The wind was still increasing, backing north-east, and it was now dark. Aided by the pilots, Scott set a southerly course to pass around Pleinmont Point for the return to St Peter Port. This course may have been incorrect, veering too far to the east, or the frigate may have been driven by the gale and the mountainous seas off her line. Some time around 6 p.m. a lookout yelled out that there were rocks ahead, the helm was instantly put up, but there was no room to come about on the other tack, and she struck hard on the port side and slammed to a halt. Scott raised more sail to drive her off, and she did advance a few hundred feet, but then struck again. She was wedged fast in the middle of the Hanois reef, with rocks on all sides, and she was badly holed below the waterline. If the reports from two separate sources are to be believed, the two pilots immediately took to their cutter, cast off, and made for land leaving their rescuers to their fate.

The Hanois lighthouse was not built and lit until 1862, and in 1807 there was no marker on the reef. The light rock is just over one mile due west of Guernsey's south-west corner and is surrounded by numerous substantial rocks, ten permanently above water. All around are extensive ledges with three to eight metres of water over them. To pass safely around the corner of the island one must stay a good two miles out from the coast to skirt the reef. The two pilots would have known the angles in their sleep even if the Royal Navy men on board weren't sure of them.

The tide was high at the time of striking, but as it fell the *Boreas* was partly unsupported, and her seams began to open. She was being pounded by huge waves which were breaking right over her, and the water flooding in was too much for the pumps. Initially three boats were launched. The gig, with Lieutenant Bewick and Lieutenant Wilson (a marine), and six men, was sent towards Rocquaine. The launch with Gunner Hoare, a group of fit men and a number of injured men, total about fifteen in all, made for Pleinmont Point, their orders being to land the injured and then return to the ship to take others off. The cutter with the boatswain, Simpson, and also about fifteen men was also ordered to the point. The waves were so high that they had great difficulty keeping the oars in the water and were in constant danger of being overturned. After a long struggle the launch and cutter got to the shore, but once grounded many of the men took to their heels and disappeared in the darkness. These were later said to be pressed men, taking their chance to escape from the navy. Hoare had to put back to the wreck in the launch with only four men, and it shipped so much water that as it approached the rocks for the second time it went under. Luckily the cutter had followed them, and it was able to pick the men out of the troughs. In his official report on the disaster Admiral Saumarez thought the cutter then foundered also and never reached the ship, but since Simpson is listed among those saved, it is clear that it did make it, and his and his companions' survival explains why there is so much detail available about what happened in the two boats. However, it was apparently decided that it was too dangerous to make any further attempts to take a boat ashore. By now the gig had also reached the beach, where Bewick, Wilson and the others were pleading with some fishermen to give assistance. They met with no sympathy, being told first that they must be Frenchmen, and then that it was too rough to put to sea.

On board *Boreas* distress guns were being fired and rockets sent up, but in the howling north-east gale there was no chance of the guns being heard on shore. Scott ordered a number of rafts to be made, and because of the increasing strain on the hull he had the ship's masts cut away. As the water rose in the holds and the tide fell, the *Boreas* took an increasing tilt, and by midnight the deck was too steep to walk on, with the crew clinging on in the main and mizzen chains. There was a continual ominous grinding sound from the keel. At about 2 a.m. the ship gave a lurch and fell onto her side, partially submerged. Many of the crew were swept away, although some managed to cling to the rocks. Here those who did not die of exposure remained in the bitter cold until boats at last put out to rescue them at 8 a.m.

A fourth boat, a small cutter, had also been launched in the night. In this there was a young midshipman, Heming, and a boy, Luttrell, and two other crewmen. This was swept out to sea, and they lacked the means and the strength to control it. At dawn they were far out with no coastlines visible. Hours later they saw sails in the distance. This was HMS *Thalia*, and by great good fortune she eventually saw them and turned. They were pulled aboard more dead than alive. Sir James Saumarez wrote his account of the disaster for the Admiralty the same day:

Inconstant, in Guernsey Road, Nov 29th.
Sir, It is with deepest regret I have to acquaint you, for the information of the Lords Commissioners of the Admiralty, that His Majesty's ship *Boreas*, in standing towards this island yesterday evening, about six o'clock, run upon the Hannois rocks, the wind at the time blowing very hard at NE. I received information of this unfortunate event about 2 o'clock this morning, and immediately sent orders to the *Brilliant* and *Jamaica*…to proceed off the Hannois, and afford her every assistance [presumably these ships went as near the reef as they dared, but by then there would have been little to see]: their lordships will be very much concerned to be informed, that on the tide's flowing the ship overset, and became a complete wreck, at about two o'clock; and I am truly grieved to be obliged to add, that Captain Scott, with the officers and men, except those mentioned in the enclosed list, were lost with the ship: Lieutenant Bewick (second lieutenant), with Lieutenant Wilson, of the royal marines, and six men, were sent off in the gig, and landed in the western part of the island; and about thirty others in the launch and large cutter, were also landed, and the boats returned to the ship, but have not been heard of, and there is every reason to fear they were lost on nearing her.

Through the great exertions of Lieutenant-Colonel Sir Thomas Saumarez [Saumarez's brother] in collecting the pilots and boatmen in the vicinity of Rocquaine, about thirty seamen and marines were taken off the rocks of the Hannois at day-light, which, I fear, are the whole that have been saved.

The greatest praise appears to be due to Captain Scott, and all his officers and men, for their steadiness and good conduct, under such perilous circumstances, in a dark and tempestuous night, in the midst of the most dangerous rocks that can be conceived; and I have most sincerely to lament the loss of so many brave officers and men who have perished on this most melancholy occasion.

Saumarez lists the names of seventy-seven men saved, but he does not give a figure for the number lost. Tupper in his *History of Guernsey* (1854) gives a figure of seventy-seven saved, seventy-seven lost, but William Gilly in his *Narrative of Shipwrecks of the Royal Navy between 1793 and 1849* (1850) maintains that sixty-eight men were lost, although it is probably better not to trust his estimate since his figure for the number saved is clearly incorrect at 127. Terence Grocutt (*Shipwrecks of the Revolutionary and Napoleonic Eras*, 1997) puts a figure of over one hundred lost. By 1807, fourteen years into the war, a frigate with *Boreas*'s armament would have been carrying between 130 and 180 men, so that if seventy-seven were saved anything between fifty-three and 103 men were lost. Bodies were later washed up on Guernsey beaches and some of these men were later buried in island churchyards.

Richard Keen with a musket recovered from the wreck site.

The loss of a ship meant a court-martial, and this was held on board HMS *Gladiator* at Portsmouth on 19 December 1807. All officers and crew were cleared of any possible negligence except for those who had run away once they had landed. These men were liable to individual court-martial and hanging if caught, and their situation was not one to envy.

The story of the wreck caught the imagination of Richard Keen, and in the late 1960s he began to research the background papers at the Public Record Office. Knowing the direction of the wind, the state of the tide and the course *Boreas* was trying to establish at the time, he was able to make an informed estimate of her position at striking, bringing his own considerable experience of the west coast waters to bear. He also knew that she had struck 'in the middle of the rocks', probably not on the light rock, but near it. He was aided by a discovery made by Guernsey maritime historian Eric Sharp, who came across a small item in the *Guernsey Comet* newspaper for July 1847. This described how a diver, working out on the reef in search of the recently lost barque *Rose*, had found fifteen guns, shot and iron ballast in less than twenty feet of water, which he had reported but left untouched. Convinced that this was the remains of the *Boreas*, Richard set out with colleagues Mike Rogers and David Archer to try to locate the site. On 28 October 1969 they went out from St Peter Port to follow the path of the *Boreas* around the south coast, and in the afternoon began a series of shallow dives within the reef in what seemed a likely area north-west of the light rock. With his permission we quote from Richard's diving log:

October 1969, the 28th

Mike started off doing spot dives in an area I fancied. I started getting warm and impatient in my suit so I went in and worked an area. I kept on seeing lobsters and congers. I had a go at three lobsters but only had one. When I surfaced Arni and Mike were looking for me. On board I found Mike had picked up two pieces of lead sheeting and a conglomerate of iron and stone. Arni broke this in two to reveal some badly rotting iron. The search was on in earnest. Mike showed me where he had them and I dived a little further north-west. After 20 seconds I found a green piece of copper or bronze slightly ornamented which we left to be photographed later. A little distance away I found an iron and stone (wood?) conglomerate, and further up the gully a copper keel bolt 3-foot to 3.5-foot long, badly bent. We had found the wreck.

After more searching Mike found a cannon, 2 cannon balls, and 4 iron pigs. I went to look for it and found the two spades of an anchor but no shank, and a large cannon. The tide by now was running strongly and the groundswell was getting worse, so we pushed off home.

They went back a week later, when they photographed one of the cannons. The markings on this confirmed that it was from a wreck from the Georgian period. They resumed their exploration during the following summer, 1970, and as well as finding two more cannons, came across a large piece of iron-bound timber sticking out of the stony seabed. When they dug down at the spot they discovered a very large mass of conglomerate which had a cluster of musket butts projecting from one end. This was extracted from the seabed with some difficulty and then with the help of David Roland and David Froome, they managed to lift the lump and tow it slowly into St Peter Port, where it was found to weigh three and a half hundredweight. On breaking into this mass they uncovered twenty-four iron-barrel muskets packed butt to muzzle inside the remains of a wooden case. Embedded in the conglomerate were six brass badges depicting the fouled anchor of the Royal Navy, probably originally worn on shoulder belts. The musket barrels were badly rusted, but their wooden stocks responded well to conservation treatment. Flints were also found with the guns.

The surprising aspect of the finds is the shallow depth at which they were lying combined with the violence of the waters through this part of the reef. A hundred and fifty years of storms over the Hanois rocks should, in theory, have destroyed anything lying close to the surface, yet the muskets were intact and complete. Five metres away from their position, in another shallow gully, are heaps of large granite boulders, ground into egg shapes by the ferocity of the constant tide action. Somehow the remains of the *Boreas* were sheltered from this erosion.

In the summer of 1974 the Guernsey Museum was preparing to open a maritime branch at Fort Grey, a martello tower and battery standing on a high rock islet joined to the shore by a narrow spit at Rocquaine Bay. The fort had been built in 1804–5 as a defence against Napoleon and had just come into full use at the time the *Boreas* was lost. It was decided that no better exhibit could be included in the new museum than one of the guns from the *Boreas*, but the height of the fort walls meant that it was not possible to crane the gun in, and the entrance gates and steps were too narrow and angled to allow it to be carried through. The aid of the navy was therefore requested, and after lines had been attached to the cannon under water it was lifted by a Wessex helicopter and flown the short distance to the fort, being laid down inside the walls in fresh water to begin the conservation phase. The cannon, bearing the arms of George III, can be seen today on a replica carriage, pointing out towards the spot where the *Boreas* sank.

The Wessex helicopter recovering a cannon now on display
in the Fort Grey Shipwreck Museum, Guernsey

The *Normandy* (1870)

The speed with which things can go disastrously wrong at sea should never be underestimated, and it is a commonplace that individuals may be faced with the need to make split-second decisions which can preserve or destroy them. In his fiction Joseph Conrad is fond of exploring the crucial moments when the seaman is tested and has no time to ponder or consult. The difference between right and wrong action can be the thickness of a piece of paper, but the outcomes can be fatal. The speed with which the LSWR's paddle steamer *Normandy* met her end, and the inexplicable indecisiveness of the second officer of the *Mary* – the ship that ran into her – might well be called the best Conrad story that was never written.

The *Normandy* left Southampton for the islands at a quarter to midnight on Wednesday, 16 March 1870. She was due in at Guernsey at 11.30 next morning and she carried thirty-seven passengers and a crew of twenty-eight. The weather was fine, with a very light breeze from the south-west, the stars were clear, and apart from a heavy swell once they had passed the Needles at about 1.45 a.m. the run at the night speed of 10 knots was easy and uneventful.

At 3.30 a.m., twenty-five miles south-west of the Needles and approaching mid-Channel on a course WSW1/2W, the men on the bridge saw a long black bank of cloud or rain coming towards them from the west. As it grew in size it rose up above the ship, and within six or seven minutes the *Normandy* passed under a curtain of dense fog that reduced visibility to a few yards. First Officer Ockleford, who was on duty on the bridge, at once sent a crewman to inform Captain Harvey, who was in his cabin along the deck. The ship continued to run at 10 knots for about a minute without incident but as Captain Harvey was making his way to the bridge, the first officer and the lookouts saw a blurred red light through the thick haze ahead of them about two points on the starboard bow. Ockleford instantly shouted at the helmsman to turn the ship hard to port, and blew a long warning blast on the whistle. The *Normandy*'s head began to come round, but less than a minute after the order, the men on the bridge – now joined by Harvey – watched in horror as the bow and bowsprit of another, larger vessel loomed out of the fog a few yards away pointing straight at the *Normandy*'s starboard side. There was a shattering blow as the vessel struck the *Normandy* just aft of her paddle box, bursting bulwarks and deck planking, smashing a great hole in her side, and cutting her to the waterline. The *Normandy* heeled over onto her port side, then righted again as the swell lifted the other ship up to come crashing down a second time, carrying away the main lifeboat and its davits. There was a third impact close to the stern, and then the ships fell apart, disappearing from each other in the fog.

Within the fifteen minutes remaining, the *Normandy*'s two surviving lifeboats were got away with a total of thirty-one people in them, but within ten minutes her stern deck was awash, and five minutes after that, at 3.55 a.m., she disappeared below the water taking the thirty-four unfortunates still on board. Not one of these people was ever seen again.

The *Normandy* had been the main passenger link between Southampton and the islands for seven years. She had been built for the LSWR by Ash and Co of Millwall in 1863, and was an iron-framed two-funnel paddle steamer, 210 feet long, 425 tons gross, with a top speed of 12 knots. She was well fitted out with 130 berths for the night crossings. Her master, Henry Harvey, who lived in Southampton, a married man with grown-up children, had been with the Company for over thirty years.

A contemporary painting showing the Normandy under way

The *Mary* was a three-mast, square-rigged screw steamer of 566 tons, and not only was she larger than the *Normandy* but she was fully loaded with a cargo of 5,400 quarters of maize inward-bound for the Port of London from Odessa via Gibraltar. She had left Gibraltar on 9 March with a crew of eighteen under Captain Robert Strannach. She had had good weather across the Bay of Biscay, but once in the Channel conditions had deteriorated and most of the Wednesday night she had been in a bank of thick fog which she was bringing up with her. She had been built at Gateshead in 1868, was registered at Grimsby, and was owned by a North Shields Company. At 3.30 a.m. on the 17th she was at a dead slow of 2 knots, steering E by S 1/2S and sounding her fog whistle every two minutes. There was insufficient breeze to warrant setting any of her sails. The difference in size, weight and solidity of each vessel meant that even though one of them was under way at a mere 2 knots, the impact upon the lighter *Normandy* was like an iron ball swung against matchwood.

Immediately after the collision Harvey stopped the engines and checked the stern hold. As the hatches were lifted water could be seen flooding up from below with baggage floating on it. Harvey ordered the two remaining boats, a cutter and a small jolly boat on the port side, to be lowered, and at the same time he hailed the invisible vessel with a megaphone through the fog asking her to send boats because they were sinking. Most of the women, some male passengers and some crew were put into the boats, which then pulled away in the direction where they thought the other ship was. There were twenty-two people in the cutter and nine in the jolly boat, altogether making eleven women, seven men and thirteen crew saved. Walter Kinloch, recently passed out from Sandhurst and awaiting his commission, put his sister Melina into one of the boats, and handed in their Skye terrier but refused to join them. All the passengers had been hastily summoned on deck, and some of the women were in their night clothes. Seven women and a child had been lying down in the ladies' saloon, and stewardess Mary Wilson later described how the bow of the other vessel had burst through the bulkhead, shattering a mirror and smashing the berths. Fortunately the women had all been on the other side, and the child who had been lying on the broken side was below the entry point. All of these were saved.

One of the passengers was J. Dacam, a Royal Marine artilleryman. He later described events to the *Jersey Times*:

I heard a whistle blowing and running out of the deckhouse I looked over the starboard side, when I saw the bowsprit of the *Mary* just clear the afterpart of our starboard paddlebox and striking us down about ten feet abaft the paddlebox, completely smashing the bulwarks, and causing the *Normandy* to heel over. While she was righting herself, the swell rose and the bow of the *Mary* came down with a tremendous crash, cutting our lifeboat in two and making a large hole in the *Normandy*'s quarter. The *Mary* rose again and came down, tearing away bulwarks and stanchions, ripped up two or three planks of the deck, cutting her down, and getting clear. She was soon in a sinking condition.

Some ladies were helped into a boat, but one, only partially dressed, was sitting on the bulwarks in a bewildered state. One of the passengers, a man-of-war's man, seeing her helpless condition, came behind her, and with a rush tumbled her into the boat. The quarter deck by this time was completely under water. As I ran across it I saw a lady with nothing but her linen on, when, in great haste, I took off my coat and wrapped it round her and threw her into the long boat. Rushing aft I saw the jolly boat was made fast by a belaying pin now four feet under the water. I succeeded in getting her disengaged, and we were soon rowing for the *Mary*. When about thirty or forty yards away we met the longboat of the *Mary*, and told them to pull quickly to the *Normandy*, but why they did not do so at once, I do not know, for they turned the boat around and followed us. Then we heard loud screams, and there was not the least doubt that the *Normandy* was then making her final plunge.

As the boats went away, Harvey called anxiously, telling them to return as quickly as possible to take the remaining passengers and crew off. He must have known that the ship had only a few minutes left. This promise of return actually caused the death of several of the women passengers, four according to one account. They were at the dry bow, and rather than wade through water to get to a lifeboat (the last to embark in these were almost to their waists in water) decided to stay put until one of the boats returned to take them off. There was even some evidence that they were advised to do this by a male passenger. All drowned, and the screams heard through the fog by the survivors in the boats almost certainly came from these women as the ship went down under them. Harvey and Ockleford had remained on the bridge, and they also went down with the ship. The depth of water at the point of sinking was later estimated to be 35 fathoms, or just over 200 feet.

An early photograph of the Normandy in harbour

Arrived at the *Mary*, the survivors in the boats had to climb up her port side on a rope ladder. One of the boats then promptly put back towards the *Normandy* , accompanied by the *Mary*'s own lifeboat. The *Mary* had stopped her engines, and then went slowly astern towards where it was thought the *Normandy* was drifting. Rockets were fired and blue flares burned, but nothing could be seen in the fog. The boats came to an area of disturbed water, with some planks, cushions and a chair floating on it, but there was no sign of the ship or of any survivors, and after about forty minutes they returned to the *Mary* and reported failure. The *Mary* herself was badly damaged at the bow and holed below the waterline, and was in danger of sinking. Her bowsprit and figurehead had been carried away, and the hull plates were torn off over a large area or bent over, but the watertight bulkhead fortunately held to keep her afloat.

The failure of the *Mary*'s lifeboat to go straight to the *Normandy*'s aid when asked by the survivors in the boats, and undoubtedly save other lives, is one of the mysteries of the disaster. On hearing the call for help from the *Normandy* Strannach had promptly ordered out one of his boats, with four crewmen and Second Officer John Andrews in charge. As this boat made its way in the fog it met the two boats from the *Normandy* coming towards it. George Goodwin, second officer on the *Normandy*, later described at the inquiry what happened:

> On our way to the *Mary* we saw a boat. I spoke to the five men manning it, asking them to go to our ship and save some of the souls, as the ship was going down. I received a reply, 'We must go back and receive orders from the captain.' Our boat was about five minutes' pull from the *Mary* … I requested the men to go as speedily as possible, when the men stopped and laid on their oars. I proceeded to the *Mary*, and the *Mary*'s boat followed us. My boat first reached the *Mary* and although close together nothing more was said to them to go back, as it was thought useless after the men had said they must go back to get orders. I heard someone in the *Mary*'s boat say, 'Shall I go on?' and someone on board the *Mary* replied, 'Yes, what did I send you for?' The boat then began to make its way again in the direction of the *Normandy*.

AB Henry West of the *Normandy* put it rather more strongly, telling the court that they had shouted at the *Mary*'s boat repeatedly, telling them, 'For God's sake, go quickly', and pointing in her direction.

Another witness, George Griggs, chief officer on the *Mary*, also confirmed what had happened. He had heard Strannach tell Andrews the first time to pull away to the other ship 'at once'. The boat then returned, and Griggs heard Andrews ask, 'Are we to go on?' to which the captain answered with some impatience, 'yes'.

The lack of decisiveness shown by Andrews was censured by the inquiry assessors, but they were unable to fathom what had been going through his mind. He was not even required to show initiative, since his orders had been to go to the other ship and had he done so he could have been there within minutes. Asked for his version of events he told the assessors that when he left the *Mary* he thought she was sinking. He went for about three or four minutes, then heard a cry which he thought came from the *Mary*. At that moment the two boats from the *Normandy* came up. 'On the impulse of the moment'(his words) he turned back, and ignored their desperate pleading. When his boat returned the second time, it was too late. The *Mary* stayed in the area for over two hours, but at 6.30 a.m. with the fog lifting and no sign of any survivors in the water, she began to crawl towards Southampton. A large part of her cargo was dumped overboard to try to keep the holed bow up, and she was pumping hard all the way. She reached the upper end of Southampton Water at 3.30 p.m. with the bow beginning to go under, and the survivors were taken into the docks by a tug. The *Southampton Times* reported: 'The ladies were in a pitiable condition, some of them having escaped with only their night dresses'. Many of them were without shoes, some without stockings and three or four were wrapped in blankets. They were taken to hotels in cabs. The *Mary* was later docked at 8 p.m., and the general feeling was that she had been lucky to make it.

At the inquiry, which opened at Greenwich Police Court on Monday 4 April, there was much argument as to who had run into whom. The *Normandy* was crossing the main east-west Channel traffic, and was therefore under special obligation to look out for other shipping. The Regulations for Preventing Collisions at Sea, Article 14, stated that the ship which had the other on her starboard side 'shall keep out of the way of the other'. This faulted the *Normandy* which had first seen the *Mary*'s red light to starboard.

It was said that the *Mary* had been proceeding at 2 knots, blowing the fog whistle, heading slightly south of east. Captain Strannach had been on the bridge, and he described how he had heard the sound of paddles, and then saw through the fog a green light and a masthead light about three ships' lengths away two points on the port bow. He instantly telegraphed full speed astern and ordered a hard turn to starboard. Clearly at the same moment the *Normandy* saw the *Mary*, and tried to turn hard to port. The ships were so close that Strannach heard the order 'Hard-astarboard' (go to port) shouted on the other vessel. A steamer then 'dashed across our bows' hitting them on the cutwater with her sponson (the beam and platform abaft the paddlebox). He put the time from seeing the green light to collision as no more than two minutes. Had the ships been farther apart the avoiding manoeuvre would have worked, but the speed at which the *Normandy* was travelling and the close position of the ships on sighting meant there was insufficient room for them to go clear. Thomas Park, the *Mary*'s second engineer, who had been on duty in the engine room, said that the ship had been going dead slow, and then he received an order to go astern which he promptly executed. He estimated that it took half a minute for the reversed screw to bite. Despite this prompt action by the *Mary*, at least two crew members on the *Normandy* said that as she came at them she was showing a white bow wave, in other words she had come at some speed.

There was a heated argument as to whether the *Mary* had had her masthead light up. Crew on the *Normandy* insisted that she did not, and that this delayed seeing her. Survivor AB Richard Bennett had been on the *Normandy*'s bridge and he asserted that all the men there had seen a red light ahead but no masthead light. Because of this they had assumed the approaching vessel was a yacht, and with the absence of any breeze they had also assumed that any sail vessel would be barely moving through the water. It is not clear how this affected the order to turn the ship, all the evidence indicating that she was turned immediately anyway. The *Normandy*'s helmsman, James Willis, confirmed an immediate turn and said that she had come round two or three points (23 to 34 degrees), the head coming round faster than the compass, before the collision. The evidence on the light was contradictory. The *Mary* carried paraffin lights, which needed to be trimmed every few hours. AB James English told the court that on the orders of Second Officer Andrews, who was responsible for the lights that watch, he had taken the masthead light down ten minutes before the collision, trimmed the wick, and hauled it up again a good five or six minutes before the crash. Seaman Dennis Sullivan confirmed this, adding that the light glass had been smoky, and needed cleaning. George Goodwin, second officer on the *Normandy*, said that when he got on board the *Mary* the masthead light was on the deck. George Griggs, first officer on the *Mary* then claimed that the light had been brought down by the collision; it was fastened by a line running to the bowsprit, and when this was carried away the light fell down. The arguments indicated the importance witnesses gave this piece of evidence in apportioning blame.

A fine Ouless painting of SS Normandy passing Corbière

Second Officer Andrews told the court that he had ordered the masthead light to be taken down and pricked up a few minutes before the impact. It was being hauled up again at the moment they saw the *Normandy*'s lights, and was then about 20 feet off the deck (it normally hung at 40 feet). James English was called again to explain the contradictions between his and Andrews's stories, and said that Andrews was lying.

There is a further dramatic issue connected to the light. T. W. Traill, a Board of Trade surveyor, then explained that masthead lights must show a beam twenty-two degrees either side of dead ahead. The *Mary*'s light was produced in court, and Traill asserted that after inspection he found the light was not doing this, and that he would not pass it for use on a passenger vessel.

Assessors Patteson, Harris and Hight then delivered judgment. In their view the blame lay solely with the *Normandy*. She had failed to take sufficient care crossing the main shipping lanes, and despite quick evasive action she had failed to slow or stop her engines. This should have been done the moment she entered the fog. They accepted that the *Mary*'s masthead light might not have been in position, but discount the relevance of this because she was clearly showing her red, port light and this was seen on the *Normandy*. The *London Times* called it a good judgment, but the *Jersey Times* and the *Hampshire Advertiser* called it thoroughly bad. Both journals made the point that Ockleford on the *Normandy* had sent at once for the captain on hitting the fog and had turned the moment the *Mary*'s light was seen. He had a few seconds to make his decisions, and had no time to stop the engines. In Jersey the view was that it was a terrible accident that no one could be directly blamed for, in Hampshire it was felt that the *Mary* was more at fault.

One Guernsey resident who took particular notice of the tragedy was Victor Hugo, who had travelled on the *Normandy* previously and met Captain Harvey. In 1869 government control of newspapers in France had been relaxed and many new publications started up. One of these was *Le Rappel*, actually named by Hugo ('recall, repeal'), and he was in the habit of sending regular impromptu reports from Guernsey for its readers. After the *Normandy*'s loss he wrote (in French):

I am oppressed as I write to you. There has been a catastrophe here. The island is in mourning, the flags at half-mast, the houses shut up. The captain died like a stoic. Three years ago I was on board his ship and the English fleet was at Sheerness for the Viceroy of Egypt and Queen Victoria. Some ladies who were on board the *Normandy* wished to see the fleet and begged me to express this desire. It was two hours out of our course, and I replied, 'But, ladies, a French ship would not do such a thing for me'. When Captain Harvey heard this he exclaimed, 'What a French ship will not do for Victor Hugo an English ship will', and he put up his helm and showed us the fleet. This amiable man was a hero. He saved the people he could and remained behind to perish.

Hugo then wrote a second letter to the *Guernsey Star* on 5 April:

Rich companies like the South Western should remember that human life is precious, and that if the *Normandy* had been equipped first with water-tight bulkheads; secondly with lifebelts for the shipwrecked; thirdly Silas appliances which light up at sea and which give clear vision in disaster; if these three conditions had been met probably nobody would have died.

(There was some puzzlement as to why no survivors had been found floating in the water after the ship went down, and a rather wild rumour that there had not been enough lifejackets.)

Hugo gave fifty francs to the relief fund, and went further, donating his personal lifebelt and lifebuoy (made for him by a Sunderland firm) for presentation to the islander with the most rescues to his name. This was to publicise the importance of belts and buoys, and to bring sea safety into the minds of everyone. The articles were duly presented to Captain Abraham Martin, and today are kept at Castle Cornet in Guernsey's Maritime Museum.

On Tuesday 22 March, five days after the disaster, a public meeting was held at the Lyric Hall, St Helier with the Bailiff present. Here it was agreed not only to open a relief fund but also to collect subscriptions for two memorials, one to Captain Harvey and the lost crew members, and one to Mr John Westaway, a Jerseyman drowned on the *Normandy* who had refused a seat in one of the boats to ensure that the women got away

first. The two memorials were duly set up in the Weighbridge area in March 1871, later being moved to Mount Bingham, above the harbour to the south of St Helier, where they can be seen today. Henry Harvey had been a member of the Ancient Order of Foresters, and his and the crew members' memorial bears the inscription of the Order. The monument is topped with a granite obelisk. Just to the left is John Westaway's fountain memorial. This has his name on a metal plaque, a representation of him, and above the stone circle of the fountain bowl is a fine bronze dolphin curving around an anchor.

The memorial erected to Captain Harvey and his crew, situated at the base of Mount Bingham

The *Waverley* (1873)

Fog was also the cause of the *Waverley*'s loss, though this time it was an early morning summer fog that quickly blew off to give a hot, sunny day. The *Waverley* was a two-cylinder paddle steamer, built at Glasgow in 1865, 593 tons gross, and 222 feet long with a top speed of 13 knots. She had been built for the Dublin service, but was purchased by the LSWR for use on the Southampton-Channel Islands route in 1868. Passengers spoke highly of her amenities and comfort, and she was noted for steadiness in rough seas.

The Waverley steaming across St Aubin's Bay, outward bound to Southampton

Just after midnight on Thursday, 5 June 1873, the *Waverley* left Southampton for the islands carrying about eighty passengers, cargo and the mail. The master that night was Captain Robert Mabb, and she carried a crew of thirty-one. The sea was calm and the weather fine, and passengers were congratulating each other on what seemed to be one of the best crossings of the year. They reached the Casquets at 8.10 a.m., and about a quarter of an hour later Mabb and the officers on the bridge saw a low bank of haze several miles ahead of them. This thickened as they approached, and within a short while the ship was enveloped in a dense fog which reduced visibility to a few hundred feet. Mabb immediately slowed the ship, put two men at the helm and two at the bow as lookouts, and began to sound the fog whistle. He then gave orders to stop, and cast the lead. This showed 'deep water'. Perceiving a slight thinning in the murk, he ordered the *Waverley* ahead at dead slow, and they proceeded for a while without incident on the south-westerly course which was intended to take them into the Little Russel channel for St Peter Port. All seemed to be proceeding satisfactorily when there was a sudden bump, a dreadful rasping at the keel, another bump, and the *Waverley* came to an abrupt stop, leaning over to port. She was jammed on the Platte Boue rock.

The Platte Boue is a particularly nasty obstruction which sticks three heads out of the water to the east of the recommended line into the Little Russel. It is an isolated peak with 60 feet of water all around it. It is particularly dangerous to ships coming down the Race to the east of Alderney, when it stands on the line towards Guernsey, but anything coming down from the Casquets should be able to leave it well to port. For some reason the *Waverley* had steamed or drifted much too far to the east. Mabb had not been helped by the fact that there was no marker on or near the rock.

The Waverley fast on the Platte Boue rocks from a painting by P. Ouless

The ship had sustained severe damage and water was coming fast into the forward compartments. A letter to the *Guernsey Star* on 10 June from 'C.H.W', a passenger, described how he had immediately gone below to wake his son who was sleeping in the fore state cabin; he managed to rouse him in time, but water was then beginning to cover the cabin floor. The three boats were immediately ordered out. The fog now began to thin, revealing the Grande Amfroque not far away, and Mabb ordered the boats to take the passengers there. The Grande Amfroque lies about three-quarters of a mile south-east of the Platte Boue, and is a substantial rock islet about 150 yards long, permanently above water and 55 feet high at its highest point. It is the most northerly of the substantial reefs that run out from the north of Herm, a group known to the locals as the 'Humps', and lies just over two miles north-east of Herm's Shell Beach point. On the Grande Amfroque were (and are) two substantial conical stone towers, one 11 metres (36 feet) high, the other 6 metres (20 feet), both with masts and the taller with a cage top.

Fortunately it was a fine day and the sea was calm with the usual fierce eddies around the islet much moderated, and the first group of passengers was duly transferred and landed without danger. One of the boats then set out to row the four miles to St Sampson's harbour to raise the alarm, and the other boats returned to the ship to take more passengers across. Those left on board were waiting anxiously, frightened that the ship would tip over before they could be rescued, and there was some panic when she heeled further over. She did not however slip off the rock, which would certainly have caused a loss of lives. The *Waverley*'s steam whistle was tied down to produce a continuous blast, though some survivors later claimed that no distress rockets were fired, which should have been another aid to rescue. Once all the passengers were landed on the Grande Amfroque a clergyman proposed a short impromptu service of thanksgiving, and this was held. The two remaining boats went back to the ship to recover the mail and as much luggage as they could. The task was made difficult by the rising water in the hull, and the fact that the ship was settling further down on the rock.

Before the third lifeboat could reach Guernsey the alarm was raised in St Peter Port. By 10 a.m. the fog had burnt off, and it was possible to see the wreck with telescopes. The signal stations at Fort George and Castle Cornet both indicated 'mail boat in distress', people began to assemble at the White Rock, and a telegram was sent to Jersey. The LSWR's passenger steamer *Brittany*, also a paddler, was about to depart from Guernsey for Southampton. She had been delayed nearly an hour by the large number of potato baskets she had loaded. The LSWR's local agent, Mr Spencer, immediately took a gang of workmen with him, boarded the *Brittany* and told the captain to head for the Amfroque, where they arrived about thirty minutes later, anchoring half a mile off. On the way up they met the *Waverley*'s lifeboat coming in, and took it in tow. The *Brittany*'s boats were then put over and rowed to the islet, and Spencer distributed fresh water in buckets to the passengers, together with brandy, sherry and captains' biscuits. It was now a fine summer's morning, and some of them were beginning to enjoy themselves.

The passengers were now transferred into the *Brittany*, which took them and the rescued mail back to St Peter Port, and were landed in the early afternoon much to the gratification of the large crowd which had gathered on the quayside. The *Brittany* then left for Southampton, calling at the rock on the way up the Little Russel to check the situation. Mabb and crewmen had remained out near the wreck, doing as much as possible to salvage luggage and cargo. At the 3 p.m. high tide the ship's bow was under water, the stern was lifted slightly in the air, and she was flooded for over half her length. In the course of the afternoon she split between the paddle box and the foremast, the two sections twisting in opposite directions, so that her funnel went one way and the foremast another (a painting of her in this condition by Philip Ouless can be seen in the Guernsey Maritime Museum). It was clear at this point that she was beyond salvage, and Mabb did little to stop the local boatmen, now getting aboard as the tide fell, from removing as much of value as they could find. The following day, Friday 6th, her stern swung round as the tide was rising, and shortly afterwards her two sections fell apart. The LSWR's senior manager had come over that morning from Southampton with the company's chief engineer, bringing a salvage team equipped with hydraulic pumps, but it was obvious that there was nothing they could do, and the wreck was officially abandoned. Despite being only eight years old and recently refitted, the vessel was uninsured, and estimates put the cost of her loss to the LSWR at over £40,000.

There was much discussion of the master's conduct. Some said that he had had no chance, and that he had done everything he possibly could in the circumstances. The opposing view was represented by an anonymous correspondent to the *Jersey Times* who maintained that if the alternatives in fog were to go slow ahead sounding the whistle, or anchoring, the latter was infinitely preferable since blowing the whistle 'did not frighten the rocks away'. The States of Guernsey had positioned a buoy at the Platte Boue in 1861, but it had been swept away seven times in seven years, and had not been replaced. The inquiry assessors completely exonerated Mabb, declaring him 'most cautious' and finding that the accident had not been occasioned by any failure on his part. In their view, had the buoy been replaced, the disaster might not have happened.

The *Havre* (1875)

Two years later the Platte Boue struck again. At 9.10 a.m. on Tuesday, 16 February 1875, the LSWR's passenger steamer *Havre* ran at full speed onto the rock. The extraordinary course set by the master was solely responsible, and one might almost say that on this occasion the rock was the innocent victim.

The *Havre* was also a paddle steamer, iron-hulled, three-cylinders, 387 tons, and 185 feet long, built at Blackwall in 1856, and since the loss of the *Normandy* she had become the LSWR's main boat to the islands. She left Southampton at fifteen minutes after midnight on the 16th with twenty-seven crew, sixty-five passengers, cargo and the mail. Her master was Captain Robert Long. The sun rose at 7.14 a.m. and at 7.30 Alderney was sighted, Long then setting a course to pass down the Ortac Channel between the island and the Casquets. The weather was good apart from a slight haze that restricted visibility to five or six miles, and there was a light breeze from the south-east.

The tide was ebbing down-Channel. At 8 a.m. they passed abreast of Ortac, leaving it about three-quarters of a mile to port, and Long then set the correct course of SSW1/2W for the Little Russel and St Peter Port. What went wrong during the next forty-five minutes is not clear. At about 8.45 Long saw, much to his surprise, that the two conical beacons of the Grande Amfroque, not far ahead, were half a point on the wrong (starboard) side. This meant that the ship was a good mile to the east of her correct line. Had she continued she would have left Herm to starboard (and, incidentally, had she done this she would probably have survived).

Long now ordered a hard turn to starboard on full power – 11 or 12 knots – to swing the ship in a circle and put her on a NW course. His intention was obviously to backtrack for a mile or so, then turn south-west back down the Little Russel to complete a figure 'S'. Three-quarters of a mile from the Grande Amfroque and north-west of it was the Platte Boue, still unmarked after the disaster with the *Waverley*. Moving in a northerly direction, the *Havre* hit it at full speed with a tremendous shock that threw passengers out of their bunks and tore a large section out of the hull.

One male passenger (his name was not given), a commercial traveller who made the crossing regularly, told the *Jersey Times* what he had seen. Near Alderney he had actually chatted to Captain Long on the deck, and been told they were making good time. A little later this gentleman was 'astonished' to see the Grande Amfroque to starboard – in his experience this was an 'extraordinary' position assuming that they were trying to get in to Guernsey. At this point, he insisted, it was not foggy, although there was a haze at some distance. The vessel was then turned 'completely around' to go back the way it had come. He then clearly saw surf breaking over the Platte Boue (which dries at lowest

The Havre, suffering the same fate as the Waverley, stranded on the Platte Boue reef

tide) and realised they were going to pass very close to it. He remarked to a companion that this was where the *Waverley* had struck two years previously, but he was not too concerned since he believed the captain knew his job. As he watched the rock, the ship altered course slightly to head straight for it, and a few minutes later struck violently. He heard the captain on the open bridge order her astern, and also heard the chief officer, also on the bridge, say, 'For God's sake, don't move her', and the captain replied, 'All right'. (This countermanded order almost certainly saved the passengers' lives; had she gone astern it is highly likely that she would have sunk at once in deep water.) The navigation requirements are the same today as they were then; to quote K. Adlard Coles (*Channel Harbours and Anchorages*): 'Note. Platte Boue (dries 1m8 LAT), 8 cables NNW of Grande Amfroque is the most northerly rock of the Herm group and the two Grande Amfroque towers in line lead on to it.' At the *Havre* inquiry this point about the two beacons was dealt with at length, and it was the assessors' view that by disregarding the need to keep them open of each other until after the Platte Boue was safely passed, Long had guaranteed disaster. The passenger witness claimed a second, small adjustment of course. This may have come about because Long thought at that point he had passed the rock, and could bring the beacons in line, although it is incredible that while the white water over the danger zone was plainly visible to a passenger no one on the bridge saw it.

The *Havre* had sustained major damage below the waterline and her engine room was flooded. Some passengers had been below in their cabins, and they now rushed on deck terrified by the massive impact. Some were partially dressed and some women were barefoot. Long ordered the three boats out, fired distress rockets and blew the ship's whistle. Luckily, the disaster had been seen by some quarrymen working at the north of Guernsey three miles away, and they immediately raised the alarm, getting a telegram sent to alert the harbourmaster at St Peter Port. The *Havre*'s boats were out very quickly, but there was some altercation among the passengers. On board were a number of soldiers, and a group of these were reported to have swung themselves over the ship's side, waiting to drop into the lifeboat as soon as it was launched before any of the women and children could get in. A retired military man, Colonel H. Travers of Jersey, then intervened angrily, telling the men he would knock overboard anyone who tried to go before the women. This apparently worked, and they desisted. One of the survivors, Nathaniel Driver, later wrote a letter to a newspaper describing this event, but a further letter from another, anonymous, correspondent claimed that the trouble had been caused by only two men, neither of them being soldiers. It was later claimed that in the confusion prior to abandoning the ship, some thieving had taken place of some passengers' personal possessions. One young girl refused to leave her father and get into the boat, but he gave her his watch and other personal effects and made her go without him.

Eventually all the passengers were put into the boats, and rowed in relays the three-quarters of a mile to the Grande Amfroque, no easy task given the speed of the tide. Here they were landed with some difficulty because of the swell. One elderly lady had been in a state of faint since leaving the *Havre*, and she had to be carried onto the rock. Access was made more difficult because it was nearing low tide, but everyone had been safely transferred by 11 a.m. Guernsey and Herm were clearly visible and there was no panic. One of the boats went back to the *Havre* to secure provisions, and loaves and cold meat were distributed to the marooned passengers. A collection was taken for the benefit of the crew.

By now the news was known in St Peter Port and had been telegraphed to Jersey, and a number of fishing boats were heading out to the wreck. There was much consternation and disbelief that this could happen again so soon after the *Waverley*'s loss. The LSWR's screw passenger steamer *Honfleur* was in Guernsey on her way from Jersey to Southampton when the news broke, and she now went out to the rocks, anchoring nearby and sending her boats across. A second evacuation in relays now took place, as the passengers were transferred to the *Honfleur*. One young boy missed his footing and fell into the water between the rock and the boat, but he was not badly injured. In all they had been about two hours on the rock in chilly conditions, many lacking outdoor clothes. Crew had managed to get the mail out of the ship, and this was put onto a local pilot boat, the *Flying Fish*, and carried into St Peter Port at about 12.30 p.m. Long and his officers stayed out near the wreck in a tug for the rest of the afternoon trying to get some of the luggage off, and the *Honfleur* returned to harbour, landing the passengers at the

White Rock at 3 p.m. As with the *Waverley*, a large crowd had gathered to witness their arrival.

As the tide rose to fill and then submerge the larger part of the vessel, it was clear that she was a write-off, and before the end of the day she had slewed right around on the rock pointing back the way she had come with her starboard paddle box under the water. In the evening boats went out to pick up some of the luggage that was floating in the water, and men from the tug *Rescue* got back on board and stripped out some of the fittings. Most of the cargo could not be salvaged, and the Keiller Company suffered a serious loss of fruit and sugar which was being transported to their marmalade and confectionery factory on Guernsey. There was a strong wind that night, and the ship split in two, her forepart going under the surface so that only the mast showed. A team of LSWR engineers and managers arrived next morning to assess salvage possibilities, but saw at once that there was nothing that could be done. In Guernsey rumours spread rapidly to the effect that while Long held a Board of Trade master's certificate, he did not have a pilot's licence for Guernsey and Jersey. Further, he had been in command of the *Courier* not long before, when she became disabled in the Channel on a journey from Cherbourg to Southampton, and went missing for several days. And further again, that not only had the *Havre*'s chief officer, Usher, been an AB on the *Normandy* when she was lost but he had also been chief officer on the *Waverley* when she hit the Platte Boue.

Arrived on shore Captain Long reported that there had been a sudden fog which had obliterated all the marks, and he had seen nothing until he caught a glimpse of Tautenay just before seeing the Amfroque. This claim was flatly contradicted by several passengers who maintained that visibility had been good, and four survivors later wrote a collective letter to the *Star* insisting that there had been no fog. Certainly conditions were good enough for the quarrymen to see as far as the rock and raise the alarm. For over a week the Guernsey papers were filled with discussion (some of it angry) regarding the weather conditions at the time and the extent to which Long was familiar with the Russel. In his defence, one correspondent maintained that the LSWR's policy of switching masters around the various routes was unfair to them.

The day after the wrecking the States of Guernsey met to consider the Platte Boue and what should be done about it. Since the buoy had last been carried away in 1868 there had been no mark at the rock. After two proposals had been put forward – to replace the buoy, or to blow the rock up – it was decided to proceed cautiously and set up a subcommittee to investigate further. The next day (the 18th) a letter was printed in the *Jersey Times* from 'RN' beginning, 'As the Guernsey authorities seem at a loss about deciding on a practicable method of marking this dangerous rock...' and going on to propose the anchoring of four buoys around it at the cardinal points, painted in variations of red and black horizontal and vertical stripes on a white background. Nothing was done.

At the inquiry, held at Greenwich on 2 and 4 March, it was pointed out that not only had Long previously saved the *Courier* in very difficult circumstances, but he had been rewarded by the Company for his efforts. But the assessors were unable to establish what had been going on between Ortac and the Grande Amfroque on the morning of the 16th. It was accepted that there might have been some light haze, but nothing worse. The ship's compasses were in good order, the master had been on the bridge, yet the ship had continued for a good ten miles seven degrees off course and this in a position where numerous visual marks were available. A fast ebbing tide will exert a strong pull towards the east in that area, but both master and chief officer were familiar with the approach channel and its conditions. The assessors found that although master and crew had acted promptly and professionally in saving the passengers, great neglect had been shown by the master in setting the course after the Casquets. Getting east of the Amfroque was inexcusable, and error had then been compounded by ignoring all the warnings about the need to keep the Amfroque beacons apart. Long's certificate was suspended for twelve months.

It is usual to report the wreck by saying that there was no loss of life. In fact one man died soon afterwards as a direct result of what he went through. On board was Colour-Sergeant Dawson of the 1-16th Regiment, just back from a long spell in India, travelling to Jersey. The exposure on the Grande Amfroque gave him a severe cold, and this coupled with nervous prostration from the wrecking led to complications, and he died on 22 February, six days later.*

---

* Was Elinor Glyn on board the *Havre*? The Jersey-born writer of sensational romance novels, femme fatale, mistress of Lord Curzon and Hollywood socialite, describes in her 1937 autobiography how in 1875, at the age of 11, she was returning from a visit to the mainland with her mother and sister when their boat was wrecked 'on the Casquets'. Waves pounded the sloping deck, distress rockets were fired without response, and it was some hours before the passengers were taken off by a tug from Guernsey, after which the wreck broke in two. No passenger steamer was lost on the Casquets in the 1870s, and the only disaster in 1875 was the loss of the *Havre*. Was this what the writer was describing – with some licence – over sixty years later?

The *Caledonia* (1881)

The *Caledonia* was a single screw, iron steamer of 566 tons gross, 195 feet long, built by Cunliffe and Dunlop of Port Glasgow in 1876. She was launched as the *Hogarth*, and for two years was used by the Aberdeen Steam Navigation Company. In June 1878 the LSWR chartered her for use on the Southampton to St Malo run, and in November of the same year they bought and renamed her. She continued to run to St Malo, but was also used regularly to the islands. Her loss just off St Helier on 19 February 1881 provides interesting evidence of the inadequecy of the navigation aids available to the late Victorian steamers.

The *Caledonia* left Southampton at half past midnight on the morning of Friday 18 February with twenty-three passengers, twenty-six crew and thirteen tons of cargo, and was due in at Jersey at noon. The master that night was Captain Thomas Lainson (later to command the *Stella*). There was an increasingly thick fog as they proceeded down Southampton Water, and Lainson decided to anchor off the Calshot light-ship until conditions improved. At 11.40 a.m. they got under way again, and after calling first at Sark, the *Caledonia* reached Guernsey at 9.40 p.m. Weather conditions had again deteriorated, and because of the fog and the problem with the tide at Jersey, Lainson remained at St Peter Port until 4.25 a.m. on the Saturday morning (the 19th). The *Caledonia* rounded the Corbiere at 5.55 a.m., and at 6.10 was passing Noirmont Point. Visibility was varying from poor to moderate, and it was still dark. At Noirmont rockets were fired to give warning that the ship was coming in, but possibly because of damp these failed to fly and merely exploded.

The tide was approaching half flood, and Lainson decided to take what was then called the western channel entrance to the harbour, passing between Elizabeth Castle breakwater, which projects out some distance due south, and the Oyster Rock, lying across the passage from the breakwater. At Noirmont he ordered a course E3/4S, to take him south of the breakwater one and a half miles away, from where a turn to NE could be made between breakwater and rock straight for the harbour entrance. The recommended course (which Lainson informed the inquiry he had taken on at least 170 previous occasions without incident) recommended that vessels maintain the E3/4S line until the white light on the Victoria pier came in line with the upper red light on Fort Regent above St Helier. With the lights together, the NE turn could be safely taken and held up to the pierhead (the 44-degree course on the modern Admiralty Chart) although the line just skims both the rock, covered at half tide, and the end of the breakwater.

The approach was made without slowing. Lainson saw the white pierhead light and made his turn. He conceded at the inquiry that he had not seen the upper, red light at the same time, but thought it might have been obscured in the mist. He next saw the castle breakwater, but realised it was very wide on the port side, and ordered first a turn, and then a hard turn to port to improve his angle towards the harbour. At this point the forward lookout called that he could see something ahead, a little on the starboard bow. Lainson on the bridge did not hear this properly, and he shouted down for clarification. The lookout repeated his warning, and at the same moment Lainson saw a beacon pole very close and fine to starboard. He signalled 'Stand by' and 'Half Speed' to the engine room, but there was insufficient time to slow and the ship hit the Oyster Rock with a force that stopped her in her tracks and cut a forty-foot gash in her hull.

The SS Caledonia fast aground on the Oyster reef, a quarter-mile south-west of St Helier harbour, Jersey

Water began to rush in. Three boats were got away quickly and all the passengers and crew put safely into them. There was no panic, and every effort was made to see that the women went into the boats first. Within ten minutes the ship's bow was nearly under. Captain Lainson was the last to leave, jumping down over the ship's stern into the water where he was picked up by a fishing boat. Within half an hour the *Caledonia* was completely submerged, swinging round and slipping off the rock into deeper water. Here she settled, her upper deck, masts and funnel left uncovered at low tide. The news was telegraphed to Southampton, and the *South-Western* under Captain George Allix immediately set sail with a party of company engineers and shipwrights to assess the salvage possibilities. Luggage, mail and some parcels were found floating near the wreck, and these were brought ashore. A diver went down the following day, and more mail bags were recovered. When these bags were cut open, a mess of water and pulped paper poured out, but surviving letters were dried by a number of large fires and delivered. On ensuing days, divers managed to get more of the cargo out, but the damage to the ship was such that salvage was not practical. Within days the hull began to break up, and it was clear that she was a total wreck. She was sold on 2 April for scrap to Mr G. De St Croix of Jersey, who raised her engine and boiler and removed her wooden deckhouse. The deckhouse was carted to a quarry at St Brelade, where it was used first as a shelter by quarrymen, and later – with additions – as a house for many years. A pitched tin roof was put on, and the walls clad in asbestos before being rendered and pebble-dashed.

The Caledonia's engine salvaged from the wreck, lying on the beach just outside St Helier harbour

A fierce argument about the adequacy of the lights and beacons around the harbour developed in the press. Another letter from 'RN' to the *Jersey Times* (assuming this was the same 'RN' who had written in about the *Havre* six years before) pointed out that the Oyster Rock was marked by nothing better than a broomstick, and that the character and reputation of a good master was now being destroyed 'because the guiding lights were not sufficiently strong to pierce the mist, and the mark on the rock, which can only be seen by daylight, was invisible till the ship was right upon it.' Others criticised the weakness of the red light on the top of the fort, claiming that it was powered by only two small gas burners.

The inquiry was held in London on 24 March before the Wreck Commissioner, Mr H.C. Rothery, and two assessors. Their conclusion was that Lainson, either by passing Noirmont Point too far to the south before taking his approach line, or by delaying his final turn for the harbour entrance too long, had got onto the wrong course through poor navigation. George Allix, Lainson's fellow master, gave evidence, and told the court that whereas a correct turn towards the harbour on a rising tide would help keep the vessel on line because of the north-east flow, any delay in the turn would encounter an adverse pull to the south-east, increasing the danger of striking the rock.

Lainson was found negligent on two counts – making the turn before he had both white and red lights visible, and not slowing the ship, and his master's certificate was suspended for three months. The assessors recommended that the Oyster should be marked by a bell buoy, but refused to condemn the upper light, only saying that it might be a bit weak, but they didn't feel the need to recommend its replacement. It is hard not to conclude that the aids around St Helier harbour at this time could scarcely be described as generous.

Little remains today of the *Caledonia* that is recognisable. The tides have left only scattered pieces of plating and shapeless metal debris on the bottom. Some isolated portholes in plating have been seen in recent years, but her site to the east of the Oyster is covered with a thick carpet of kelp, and it is necessary to dig down through this to see anything. The water is 10 metres deep at the position where she must have finally come to rest.

The remains of Caledonia's deckhouse in 2001

The *Brighton* (1887)

The loss of the *Brighton* off the north coast of Guernsey on the morning of 29 January 1887 played a significant part in committing the Great Western Railway (GWR) to the running of its own passenger steamers. When the railway reached Weymouth in 1857 it became obvious to the GWR that an integrated rail and steamer service to the islands had to be developed. Initially the Railway Act prevented the railway companies from owning or operating steamships, but in 1848 the London and South Western Railway (LSWR) had applied for and been given permission to run its own ships. Despite this the GWR did not make a similar application at this time, but encouraged the formation of an independent steamer company which would run the ships with its support. A group of Weymouth and island businessmen therefore came together,

and the Weymouth and Channel Islands Steam Packet Company was formed in 1857. The GWR held 25 per cent of the shares, and gave an annual subsidy of £2,000 to the company. Two paddle steamers, the *Aquila* and the *Cygnus*, were chartered, both three years old, and these began a successful service to the islands, linking to the boat train from Paddington. A year later, in 1858, the Steam Packet Company decided to add a Weymouth–Cherbourg service, and purchased the paddle steamer *Brighton* for this purpose. The *Brighton* had been built by the Palmer Brothers at Jarrow in 1857 and had been for a short time running between Jersey and Shoreham. She was 286 tons gross at launch (she had been modified to 316 tons by 1887), and was 193 feet long with two funnels.

The Cherbourg service with a weekly call at Alderney began with moderate success, but was soon losing money and in 1859 the route was suspended. The Steam Packet Company decided to cut its losses, and put the *Brighton* up for sale, but then changed its mind, and began to run the ship intermittently to the islands. During the 1870s she was used on a variety of routes but in the 1880s she became the principal link between Weymouth and Guernsey/Jersey. Between them the Weymouth and Channel Islands Steam Packet Company's ships managed to keep up a daily service to the islands during the summer seasons, but the Company was struggling to balance the books and was falling behind the LSWR's Southampton service with its new generation of screw steamers.

A rare early photograph of the Brighton laid alongside Albert Pier in St Helier harbour

The sinking of the *Brighton* was the result of thick fog; no lives were lost, but the loss of the ship put the Steam Packet Company – already under considerable financial pressure – into such serious straits that the GWR decided to step in and take over, something it had had the power to do since 1871 when it had applied for permission to run its own steamers. The Steam Packet Company struggled on for two more years, using the *Aquila* and chartering a replacement ship, the *Great Western*, another paddler, but in 1889 steps were taken to wind up the Company. In the final balance sheet presented to the shareholders, the *Brighton*'s loss is estimated at £3,122 in the debit column. In the same year the GWR assumed direct responsibility for its own ships between Weymouth and the islands. The immediate result was the updating of the Weymouth vessels to match the luxury service of the LSWR. The *Aquila* was sold and a new fleet of twin-screw steamers was ordered. The Packet Company was finally dissolved in 1891 and with it went the whole paddle steamer generation on the Channel Island route.

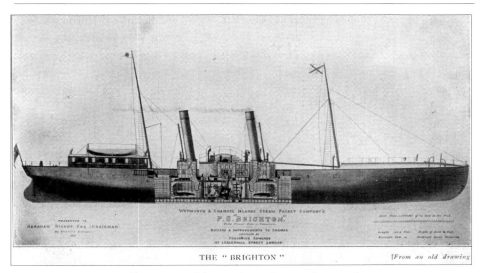

THE "BRIGHTON"   [*From an old drawing*]

A cutaway illustration of the Brighton showing her machinery spaces

The GWR paddlers made between 9 and 12 knots, and the crossing from Weymouth could take six to eight hours depending on how hard the ships were driven and whether the crossing was made by day or at night. On Friday 29 January the *Brighton* left Weymouth at 12.10 a.m., due in at Guernsey at 8 a.m. She carried twenty-three passengers, twenty-four crew, cargo, some mail and a coffin. In command was Captain Thomas Painter who had been master for five years and made the crossing many hundreds of times.

There was fog at Weymouth harbour, but as they passed along Portland Bill it cleared, and for a time Painter ran the ship at full speed. After a few miles – the point where he had the two main lights of the Bill end on – the fog thickened again, and he reduced to the 'half' speed of 8 knots (the *Brighton*'s top speed was 11 knots). From this point the fog remained dense and the vessel was kept at half speed all the way across, blowing her fog whistle and with extra lookouts on both sides. There was no incident during the crossing, and at 6.30 a.m. Painter ordered the log to be checked. This showed that the ship had run 48 miles – putting them just about level with the Casquets. They listened for the sound of surf on the rocks, but heard nothing, and another check on the log at around 6.42 showed a distance run of 50 miles, putting them just past the reef. Because the *Brighton* was somewhat antiquated (she was by now thirty years old) there was no device to count her engine revolutions, and Painter had only the log pulled along behind the vessel to tell him the distance travelled. He also had the sounding lead, but – as was later maintained at the inquiry – he made insufficient use of it.

Within a minute or two of the log check, and with visibility down to less than 50 yards, lookouts shouted that they could see rocks on the port side, and then all around the ship. Painter immediately ordered full astern, but before the way could be got off her, the *Brighton* ran head-on onto a large rock, driving a hole in the bow. Painter reversed the ship off, but she was already filling rapidly. Mr Thomas Dixon, a passenger, ran onto the deck from the saloon when he felt the crash, and asked a crewman if she was holed. The crewman's answer was yes, forward. Dixon then went quickly down to his cabin to recover some valuables, but was driven back by the power of the inrushing water. Three lifeboats were got out very quickly, and all the passengers and crew put into them. There were five women among the passengers and a small child, and it was estimated that within ten minutes of striking all the boats were safely away. Painter was the last to leave, dropping heavily into a boat in grim silence. About ten minutes later, twenty minutes after striking, the *Brighton*'s bow went under and her stern rose up to an angle of 45 degrees. Passengers in the boats reported a big explosion under water as a boiler blew up, her stern projected for a while and then she slid rapidly under and disappeared in a great swirl of foam. She was in over 100 feet of water.

Painter had no idea where he was. The inquiry established that he was at least ten miles ahead of where he thought he might be, and that the ship had actually been maintaining near full speed all the way across rather than the 8 knots he claimed. They were, in fact, just off the north-east of Guernsey, but it was not possible to say which rock she had hit. In the days that followed several possible candidates were put forward as the one that did the damage – one of the Brayes, the Platte Fougere, the Platte Boue and the Boufresse, but all assertions remained at the level of speculation. None of these put Painter far off his proper course, but the problem was that he had arrived at the danger zone before he was ready for it, either having been misled by a faulty log, or through an inability to gauge the real speed of the ship (the assessors expressed incredulity that a man with Painter's experience should have been unable to judge the difference between 8 and 10 knots over a period of several hours).

At first the boats did not know which way to go, and they drifted with the north-moving tide, but then a break in the

Richard Keen with the bridge telegraph recovered from the Brighton, and opposite a plate from the Weymouth and Channel Islands Steam Packet Company

fog revealed distant familiar shapes, and they realised where they were. Painter then ordered the boats to pull south against the current towards Guernsey. There was no way of reporting the accident to the shore. Someone at L'Ancresse later said that a ship's fog whistle had been heard at around 6 a.m., but there was no other evidence of the disaster. There was no light or fog warning on the Platte Fougère in 1887.

The tidal pull was strong, and they made very slow progress against it. Land was regularly glimpsed through the fog to the south-east – one passenger thought it was Sark, but it was probably Herm – and after about three hours the tide slackened and the fog thinned sufficiently for them to be able to see the coast at Bordeaux. They landed on the beach at Banque Imbert under the Vale Castle at around 10 a.m., where they were met by some local people and escorted to St Sampson's and the tram for St Peter Port. Some of the women survivors were in indoor clothes, and one man had no boots on, an indication of the rapidity with which they had been evacuated. No one had been lost, but all cargo, mail, crew possessions and passenger belongings had gone to the bottom with the ship. A Mr Wood, travelling to Jersey from Cardiff after several years abroad, had lost £500 in cash and bonds. A telegram was sent to Jersey, and this was stuck up in the Post Office window: 'Weymouth boat has struck rocks north of Guernsey, a fog prevailing. Vessel has gone down in deep water. Crew and passengers saved, not mails.'

The Steam Packet Company, never having had a disaster before and desperate to defend its reputation, did all it could to recover the mails, and the next day, Saturday 30th, a search was made of the supposed area of the sinking by boat at low tide. Nothing was seen. Over the next few days there were rumours that oil had been sighted off some rocks, and that the actual paddle boxes had been seen under the water near others, but there was insufficient justification for sending divers down. In fact the ship was too deep to be reached.

At the inquiry, which was held in London on 1 and 2 March, Painter maintained that in his view the ship had been at 'about' 8 knots the whole way across, but he was now willing to concede that they might have been moving somewhat in excess of half speed. Engineers Philip Elliott and John Tomkins also testified that the revolutions had been 23 per minute all night (giving half speed or less) but the assessors rejected this, dismissing the claim as being completely incompatible with the achieved crossing time. They pointed out that logs could be inaccurate and concentrated their criticism on the fact that the master had apparently not known the speed of his vessel. His course had been correct, with proper allowances made for tidal movement, but he had been too far ahead, preventing him from making the necessary changes in direction on the approach to the north of Guernsey. He was criticised for not using the lead to establish his position, and his certificate was suspended for six months.

On Saturday 5 February the *Weymouth Southern Times* carried an appeal on behalf of Annie Beale, a young woman who had been returning to service in Jersey on the *Brighton*. The daughter of a labourer, she had lost everything that she possessed in the world, and was penniless. The paper requested donations on her behalf.

The coffin being carried on board contained the mortal remains of a Miss Marechaux, going back to Jersey for burial. The coffin was enclosed in a stout packing case. Not a scrap of mail, or indeed any other important object apart from a bucket, some planks and a saloon seat surfaced from the ship, but a week later a packing case was seen floating under Essex Castle, Alderney by a fisherman. He towed it in to Longis Bay. The case was labelled for Mr J.R. Sinnatt, undertaker, Jersey, and on opening it the coffin with its nameplate was found. The case was hastily closed up again, and shipped first to Guernsey on the *Courier*, and then to Jersey where Miss Marechaux was finally laid to rest after her week at sea. None of the *Brighton's* crew expressed the least surprise at the disaster. To sail on a Friday with a coffin was asking for trouble.

For eighty years there was no sign or trace of the vessel until Richard Keen found it by accident in the early 1970s. He was approached by a local fisherman requesting help with a lost dredger and line which he had been using to dredge up scallops to the north of the island. Richard went out with him, and at the site dived in 45 metres of water. Visibility was good, and as he went down the line he saw a shadowy mass lying on the bottom. The first thing he recognised was a paddle wheel, then the shape of the long hull buried almost to the top in sand. By chance the dredger had hooked into the paddle wheel and the line had taken him straight down onto the ship.

He knew the story of the *Brighton* and was knowledgeable about her characteristics. Although she was nowhere near any of the rocks where she was claimed to have been holed, the dimensions of the wreck and its narrow beam convinced Richard that it was the *Brighton*, and this was confirmed when he found the bell. Her unpredictable position he attributes to the strong tidal pull at the time, and the fact that the paddle steamers went astern as fast as they went forward. She was in fact well north and east of any rocks. The survivors had watched her go down from their boats, and had probably underestimated the distance she drifted before going under.

Most of the hull is filled with sand (trapping whatever artefacts have not rotted) but on one visit Richard found a gigantic copper kettle sitting on top of a cast-iron stove, still somehow fixed in position. He lifted the kettle, which was extremely heavy, probably because of silt inside, and began to ascend. As he came up he began overbreathing, and for safety's sake he let the kettle go. Although he searched the area carefully on later visits, he never found it again.

On another dive he noticed a sizeable lump of concreted non-ferrous metal sticking up out of the sand on a cylindrical tube in the middle of the wreck. He cut through the tube with a hacksaw and tried to lift the lump with a rope, but it was very heavy, and in attempting to winch it up from the boat the line became entangled in the paddle wheel. At that time (1973) Richard was working with Henri Delauze, Richard Wharton and Mike Roger of Comex, looking for the *Victory* off the Casquets, and one day when the weather was bad and they were unable to get up to Alderney, Richard took them to dive on the *Brighton*. With the help of Henri Delauze, Richard moved his interesting lump a little away from the hull, and this time it was lifted successfully. Cleaning revealed that it was the ship's telegraph, of a kind Richard has not seen anywhere else. One of the earliest of steamship telegraphs, its solid shaft went directly down into the engine room from the open bridge, which was situated centrally between the two funnels with the paddle wheels on each side. The telegraph's glass was still intact, together with the side aperture for an oil lamp.

When John Ovenden dived on her in 1994, the outline of the hull could still be traced, although completely filled with sand. The two paddle wheels are in place, standing up above the sand on either side to over half their height, with the central bosses visible. The point of the bow is well defined, and a large square block between the wheels may be what remains of the boiler.

A painting of the Brighton

The *Ibex* (1897, 1900)

When the *Ibex* left St Helier for the last time on 14 April 1925 after thirty-four years' service to the islands, hundreds of people assembled at the quay for the farewell party. The ship was held in great affection, and her career had been highly colourful. She had broken the record for the Weymouth crossing, been wrecked twice (the second time spending six months under water), and had been involved on two different occasions in major collisions. She had contributed to the war effort by reporting a U-boat north-west of the Casquets on 30 November 1916, as a result of which UB19 was sunk the same day by the Q-ship *Penshurst*. Her activities were invariably hailed in press headlines of the '*Ibex* does it again' sort, and she had the modern equivalent of a fan club.

Captain Le Feuvre and officers aboard the Ibex

She was built by Laird Brothers of Birkenhead in 1891 for the GWR, to replace the *Brighton* generation of paddle steamers. She was twinscrewed with triple expansion engines, was capable of 18+ knots, and was to crown the new GWR fleet of *Lynx*, *Antelope* and *Gazelle* in their rivalry with the LSWR. She was 1161 tons gross, 265 feet long, schooner rigged, and her two funnels were painted red. She arrived in the islands on 5 September 1891 after trials at Milford, and on 7 September she made the return journey from Guernsey to Weymouth in the unprecedented time of three hours thirty-five minutes. On arrival she fired off celebratory rockets, much to the delight of the large crowd assembled to see her come in.

The Ibex hard aground, just off Portelet Bay, Jersey

Throughout the 1890s she was to play a key role in the unofficial racing that went on between the two companies on the Channel Island route. The GWR, with sailings from Weymouth, had the shortest sea crossing, but it was farther from London to Weymouth by rail than to Southampton. The LSWR had a fast rail link to Waterloo, but a longer sea journey. Throughout the decade the two companies fought an intense advertising battle, each claiming to offer the faster service. Boats were scheduled to arrive at Guernsey at the same time, and interested parties included not just the passengers but the shareholders and those who laid bets at the quayside as to which ship would be in first. From Guernsey the race was on for Jersey, where the second boat to arrive had to wait for the first to enter the narrow harbour, swing and dock, and could even fail to make the harbour at all if the tide was falling. Passengers and their luggage had then to be landed in small boats, which cost the company money. This racing contributed to the *Stella* disaster of 1899, after which the companies saw sense and ran alternate days and nights, pooling ticket receipts, but it took the death of over eighty *Stella* passengers to accomplish this. Two years prior to the 1899 disaster there was an accident involving the *Ibex* and the *Frederica* off Jersey which should have caused the companies to moderate their competitive aggression. Unfortunately, the warnings were not heeded.

At 2.55 a.m. on Friday, 16 April 1897 (Good Friday), the *Ibex* left Weymouth for the islands under the command of Captain John Le Feuvre. She was forty-five minutes late getting away because the boat train had been delayed by extra Easter trains on the line. On board were 309 passengers and a crew of thirty-four. The weather was good, and the sea condition slight. She arrived at Guernsey at 7.24 a.m., landed 109 passengers, took on sixty-one, and then left for Jersey at 8 a.m. By chance the LSWR boat, the *Frederica* under Captain George Allix, had also been delayed at Southampton, and she came into Guernsey fifteen minutes after the *Ibex*. This gap had narrowed to only ten minutes by the time the *Frederica* set off for Jersey behind her. As the two ships proceeded south, the *Frederica* was clearly catching up. The *Ibex* was running with her iron, winter propellers which actually gave her slightly increased speed, but by the Corbière the *Frederica* had narrowed the mile-odd gap to a few ships' lengths. Asked at the official Board of Trade Inquiry how he had reacted to this, Le Feuvre said that he hadn't taken 'much notice' of the LSWR boat behind him, although it was obvious to passengers that both ships were being driven flat out. The time was now just about 9.10 a.m., and the tide condition was exactly calculated to encourage maximum mischief. The tide was falling and St Helier harbour would remain open until only 9.45 a.m. After that it would have dried out too far for anything to enter. The ship that arrived first would therefore be able to take its time docking, and delay the other just long enough to make entry impossible.

As the ships rounded the Corbière, the *Ibex* was to the south on the 'outside' and the *Frederica* was gaining ground on the inside of the turn. Just off the Corbière to the south-west is the Noirmontaise Rock, and the usual route was for ships to pass outside this. It was not unknown, however, for masters to sometimes take a tighter course and pass inside the rock, and in choosing to do this on this particular morning Le Feuvre was not performing any risky manoeuvre. What made it dangerous was the fact that the *Frederica* was just behind on his port quarter, running exactly parallel with him, and that the *Ibex* was now going to cut across her bow. Le Feuvre gave two blasts of his whistle and ordered the *Ibex* to port, further tightening his turn in order to pass inside the rock.

According to him he then walked across to the other side of the bridge, the port side, and was horrified to see the *Frederica* almost on top of him aimed directly amidships at an angle of 45 degrees. At the inquiry the Board of Trade solicitor Mansel Jones asked him:

'How did she [the *Frederica*] appear then?
Le Feuvre: 'She was coming straight towards me, about midships on my vessel.'
Mansel Jones: 'Did that make you anxious at all?'
Le Feuvre: 'Yes, it did. I called out, "Good God, she is running into me", and gave the order to port sharp [go to starboard] hoping to clear the Noirmontaise and get outside again.'

At this point the *Ibex*, with no space left to steam clear, hit the rock. Le Feuvre estimates that the *Frederica* then passed him no more than 40 feet away. The time was about 9.19 or 9.20 a.m. The *Ibex* was badly gashed below the waterline on both sides of her hull, one rent being over 30 feet long, and seven of her eight propeller blades were shattered. As she passed on over the rock water was already pouring into her, and passengers were called on deck and told to put on life jackets (one man managed to put on four). Water had not penetrated the engine room and the chief engineer was able to keep the ship going sufficiently on part of one propeller to pass Le Fret Point and ground her in Portelet Bay. Here the six boats were lowered and all the passengers were landed safely on the beach, other boats being provided by the *Frederica,* which had stopped and anchored. The news was passed to St Helier by a telegram from the keeper of the Corbiere lighthouse.

In the afternoon on a rising tide there was an attempt to tow the *Ibex* to St Helier using first her sister ship the *Gazelle* and then the tug *Assistance*. They managed to get her out of the bay and off Noirmont Point, when the cables broke. She then drifted west back past the Corbière, anchoring off the point at about 7 p.m. and remaining there overnight. Next day, the Saturday, a stronger cable was used and this time she was brought successfully behind St Aubin's Fort where her holes were patched with timber and cement. The *Assistance* then took her in to St Helier harbour on the Easter Sunday. No lives had been lost, but she had suffered substantial damage which took her to Barrow for major repairs, and she was out of commission for three months until July.

The interesting feature of the inquiry, held in London on five days between 20 and 28 May, was the aggressive way in which Le Feuvre defended his actions, revealing that there was not only rivalry between the masters of the two companies but also bad feeling. Mr J. Aspinall, QC (for the LSWR) asked him why he initially starboarded his helm (went to port).

> *Le Feuvre:* 'I had a right to starboard my helm.'
> *Aspinall:* 'Had you, with the *Frederica* in that position?'
> *Le Feuvre:* 'I had nothing to do with the *Frederica*.'
> *Aspinall:* 'You had a right, having a vessel a little on your port quarter, two or three ships' lengths off, to go right across her bows?'
> *Le Feuvre:* 'I had nothing to do with the *Frederica*.'
> *Aspinall:* 'What did you expect him to do?'
> *Le Feuvre:* 'To do what he liked.'
> *Aspinall:* 'But what did you expect him to do?'
> *Le Feuvre:* 'To get out of my way, or not interfere with me.'
> *Aspinall:* 'And were you not trying to cut him out to get across his head so as to prevent him getting into harbour first?'
> *Le Feuvre:* 'No, there was nothing about that. I did not try to cut him out.'

Pressed, Le Feuvre admitted that he expected the *Frederica* to slow and give way (this of course would have lost her so much time that she would have had no chance of making the tide at the harbour). It was again put to him that he deliberately cut across *Frederica* to stop her. He denied this and also denied any suggestion that racing was taking place. If the *Ibex* was hurrying it was 'against time and tide', and had nothing to do with any other vessel. John D'Aubert, keeper at the Corbière lighthouse, then gave evidence, saying that he had never seen the *Ibex* go inside the Noirmontaise before.

The Ibex beached in St Aubin's Bay, Jersey

Captain George Allix of the *Frederica* also denied any racing, and said that his intention all along had been to go outside the Noirmontaise, and he believed that this had been the *Ibex*'s original intention also. He then found the *Ibex* just ahead on his starboard side obstructing his way round to the south, so that he had to change course himself to go inside the rock: 'I was forced to go inside. I had no alternative.' Asked why he did not slow and go astern of *Ibex* he replied that 'he did not want to'. He maintained that the *Ibex* was never in danger from the *Frederica*, and that there was ample room for the two to have maintained a parallel course inside the rock once he had made his (forced) turn.

There was a conflict of evidence about the position of the ships when Allix turned the *Frederica* to port, and about where he was when the *Ibex* struck. He told the assessors that he had moved to port in plenty of time to give room for both ships to pass inside the rock, and that he was slightly ahead of *Ibex* when she struck. Some passenger witnesses gave a different version of events, saying that the *Frederica* was within 50 feet of *Ibex*

Passengers viewing with interest the close encounter with the Frederica

at the point of striking, and definitely behind her. If true, this would indicate a more aggressive stance on Allix's part, bearing down on Le Feuvre until the last moment. Other witnesses maintained that *Ibex* moved some distance along her adjusted starboard course before striking. In view of the proximity of the ships at the point of impact (no one disputed a distance of 40–50 feet) it appears that Allix held on even after Le Feuvre had lost his nerve and turned away. A battle of wills was going on between the masters, a battle in which the several hundred passengers were incidental.

Legal counsel summed up predictably. Aspinall for the LSWR asserted that racing was not taking place, the *Frederica* never posed any danger to the *Ibex*, and that the navigation of the *Ibex* was so bad that she was going to hit the rock anyway. Sir Walter Phillimore for the GWR maintained that the *Frederica* threatened the *Ibex* and forced her

into error. After deliberation the assessors (R.H.B. Marsham, Captain Ward and Captain Ronaldson) concluded that Le Feuvre had not been justified in making his first turn to port so close to the rocks and with the *Frederica* just behind him; that he gave insufficient warning of the turn, blowing his whistle at the same time as he put the helm down; and that he was wrong to turn back to starboard to try to get outside the rock, since there had been room for both ships to pass inside. They duly found that Le Feuvre had not navigated his vessel properly, while Allix had, and suspended Le Feuvre's certificate for six months.

The assessors swallowed the plea that the two ships were racing the tide and not each other, and did not see the need to require the companies to stagger their arrival times in the islands, which simply encouraged continued foolhardy rivalry. Had they been more courageous a judgment might have been made with conditions that prevented further racing and saved the *Stella* two years later.

The Ibex after her repair from the first sinking

Le Feuvre may have made a genuine mistake. The nature of his defensive answers, however, suggests that he tried it on and then panicked. It appears that he blew a warning whistle and ordered the helm down without looking out for the ship behind. He knew the *Frederica* was close by and catching him up, because many of his passengers had spent the hour from Guernsey on deck cheering the two ships on. As leading vessel he had the right of manoeuvre, but to make the course change without being aware of the exact position of the other ship indicates carelessness, or, worse, bloody-mindedness. Seeing the *Ibex* move across his path, Allix held on long enough to frighten Le Feuvre into backing off, by which time there was no room left for the *Ibex* to clear the hazard.

The first officer on board the *Ibex* that day was John Baudins, a Jerseyman. Three years later, as her master, he was to cause the ship more grief, this time off Guernsey. No other vessel was involved, the weather was good, the sea calm, and the disaster was solely the result of strange goings on between the master and the helmsman.

As before, the *Ibex* was making the night crossing. At 2.30 a.m. on the morning of Friday, 5 January 1900, she left Weymouth with thirty-four passengers, mail, 60 tons of cargo and some livestock. The crossing was easy and uneventful and at 5.39 a.m. she was passing the Casquets. At 5.50 the master took charge on the bridge for the last forty-five minutes, intending to see the ship into St Peter Port. At this point they were about four miles north of the Brayes, the extensive and very dangerous reef with some rocks permanently above water just north-east of Guernsey. Baudins told the inquiry that at night he normally aimed to leave the reef half a mile to starboard, a little less during day crossings. In 1900 there was no light on any of the rocks, only a pole and beacon on the most easterly of the group, the Platte Fougere (the lighthouse there was not built until 1909). Sunrise was at 8.07 and it was dark throughout the ensuing events. At 6.13, while still north of the island, Baudins saw the first of the leading lights into the harbour, the Belvedere light, set up on a hill to the south of St Peter Port. Two minutes later he picked up the second leading light on the Castle Pier. Both lights were ahead, slightly to starboard and at this stage the higher Belvedere light was open to the west of the pierhead light. The recommended course for all approaching vessels (and the course laid down in the 'Sailing Directions') was for approaching ships to maintain a southerly course until the lights were on with each other, at which point a turn to the south-west could be made, keeping the lights together to the harbour entrance.

For reasons which were not made entirely clear even at the inquiry, Baudins did not trust the Belvedere light. In his view it was 'very deceptive, particularly at six or seven in the morning' and 'he had no faith in the light and did not use it.' When he had first started coming to the islands, the light was not in existence, and he was of the opinion that it had been put up only to help ships avoid the Platte Boue rather than give aid into the harbour. Because of this, it was his usual practice when entering the Little Russel to take a bearing on the Casquet light behind him. In order to do this, he would order the ship to port for a short time so that he could see the Casquets from the bridge, and then resume the original southerly course. Until now this slightly unorthodox approach had worked without incident. Baudins had been with the GWR since 1896, and had held a master's certificate since 1890. He was a valued employee of the company, and had received rapid promotion.

The man at the wheel was AB Thomas Woodland, who had come on duty at 5.45 a.m. He was in the small wooden wheelhouse at the back of the open bridge. At 6.16 Baudins ordered him to go to port while he took his bearing on the Casquets, fifteen miles astern, and after about two minutes told him to turn back to starboard and resume the original course. While on the port turn, Baudins had opened St Peter Port sufficiently to see the red light at the entrance to the Old Harbour. Woodland went to starboard, and then found that the ship was running away too far to the south-west. Without waiting for an order he turned back slightly to port. Baudins now acted to correct the south-westerly drift, and ordered Woodland to come to port. There was no immediate response from the ship, either because Woodland had misunderstood the order, or thought he had already anticipated it, or because the ship was sluggish. Baudins shouted at Woodland, who put the wheel down hard. Baudins then sent AB Francis Randall to ask John Hamon, the AB who usually took the wheel at the Brayes, to come up and see the ship into the harbour. By now not only had the red light on the Old Harbour disappeared, but the Belvedere and pierhead lights were on the port, wrong side. Baudins shouted at Woodland, 'Do you intend to starboard [go to port] or not?' Baudins then strode to the wheelhouse, put his head through the window, and yelled at Woodland, 'Where the - are you going?' Woodland replied, 'Helm is to starboard.' 'Well, hard a-starboard then,' Baudins ordered. Seeing the worsening position of the leading lights he moved quickly back to the telegraph to stop the engines, and at that moment saw the beacon on the Platte Fougere 'fly past' close by. There was a jolt, a grinding noise at the keel, and the vessel shook violently as the *Ibex* struck the southern end of the rock, opening a long gash in her starboard side. It was 6.25 a.m. give or take a minute.

117. JERSEY — S. S. Ibex

The Ibex leaving St Helier harbour

At the inquiry Second Officer William Mulholland, who had been on the bridge, asserted that the ship was badly off course for at least one-and-a-half to two minutes. By badly off course he meant 40 degrees too far to the west. During this time she had not been slowed from the 12 knots she was travelling. Questions were asked about the ship's steering mechanisms, and Joseph White, the quartermaster, told the assessors that the wheel chains had a tendency to slacken and had to be tightened every fortnight. The last check had been a week before. Other crew members said that the ship was not markedly slow to respond to the wheel, and the assessors decided that this was not a significant contributing factor. There was discussion as to whether Woodland had misinterpreted south-south-west with south-west by west on the compass, a difference of three points or 34 degrees. It was also asked whether the tide had pushed her the wrong way, but at that time the tidal stream was north–south along her intended course.

The Platte Fougere rock usually stood well above water, but with the tide particularly high that morning it was a few feet under. The *Ibex* was badly damaged below the waterline, and the forward stoke hold and engine room were filling. Passengers were being fetched on deck and given lifebelts. Many of them were already dressed because they knew they would soon be in harbour, but some of the Jersey passengers had to be roused from their bunks. The ship was still under way and Baudins telegraphed for full speed ahead, ordering Woodland to turn south-east for Herm in the hope that she would stay above water long enough for him to beach her on the north of the island. He then found that Woodland had left the wheelhouse (he later said that he had gone to assist with the passengers). Baudins now tried to steer the ship himself using the screws. Passengers described the strange sensation as the ship ploughed forward with

her bow beginning to go under. In the engine room the chief, second and third engineers and three stokers stayed put long enough to stop and start the engines as ordered, but the ship was sinking fast and the steam pressure was falling rapidly. When the water reached their waists they abandoned the engine room.

By now Baudins had changed his mind and turned south-west hoping to get near St Sampson's harbour, but before he could cover any sort of distance the *Ibex* came to a halt and began sinking by the head. She was between Roustel and the Gant Rock, north-east of the Vale Castle. It was 6.37. Ironically, after having zig-zagged left-right left-right for over fifteen minutes she came to rest a touch north of the correct line into St Peter Port

Captain Baudins of the Ibex

The *Ibex* carried two lifeboats and three cutters, and it would have been possible for all the passengers to go comfortably in two of the boats. There were also over 600 lifebelts of the cork corset variety on board. As the ship headed for Herm the boats were swung out. Once she came to rest, three boats were launched, the starboard and port lifeboats and the starboard cutter, and the women and the few children were got away first. One of the passengers, Miss Gertrude Hay, said that there was some confusion once the boats were in the water, the crew members not seeming to know which way to go. Both John Hill, the chief steward, and Joseph Jukes, after-cabin steward, went through the ship ensuring that no one was left behind. Hill then told Baudins that the ship was empty, and Baudins himself called out loudly three or four times asking if anyone was still on board before taking to the starboard cutter himself as the last to leave at 6.42. The bow was then completely under, and the stern deck was level with the water.

As the boat pulled away, the crewman Francis (Jim) Randall appeared on the tilting deck calling out for help. Baudins shouted at him to climb one of the masts while they put back for him, but Randall ran to the stern and climbed the jackstaff, the ship sinking underneath him. Baudins then ordered the first officer, John Burnand, to go to Randall's assistance in the port lifeboat. As the boat came near to Randall he was clinging to the flag staff about four feet above the water, obviously terrified and shouting that he couldn't swim. The tide was running fast, and Burnand had great trouble getting close and holding a position. Several times his boat was swept away, and there was a danger of being struck by the submerged deck of the *Ibex*, which was lifting and falling in the swell. A second lifeboat then came to give assistance, but the two boats collided, and with the danger of one or both tipping over, it withdrew.

Someone in Burnand's boat managed to touch Randall with an oar, urging him to jump into the water and grab hold of it. Randall, seemingly irrational, refused. The tide then swung the lifeboat away again. When it got back into position Randall was seen in the water being carried off, and shortly afterwards he went under. Burnand's boat was then taken in tow by a pilot cutter, and taken in to St Sampson's harbour where Baudins had preceded them in his boat. The starboard lifeboat was making its way into St Peter Port.

Shortly after 7 a.m. the deputy harbourmaster at St Sampson's was roused from his bed to take charge of the landed survivors, including four small children. Passengers were sent to the Victoria Hotel and on the tram to Gardner's Royal Hotel in town. Some passengers, anxious to go on to Jersey, chartered the tug *Assistance* to take them down. On the quay at St Sampson's the enormity of what had happened must have come home to Baudins; when Randall's death was reported to him he tore the gold stripes off his uniform sleeves, although one passenger witness, a Mr Dupré, said that this was not done in a 'dramatic' way, and the motive might have been a wish to avoid public recognition.

The Ibex beached in St Peter Port harbour for temporary repairs

The *Guernsey Evening Press* that day was puzzled. 'It is inexplicable that in calm weather, with all the leading lights shining clearly, and at high water, there being no fog, this fine ship should have been run to her destruction. We think a good deal of explanation is necessary.' The paper also reported that Mr Alfred James of the Vauxbelets, Guernsey, had been on board, and that this was his third shipwreck in two years. Previously he had escaped from the *Stella* (where the LSWR listed him among the drowned) and from the liner *Paris* when it had gone onto the Manacles. He was none the worse for his ordeal and told the reporter his story with much enthusiasm.

The *Ibex* was in about 40 feet of water, and the tops of her masts and funnels were still visible at high tide. Divers arrived from Plymouth on Saturday 6th, but the sea was too rough for them to go down. They tried again on Sunday, and this time one diver got as far as the mail room, but he was unable to get inside to recover any of the mail bags. Cabin furniture was floating near the wreck, and also the carcass of a dead cow (the livestock being carried). The sea continued rough, and by now the funnels had gone but the ship had not shifted her position on the rocky bottom. Over the next week, more mail was recovered by the divers, and two baskets of parcels were found floating in the sea by a fisherman. In all, the divers managed to recover thirteen of the forty-four bags the ship had been carrying. What had not been pulped was dried out and delivered. The GWR had already issued a warning to would-be looters, but as most of the ship was under water it was not possible to get inside her.

A week later a grim discovery was made as the divers moved further back through the ship. The body of a young man with a rug wrapped round his legs was found inside the stern saloon. This was George de St Croix, a Royal Navy rating, who had been going home to Jersey on leave. He had apparently slept through the collision and become trapped as the water rose to the ceiling in his compartment. At the inquiry Joseph Jukes maintained that he had been into the saloon, but saw only rugs on the seats. It is possible that St Croix was lying concealed under some of these asleep. When he failed to return to Whale Island, Portsmouth, at the required time, he was posted AWOL and enquiries made at Jersey as to his whereabouts.

The inquiry was held in the first week of February 1900, and when asked why he had altered course to get the Casquets bearing, Baudins replied that he had to do this because the funnels were in the way. He was then asked why he hadn't taken the bearing from the stern of the ship without altering course (the *Ibex* had three compasses). He replied that he didn't want to leave the bridge, and that he wasn't happy sending other officers to take this bearing for him. Asked several times why he felt he needed to consult the Casquets light anyway when the Guernsey leading lights were clear, near and sufficient for everyone else entering St Peter Port at night, his answer became positively eccentric: 'Because the lights were only just on the bow. It is not practicable to navigate with a light only on the bow.' (In fact he was looking at two lights, but of course paid little regard to one of them as being 'deceptive'.) It is clear from Baudins's testimony that he regarded Woodland as the sole cause of the disaster, and this view was taken by the GWR's barrister. The assessors, however, thought otherwise. They agreed that the helmsman had let the ship fall off too far to the west, but not through any carelessness. What they did find unacceptable was the use of the bridge compass to take the Casquets bearing, and in view of this found that the vessel 'was not navigated with proper and seamanlike care.' This put the whole blame on the master. They suspended Baudins's certificate for six months, but he promptly resigned from the company, apparently feeling that he had been victimised.

The possibility of raising the ship was discussed from the outset, and the Northern Salvage Company of Hamburg sent representatives to the island the following week. Their initial estimate was a cost in the region of £8,000. The *Ibex* lay in the main channel into both harbours, and represented a significant danger to other vessels. Despite this, the speed of the tides at her position and the need for the salvage team to have good weather meant that any attempt to move her was abandoned until the spring. Red lights were put on her, and all shipping was warned.

On 5 May, with tide and weather right, preparatory work began. As the team was able to work only at neaps it was not until 9 July that an attempt was made to lift her with cables under her hull and support vessels on either side. Attempts failed on the 9th, and again on the 20th (when a cable broke), but on 21 July she was raised off the seabed and towed into St Peter Port where she was left on the bottom in the pool.

Large numbers of islanders went to see her, and there was competition for souvenir pieces of the seaweed which had grown over her in the six months. A gang of GWR workmen began to scrape the weed off and empty her of sand. Strange objects came to light – three dead pet dogs, an empty parrot cage, boxes of oranges, and the workmen spoke of an unpleasant stench below decks. A packet of diamonds was recovered, much to the relief of the owner, and more mail emerged. The *Guernsey Press* reporter wrote:

> The appearance of the *Ibex* is most weird. Everywhere is seaweed, sand and water. Inside can be seen doorways without doors, water washing in and out of empty bunks, and small articles floating from side to side ... on the deck rails are bent and broken.

Her holes were patched, the water pumped out, and after two failed attempts she was floated and towed to St Sampson's harbour on 31 July all flags flying. Here she was given more substantial repairs and then taken to the yard at Birkenhead. Her salvage eventually cost nearer £15,000 than £8,000. At Birkenhead she was restored to a working condition, with an extended bridge deck, and she was back in the islands for the Easter of the following year.

TBD *Viper* (1901)

The wrecking of Torpedo Boat Destroyer (TBD) *Viper* off Alderney on 3 August 1901 in thick fog ended the short career of the Royal Navy's fastest and most technically advanced Torpedo Boat Destroyer. Because they were the first warships in the world to be powered by turbines, *Viper* and her sister ship *Cobra* were experimental prototypes. In 1894 Charles, later Sir Charles, Parsons had fitted turbines to a small yacht called the *Turbinia*, and after modifications got 34 knots out of her. The Royal Navy did not at first take this seriously, until Parsons demonstrated what turbines could do at the Spithead Review of 1897 when he left the navy's fastest ships standing. The navy then decided to trial two turbine-drive torpedo-carrying destroyers, and the *Viper* was duly launched on 6 September 1899. Her hull was built by Hawthorne, Leslie and Co, and her engines were made by the Parsons factory at Wallsend on Tyne. She was 210 feet long with 345 tons displacement, and officially capable of 31 knots. At her trials she achieved 35.5 knots (41 mph) and once commissioned reached 37 knots. These speeds for a destroyer-size vessel were astonishing. She had four turbines driving four propeller shafts, each shaft with two manganese bronze propellers on it, set one behind the other.

HMS Viper

The high power of the turbine engine came from the fact that the steam acted directly on the propeller shaft. In conventional engines the shaft is driven by pistons and cranks

13. DESTROYERS AT ALDERNEY. JUNE 1906.

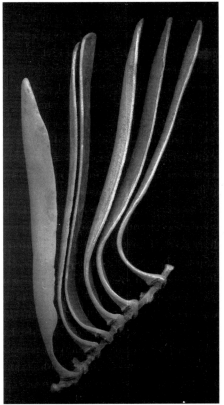

Sir Charles Parsons together with some surviving turbine blades from the Viper

moving in steam cylinders. In the turbine the propeller shaft is turned by fastening several collars of slanted blades around one end and driving the steam through them to make them – and the shaft – spin, or, to be more precise, a sequence of large flywheels is fixed along the shaft, each wheel having many small angled blades set around its rim like petals round a flower. A typical arrangement in the early turbine warships was to have two high pressure turbines driving two propeller shafts, and two at low pressure to drive two others for slower speeds or reverse. The *Viper's* two outer shafts were for forward propulsion, the two centre for going astern. Her engines used 250 pounds per square inch steam pressure to get 1050 revolutions per minute, driving shaft wheels set with thousands of phosphor-bronze blades around their rims. Total wheel and blade diameters were 29.5 inches in the high pressure turbines, and 44 inches in the low pressure. The high spin rate was controlled by a system of gears. The advantages of the turbine were not only greatly increased speeds, but also a need for fewer boilers, fewer working parts, and – in theory – a saving on coal at high speeds. The later turbine vessels did show considerable fuel economy, but the *Viper* was notorious for her high consumption, using a massive 6 tons an hour at 22 knots. This explains the fact that on the day she struck she was carrying sixty-eight crew, thirty-four of whom were listed as stokers. This heavy coal consumption was actually restricting her operational range, and it was taking thirty stokers working flat out to maintain her for any length of time at above 30 knots. Both *Viper* and *Cobra* were lost in accidents; shortly after *Viper* came to grief off Alderney, the *Cobra* broke up off Cromer in the North Sea with loss of life. Speed was not the cause of the disaster in either case, and after 1905 with turbine marine engines satisfactorily modified and proved, the Royal Navy built their ships with turbines as standard.

The *Viper* was – appropriately – a rather sinister looking ship. Long and low, she had three large, squat funnels, with two huge cowled ventilators between them. The short forecastle ending in a vertical bow was covered over with curved plating, and the high, open bridge was set almost on the bow. There was one stumpy mast rising just behind the bridge and in front of the funnels. Photographs exist of her at speed, showing a superb bow wave. She carried five six-pounders and one twelve-pounder gun, and two torpedoes with two spares. Her hull was made of nickel steel.

During the week commencing 29 July 1901 the Royal Navy staged the most extensive peacetime manoeuvres ever held in the English Channel. Over 150 large ships were involved, including battleships, cruisers and destroyers, together with numerous support vessels, and *The Times* carried extensive reports each day on the progress of the mock battle. The *Evening News* commented: 'At the present moment one of the greatest fleets ever collected off the treacherous coasts of the Channel Islands is manoeuvring', and *The Globe* called the exercises 'the most interesting and exciting which have ever taken place'. Tactics and weapons were tested, and the experiment was tried of painting

*Torpedo Boat Destroyer
entering St Helier
harbour in 1901*

some of the ships black to find out whether this made them harder to see (it didn't). Fleet 'B', under Rear-Admiral Sir Gerard Noel in *Revenge*, with thirty-two destroyers and ten torpedo boats, was ordered to defend the Channel Islands and their trade. Fleet 'X', under Vice-Admiral K.Wilson in *Majestic*, with twenty-eight destroyers and ten torpedo boats, was ordered to attack the islands and all the ships belonging to them. The cross-Channel railway boats were included in the games, and were subject to 'attack' by 'X' fleet. At one point the cargo carrier *Gazelle* was captured by a destroyer on her way from Guernsey to Weymouth with a load of fruit (capture was effected by the aggressor taking up a position one mile astern of the victim, then overhauling and circling her) and the *Ibex* was also attacked, but managed to escape with her superior speed. The action extended as far west as the Scillies, and civilian yachtsmen wrote letters to the newspapers commenting on what they perceived as bias (or not) on the part of the umpires who were charged with deciding who had been captured or sunk and by whom. A photograph taken at the time and reproduced in Coysh and Toms's *Guernsey Through the Lens* (1978) shows fourteen Royal Navy vessels anchored in Braye Bay during the week of the manoeuvres.

HMS Viper

On Thursday, 1 August, part of Fleet 'B', including HMS *Viper*, was blockading a section of Fleet 'X' based at Alderney. A detachment from the main Fleet 'X' was sent to the island to raise the blockade, and when the 'B' Fleet saw the superior 'X' numbers coming down on them, they turned and fled down the Swinge, pursued by 'X' torpedo boats and destroyers. In this pursuit *Viper* and *Bullfinch* were 'captured', and one of the pursuing 'X' torpedo boats, TB81, struck the submerged part of the Alderney breakwater and was sunk in reality. The umpires declared that the *Viper*'s penalty was to be out of the game for forty-eight hours, and she was sent back to Portland.

Two days later, on Saturday, 3 August, the *Viper* re-entered the exercise and was sent from Portland to reconnoitre Alderney and Guernsey to determine the latest position of 'X' Fleet in their waters and return with the information that evening. After crossing the Channel and sighting the Casquets, the *Viper* was caught in dense fog. The captain, Lieutenant William Speke RN, steered what he believed were various prudent courses, but navigational errors and the combination of thick fog and tide rip was too much for him, and at 5.25 p.m. the *Viper* went onto the Renonquet Rock, just north-west of Burhou. She suffered major damage and within hours she had broken in half and was a total wreck.

Renonquet Rock today. Opposite top right, the same view at the time of the Viper's loss

The Renonquet is a rock islet, nine metres high. Extensive ledges spread out from its base, and it is part of a complicated, partly submerged reef half the size of Alderney,

*Present-day underwater views
of the Viper site*

lying a mile and a half across the Swinge. It includes Burhou, Little Burhou, the Great
Nannel and Verte-Tete. There are passages through this mass, but they are tortuous and
the tide sweeps through at anything between 5 and 9 knots. *The Channel Pilot* advises
extreme caution: 'Owing to the very great strength of the tidal streams which often set
directly onto and across the numerous reefs and drying rocks, passage through these
channels is extremely dangerous and should not be attempted without local knowledge.'
Not only did Speke and his officers lack local knowledge, but their general knowledge
appears to have been shaky as well. The *Viper* should never have been anywhere near
this danger zone. The destroyer struck with a force that took off a spur of rock the size
of a waggon, toppling it into the sea, and one local visitor who went out to the site a few
days later declared the granite to be cut 'clean and spank' as if by a stonemason. Needless
to say, huge rents were made in the ship below the waterline, and the damage to the hull
was so great that within twelve hours she split in half. Speke described what happened
next in his report:

After the ship struck, it being impossible to work her out by means of the port screws and the tide setting her strongly onto the rocks, my first endeavour was to get out a bower anchor on the port bow and the stream anchor on the port quarter to keep her firm from drifting further on. While this was being done, water was reported making in the foremost stokehold and soon after in the engine room. Then the stream anchor carried away and the ship swung with her stern inshore. As soon as the anchors were out an attempt was made to get the collision mats out abreast the engine room and stokehold, but it was found of no use as the bottom lines were at once chafed through and the mats being small it was impossible to get them properly placed. About 6.15 – the engine room and both stokeholds being full of water, the foremost compartments rapidly filling and the ship bumping very heavily on the rocks – considering it impossible to keep her afloat if she drifted into deep water with the turn of the tide, also taking into consideration the danger of crowded boats after dark with a strong tide running, I ordered all the boats to be got out and provisioned.

Recovery of the Viper wreckage on the Renonquet Rock

During this time the *Viper* had been sending up distress rockets and firing her guns, but the fog was still too thick to see or be seen from Alderney and no one appeared to hear her, or at least not for some time. Speke had no idea how close he was to the island.

The starboard propellers had been smashed in the impact, and when the anchor line gave way the *Viper's* stern swung round hard against the rock, causing further damage. The pumps were activated, but the rising water put the fires out, and steam pressure to drive the pumps was lost. The stokers stayed at their posts until the water was up to their waists. The three boats left at 6.45 p.m., and began to make their way north up the Little Swinge on the north-west side of Burhou. At this time the fog began to clear, and Alfred Gaudion, the Alderney postmaster, saw the wreck from the top of his house. He immediately phoned the Fort Albert signal station, which in turn signalled the cruiser *Thames* (captain A. Clarke) which was lying just inside the harbour. *Thames* raised the alarm and the Alderney pilot cutter *Volage* put out, together with the destroyer *Mermaid* and two cutters from the Thames. As they went out they met the *Viper's* boats coming in, struggling with the tide, and some men were transferred into the *Volage* while the rest were towed into the harbour. There were no accidents, and everyone was taken off safely including the ship's two kittens.

The next day, Sunday 4th, Captain Frederick Morgan of HMS *Latona* went out on the *Volage* to the wreck to prepare a report for the Commander-in-Chief in Portsmouth. By this time the *Viper* was broken clean in two, split between numbers three and four boilers. The 100-foot stern section was upside down, so that her rudder and four propeller shafts were exposed to the sky. The two ends of this section were lying on rock, but it was unsupported in the middle, so that cracks were beginning to appear midway. The forward section of the ship was partially submerged and lying a short distance away, upright, but pointing outwards at an angle of 90 degrees to the stern part.

In his report Captain Morgan informed Portsmouth that it would be too difficult to get the engines out, since this would mean cutting into the hull and rigging shears to lift them, and by the time these had been set up, the rising tide would force them to be taken down again. He also described the extreme difficulty of getting large salvage boats anywhere near the spot and more or less indicated that she should be written off.

On Monday 5th the Admiralty put out a very brief press release. 'HMS Destroyer *Viper* grounded on the Renonquet Rock, near Alderney, during a fog on Saturday evening, and has, it is feared, become a total wreck. No lives were lost.'

Men from HMS *Thames* and two navy divers, Albert Lake and William Stacey, then began work to recover her guns and torpedoes, going out every day until the 6th, when men from the *Latona* took over. Eventually four guns were retrieved – three six-pounders and the twelve-pounder. One of the six-pounders was still in position underneath the upturned stern section, and the twelve-pounder had been shed at the collision and was lying 30 yards away in 3 fathoms of water. A fourth six-pounder was visible to the divers at the bottom of a deep and very narrow underwater gully, but was considered to be in too dangerous a position to retrieve. They could work only at low tides and were greatly hindered by the speed of the current as it raced through the channels. One of the torpedo tubes, with a torpedo in it, was lying in 2 fathoms close to what was left of the ship, and this was also recovered, together with the two anchors. All this was done in small boats, pulling the heavy objects out of the water by hand, whilst fighting against the current, and trying to stay steady with warps to the rock. Warheads, gyroscopes and confidential books were also recovered. Most of the *Viper's* crew were taken back to Portsmouth on Sunday 4th on the *Albatross* and *Conquest*, but Speke, Chief Engineer Charles Hill, and William Westbrook, the gunner, stayed behind to help with the salvaging. Captain Morgan particularly commended the efforts of Speke and one of his own officers from the *Latona*, Ernest Taylor, in the work. This may have helped Speke at his court martial.

Morgan went out again on the 7th, and found that the stern section had sagged in the middle. On 9 August the *Guernsey Evening Press* carried a report by an Alderney correspondent who had also been out to the wreck. It appeared to him 'as if she had been cut through sharply and swiftly with a giant's knife' straight up and down. The exposed underside of the stern section was peppered with holes, some so large that the internal red-painted ribs and white bulkheads could be seen. Where not holed, the hull was full of dints 'like a battered Guernsey can'.

Given the impossibility of a thorough salvage, and given her experimental specifications, it was then decided to blow her up. On Saturday, 17 August, navy demolition men from HMS *Vernon* and *Australia*, using the tug *Seahorse*, put two big charges under her hull, but were driven off by the tide before they could wire them. Charges were then fired on the morning of Sunday 18th, and again in the evening, and again early on the morning of the 19th. These were detonated at high tide. Each charge lifted a plume of water 80 feet high, and these were much appreciated by the many Alderney residents who came out to watch, although some complained at the violent shaking of their windows. On Saturday and Sunday the demolition men had to stay out on the rock overnight where they survived with an ingenious stew made of seagull and bacon bits. In all over 2,000 pounds of gun cotton were used in the form of sixteen-pound canisters placed under parts of the hull. Two-and-a-half pound primers were connected by line to a battery several hundred yards away. The first explosions threw the boilers and steam tubes into the sea in large chunks, together with pieces of shattered turbine. The Admiralty seemed to want total dismemberment, because an attempt was also made to cut the stern section into pieces by laying gun cotton hoses across it. The leader of the team was Lieutenant Pound of the Torpedo School of Instruction, and the work involved divers going into the hull to place explosives under water.

On 31 August, HMS *Raven* reported on what was left at the scene, describing boiler and bulkhead debris visible on the rocks at lowest tide, but advising that there was no need to proceed any further with these since 'they were not likely to be meddled with.' The *Viper's* remains were then sold to a salvage yard in Southampton for £100. Some of her metal was lifted, but some was left and remains in situ today.

Speke and his crew were court-martialled at Portsmouth on 16 August, and had the dubious privilege of a court held on board HMS *Victory*. The president was Captain E.G. Shortland RN of the *Narcissus*. Speke's version of events had already been submitted in a report written immediately after the disaster, and he now offered a sketch map showing the course of the *Viper* from 4 p.m. to the striking.

Left: Salvage crew at work on the remains of the Viper
Above: Tread plate once stepped upon by Lt Speke and the crew of the Viper

According to his account, the *Viper* had left Portland at 2 p.m. on the 3rd with orders to reconnoitre the waters around Alderney and Guernsey and return to base the same evening. He crossed the Channel at 20 knots on a S 3 degrees E heading, and at 4.15 saw a destroyer to starboard. He altered course a few degrees to the west for a few minutes to get a better look at her, then seeing that she was 'hostile' he resumed his original heading and cleared for action. He thought visibility was then about four miles in the haze, with no horizon. At 4.30 he sighted the Casquets, in his estimate about two miles away to the SW – he didn't take a bearing – and altered course to the east to avoid the destroyer and make towards Alderney harbour. He then decided to pass north of the island, and altered course to E by N to ensure that he cleared it. The destroyer was still in sight, so at 4.40 he altered course again to N 60 degrees E, and on this heading soon lost her. He admitted to the court that his main preoccupation throughout this time had been with the destroyer rather than with his own position. At 4.50 the fog closed in and became thick. At 4.55 he turned SSE, still doing 20 knots, aiming to go down the Race which he believed was now open on his starboard side in order to proceed to Guernsey. At 5.10, with visibility down to a few hundred yards, he slowed to 10 knots, realised that his mission could not be accomplished that day, and turned NE intending to wait in open water until the fog cleared, or if it did not, to return to Portland. At 5.23 rocks were seen to starboard, and he ordered a hard turn to port. More rocks appeared dead ahead, and he first stopped the engines, then went ahead on starboard with port reversed to tighten the turn. At 5.25 the *Viper* struck a substantial rock at a speed – in his estimate – of 8 knots.

Given the *Viper*'s final position on the Renonquet, the sketch map Speke submitted to the court based on these courses was incomprehensible. It showed the ship travelling eastwards well to the north of Alderney, turning briefly SE down the Race, then heading NE away towards France. At no point do the courses shown come within two miles of the Renonquet, and at 5.25 p.m. the ship is depicted as being on the other side of Alderney, seven miles from the rock, and heading away from the island for the Cherbourg Peninsula. Lieutenants Dannreuther of HMS *Ariadne* and Grant of *Intrepid* had been asked by the court to prepare charts based on Speke's claimed courses, and their attempts to make sense of his bearings were submitted. They did this very thoroughly, offering three versions in different colours, one calculating by dead reckoning, one taking magnetic variation into account, one allowing for magnetic variation and tidal pull. Since they had only Speke's data to go on, their versions are equally incomprehensible, differing only very slightly from Speke's and putting the *Viper* far away from the Renonquet at 5.25.

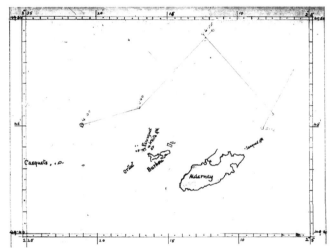

Lt Speke's chart showing his imagined track prior to striking

The assessors came at these discrepancies obliquely. They questioned AB Isaac Lee, who had been at the helm from 4 p.m. onwards. Lee appeared to be suffering from severe memory loss, and at first could not remember any of the courses he was ordered to steer. Pressed, he admitted that E, N 60 E, and SSE were all there at some point, but he couldn't remember the order in which they came. Various crew members were then asked if it was the Casquets that was seen at 4.30, or some other rock. All confirmed that it was the Casquets, but one can see that the assessors were trying to explain the strange courses by establishing an incorrect starting point.

Speke was then asked why the ship's log contained details of a completely different set of courses, and why the log hadn't been signed. Speke immediately disclaimed all responsibility for the log after 4 p.m., saying it was written up by Sub-Lieutenant Kenneth Mackenzie Grieve, and that it contained details that 'did not correspond to his orders'. All he had done was to 'scribble a little in' just after they struck.

Grieve was called, and some odd exchanges took place. He was not the officer of the watch, but decided to write the log up the next day from memory 'for no especial reason'. He was not asked to do this. He had not seen the compass, or questioned the helmsman, only heard Speke's orders on the bridge and entered the courses as he remembered them; 'knowing that they were not quite correct' he didn't sign the entries. He added that the courses in the log must be seen as 'very approximate'.

He was asked why two courses entered in the log were westerly, and differ by eight and sixteen points (90 and 180 degrees) from those submitted by Speke. Grieve's reply is odd to say the least; 'It must be my mistake. I looked at the chart and put down W instead of E in the standard course column.'

These exchanges make it very difficult to determine what was going on. Speke's alleged courses put him seven miles away from the Renonquet at the time of striking, so can be discounted. But there is no proof that Grieve's courses were correct either, and it is not possible to tell whether his motives were to help Speke with a post-strike tidying up and filling in, or to expose his errors. When the court martial papers were later sent to the Royal Navy hydrographer, so that he could comment on any navigational issues, he noted that in his view a number of erasures had been made in the log for 3 August. The facts were that the *Viper* did hit the Renonquet at about 5.25, and when she did so she was heading north-east.

It was put to Grieve that the SSE course 'was purely imaginary on your part', which elicited the response: 'Not altogether'. He added that he had seen the captain 'laying off' a course that looked like that on the chart with the parallel rulers (the chart had not survived, and Speke was no doubt wishing that the log hadn't either). In fact taking a SSW course instead of SSE might just explain what happened – bringing the *Viper* back down west of the Burhou-Renonquet group before turning NE into the rock, but Speke insisted he was looking to go down the Race, and it is all guesswork.

The court discovered other problems. The *Viper* had no log spinner out, and was using only engine revolutions to estimate distance travelled through the water. The lead was not used to check depths and Speke had seriously underestimated the speeds of the currents (he admitted he had been to Alderney only once before). There was a discussion as to the reliability of various navy publications on the nature of the Alderney tides, none of which appeared to be completely accurate, but it seems not to have occurred to the navy to call on local knowledge. Despite thick fog from 5 p.m. no one on board had heard the fog siren at the Casquets – a fact which had confirmed Speke in his belief that he was at least six miles from the lighthouse at all times (the Renonquet is just under four miles from the light).

In mitigation Speke drew the attention of the court to his preoccupation with the enemy destroyer at the point where he began to go east, and offered the justification that 'he considered it his duty to take more risk whilst employed on important detached service than he would have been justified in taking under normal circumstances'.

At the end of the day the court delivered its findings: (a) a proper bearing on the Casquets should have been taken when first sighted; the fact that this was not done put all subsequent calculations into error and the courses submitted by the captain 'cannot be relied on' (b) insufficient allowance was made for the strength of the currents (c) soundings were not taken, and should have been (d) but the nature of the ship's orders and mission 'necessitated taking unusual risks'.

Speke was found guilty of negligence and reprimanded, but not dismissed from the service. The court noted his exemplary work during the attempted salvage. All other crew members were exonerated, but when the Commander-in-Chief in Portsmouth later forwarded all the relevant papers to the Admiralty he included a covering note in which he declared Grieve's insertion of 'guesswork courses' into the log to be 'reprehensible', and their Lordships' displeasure was later conveyed to him formally.

After the court martial the papers were also sent to the navy hydrographer who again tried to work out the actual courses of the *Viper*, using all the information on tide movement and speed available to him. The tide was ebbing down-Channel as the *Viper* crossed, it was low tide at Alderney at 2.52 p.m. – one day after the high spring – and she struck near half flood. The hydrographer's calculations come to a surprising conclusion: in his view when the *Viper* sighted the Casquets she was nearer twelve than two miles off. He checked the log of the destroyer which the *Viper* saw – the *Spitfire* – which indicates that *Spitfire* saw *Viper* well north of the reef, considerably more than two miles from it, although no exact distance is given. The *Viper*'s reported speed crossing the Channel tends to give credence to this; on the other hand at least four members of her crew questioned at the court martial put the distance to the Casquets as between two and three miles.

The hydrographer is critical of Dannreuther and Grant for accepting Speke's starting point just north of the Casquets, from which all the errors stem, but his own versions of the course are no more helpful, and fail to get the ship anywhere near the Renonquet. In desperation he manages in one version to do this, but only by having the ship go through the middle of Burhou. His conclusion is that the cause of the accident 'was owing entirely to the neglect of the ordinary principles of navigation'. No accurate record was kept of the courses steered and no attempt was made to check the assumed distance from the Casquets using a simple elevation.

The other casualty of the war games fared better. After striking the submerged part of the Alderney breakwater on Thursday 1 August, torpedo boat T81 of 'X' fleet went to the bottom leaving her upper deck exposed at the lowest tides. Divers were called in and they reported that she was holed near the engine room but that the rest of her hull was sound. The navy put lighters either side of her with slings under her hull fore and aft, patched her, pumped her out, and managed to raise her on the 12th. She was towed to the New Jetty, patched further, and then towed to Portsmouth.

In its leader for 6 August the *Guernsey Evening Press* was highly critical of the navy's apparent inadequate knowledge of the Channel Island sea hazards, and on Saturday the 10th the *London Times* carried an extensive post-mortem on the success of the naval manoeuvres covering an entire page. This included the comment:

'The waters surrounding the Channel Islands are notoriously beset with perils. They are studded in all directions with rocks and reefs visible and submerged, and these are washed by some of the heaviest tides and most furious currents to be found within the four seas…it may well be a question whether they are not too treacherous for the evolutions of such very frail vessels as torpedo craft.'

Above: Underwater view of Viper's resting place with Fred Shaw and the wheel

Below: Recovered nameplate

Right: Fred Shaw

The paper then puts in a good word for Speke, suggesting that he should not be blamed for being placed in extremely difficult circumstances.

The remains of the *Viper* were visited by French divers in the 1930s, and she was then left untouched until 1967 when Fred Shaw, Peter Oselton and Don Longdon of the Seasalter Company of Alderney began diving regularly at the low springs to recover pieces of her metal fragments for scrap. The rights to the remains had originally been bought by an Alderney fisherman, John Quinain (Senior), who then sold them to Shaw, Oselton and Louis Jean. The fragments mostly lay in ten metres of water, and fishermen had reported seeing light reflecting off metal on the seabed. Fred and his partners dived regularly on the site for four years and recovered four tons of scrap which they sold to a dealer in Portsmouth. They also found the ship's second bronze torpedo tube with the torpedo still in it, wedged in the rocks, and informed the Royal Navy who sent a diving team over to the island to blow it up. This team then found two more torpedoes – the *Viper* had been carrying both her spares – and these were blown up as well. Other small items have been raised over the years – portholes, a lantern, the ship's whistle, a small nameplate, cutlery, the ship's wheel with much of the wood preserved, and turbine blades. These blades, shaped like old-fashioned razors, were scattered singly and in clumps over a wide area when the ship was first blown up. Blade pieces have been found in the nests of cormorants along the Alderney cliffs, the birds being attracted by their glitter under water.

The area is extremely dangerous for diving, and presents even experienced locals with major challenges. Most of what is left of the ship lies in a number of connected deep rock gullies full of weed, with the tide streaming through at 8 knots. Diving is only possible at slack water, and an added complication comes from the fact that the time of slack and almanac low tide time do not always coincide. On one occasion Fred and Peter were working at the bottom of a gully when a crowbar they were using to prise out a lump of bronze slipped, smashing Peter's face mask. He made for the surface, lost his direction, and was whipped away in the current between the rocks. Luckily Fred was able to catch him and get him to the surface, badly bruised. The Royal Navy divers also had difficulties at the site, suffering injuries and loss of some of their equipment in the fierce currents. On another occasion Fred and Peter were anchored just off the rock with a load of scrap in their boat. The combination of weight and tide speed snapped their anchor chain and they were swept down through a gully like a mill race. There

is still a quantity of ammunition lying down there, and recent dives (May 2000) have revealed coal from the ship's bunkers still recognisable on the bottom.

No 4 boiler test plate,
dated April 29th 1899

The *Liverpool* (1902)

Of all the numerous photographs taken of ships that have come to grief around the islands, few can match the spectacular image of the four-masted *Liverpool*, lying level and upright on the rocks just beyond Fort Homeaux Florains on the north-east of Alderney, where she ran aground on 25 February 1902. While the *Viper*'s turbines represented the future for marine propulsion, sailing ships were still working in significant numbers at the beginning of the century. At that time the *Liverpool* was the largest sailing vessel in the world, built of steel with metal spars, 3,396 tons gross and 334 feet long. She was ship-rigged, carrying squared sail yards on all four masts (as opposed to barquentine-rigged, where yacht-type sails were carried on the fourth mast). Built in 1888–89 by Russell and Company at Port Glasgow, she was owned by R. W. Leyland of Liverpool, and she was bound from Antwerp for San Francisco with a 6,000-ton cargo that made her a floating cross between Fortnum and Mason and a royal dockyard. She carried sardines, flour, cognac, wines, whisky, liqueurs, gin, claret, sherry, mineral waters, vinegar, mustard, olive oil, curry powder, chow (a Chinese condiment), caraway seed, preserves and vegetables. She also had substantial quantities of marble, cement, glass, silk, soap, wrought and sheet iron, coke, candles, sulphur, rope, sheep dip, steel girders, whitelead, naphthaline, clay crucibles, iron bottles for quicksilver, and sumac. Most of this cargo was recovered after the stranding. Some of it was auctioned in Guernsey, some of it was shipped back to the mainland, and some of it mysteriously disappeared into the corners and byways of Alderney. The *Liverpool* was a windfall that islanders still talk about fondly today.

She left Antwerp on 23 February with a crew of thirty-five. The master was Captain Owen Lewis, who had been with the company for fifteen years. Having passed through the Straits of Dover, he dropped his pilot at 1 a.m. on the 24th near the Varne lightship, and at 3 a.m. passed Beachy Head, bearing NNE, about nineteen miles distant. The wind was then SSE, very light, and setting full sail to catch every bit of breeze he took a WSW course at about 4 or 4.5 knots. By 8 p.m. the Barfleur light was in view on a bearing S by W1/2S, and Lewis estimated that he was sixteen to eighteen miles off the point. The light was still in sight at midnight, bearing SSE, again at an estimated distance of sixteen miles.

The wind was now decreasing, and the *Liverpool* was crawling along at no more than 2 knots. Lewis had difficulty reading the ship's speed from the log, which was known to be unreliable at anything under 4 knots. He lost the Barfleur light at 1 a.m. in mist, and soon after that a thick fog began to come down. The wind had shifted to ESE, and was very light. At 3.30 a.m. Lewis took soundings, and got no bottom at 60 fathoms. When he checked the chart it was seen that no such depth existed where he estimated the ship to be. At 4 a.m., calculating that they had covered about seven miles since midnight, he adjusted the ship's course a point from west to west by north to ensure safe passage past the tip of the Cherbourg Peninsula. He took soundings again at 6 a.m., and got 40 fathoms on rock, which now agreed with his estimate of the ship's position. At 8 a.m. he got 36 fathoms, and again adjusted the course one point westward to give what he estimated would be a clear line along a co-ordinate passing through Prawl Point on the south Devon coast. The fog was now very dense and it was not possible to see the length of the ship.

The Liverpool shortly after grounding on the rocks by Fort Homeaux Florains

The sounding at 10 a.m., 35 fathoms on rock, again confirmed that the ship was apparently proceeding properly. Lewis held the course, blowing the foghorn at regular intervals, and trying his best with every available sail to improve the 3-4 knot speed. As he was giving orders for the noon sounding to be taken, the lookout yelled back that he could see breakers ahead. Lewis instantly ordered the ship's helm to be put up, but she didn't respond, and a few minutes later with all sails set she ran quietly onto the rocks. The tide, a high spring, was up, but had been running out for about an hour.

Lifebelts were handed out on board, but there was no necessity to abandon the ship at that stage, and an inspection was made of the damage. As the tide fell the vessel was put under increasing strain, and some ominous cracking was heard from the deck area by the mainmast. At this point the captain ordered one of the boats away with crew and crew belongings, and shortly afterwards a second boat was launched to travel the short distance to the unsubmerged part of the point. Seeing that the ship remained upright and stable, one boat then put back, and the captain and some of the crew went back on board, trying to rescue some of the transportable cargo. They worked all day, and were only driven off in the evening when the rising tide threatened them. The captain was the last to leave, on board the Alderney cutter *Volage*. The only casualty had been one man who slipped during the day and broke his ankle. Local folklore maintains that some of the crew went straight into St Anne's where they got spectacularly drunk, but this story may have become mixed up with another, verifiable event, in which some of the hands decided to sample a number of the casques of spirits which had been offloaded.

Nearby, the 24-year-old John Godfray had been working in Mannez Quarry that morning with a mate, George Sharp. Through a brief gap in the fog they had earlier seen a sailing ship moving towards the north of the island. Interviewed in 1955 about his memories of the event, John recalled that the wind had been so slight, he had assumed she was being carried by the tide. He had thought her position strange, but then the fog had blotted everything out again. At this time there was no light or fog warning at Quesnard (the lighthouse was not built until 1912). At midday he heard voices coming from the point. He went down to the beach, but the fog was too thick to see anything, and the tide was still over the causeway out to the fort. He and George then unmoored a boat and pulled out to the end of the rocks where they found the *Liverpool* stuck fast. Someone shouted down to them from the deck, asking if they were near the Casquets. Godfray climbed on board, where he found the crew dazed and incredulous, and told Lewis where he was. The master was still hopeful at this stage that she could be floated off on the next tide, but inspection then showed how badly she was holed, and on hearing the sounds of distressed and splitting timbers the decision was made to take to the boats. By 2 p.m. the fog had cleared and a large crowd had gathered, and Lewis rather unwisely asked for help unloading the cargo, which was being taken in small boats and landed to the west at Vau Trembliers below Fort Corblets. The *Liverpool* had gone aground with fore, main and mizzen upper and lower sails, topgallants and jibs set, and many islanders reported the same impression as they looked north-east across the island towards her; it looked to them as if 'an immense whitewashed house' was towering over the hill.

The ship was lying with her head pointing west on a gently shelving, uneven rock bottom. She was 100 yards from the shore proper, and as the tide receded it was possible to reach her on foot. At low tide she was dry from stem to mainmast, but the rising tide filled her and put twelve feet of water over her stern. The inrush of water from the tide was such that on the second day her hatches burst, and much cargo came out and floated around. On hearing of the stranding, the Liverpool Salvage Association immediately sent their representative over, and his initial reaction was optimistic, believing that she

could be got off. This underestimated the big tidal rise and fall, the speed of the currents, and her exposed position, all of which made any work on her extremely difficult. By 1 March a salvage crew from the Neptune Salvage Company of Stockholm on board the tug *Helios*, sent from Southampton, were expressing serious doubts about the possibility of saving her, and on days of bad weather it was not possible to get on board her at all. Special Constables were sworn in to guard the ship and to keep a tally as the cargo was landed, and permission was given to work on her on Sundays. The *Guernsey Evening Press* reported that within days much of the cement, mustard, salt and soap left inside her was ruined. Each high tide caused some of the cargo to float in the holds, and when the water receded the casks and cases wedged together to form platforms with spaces underneath, making it very dangerous for the men working on her.

Sight-seeing excursions were run from St Peter Port on the *Courier* to view the ship (depart 10.30 a.m., return 3.30 p.m., fare three shillings), and by 1 March the number of visitors (some of whom were climbing on board her) had reached nuisance proportions.

The mixed nationality crew, made up of French, German, Danes and Dutch under a British master, were taken to

Bottle recovered from the Liverpool

Guernsey, and then back to Antwerp. When they were landed at the White Rock, the *Guernsey Evening Press* reported: 'Some of the crew seem to have indulged rather freely in consuming the liquor recovered from the wreck, and when they came ashore here yesterday were in an intoxicated and quarrelsome mood, disputing over their effects that had been lost.' A knife had to be taken off one of them by a police constable.

The *Shipping Gazette Weekly Summary* reported that by 5 March 'a good lot of cargo has been salved, probably all the wines and spirits, and it is thought the cases of beer will also be salved. A quantity of soap and sardines in cases is on shore. All the glass in cases has been taken out, but the marble slabs are blocked in by the cement which is all spoilt. The vessel's sails have been brought ashore.' In all, 534 cases and casques of spirits and liqueurs were taken to Guernsey where they were put into bonded stores. The *Gazette* reports cargo being taken off on 5, 11, 12, 13, 15 and 17 March.

The inquiry was held in the Magistrate's Room, Dale Street, Liverpool on 2 and 3 May. It was established that the ship had been twelve miles SSE of her proper course when she struck, although the assessors were unable to verify the courses reported to them because the ship's log was not available. It had been taken ashore, but had then been lost. She had four compasses on the decks, and two spares, and all were in good order. The master told the court that he did not think that the 300 tons of iron he was carrying stored amidships had interfered with the compasses, and the checks he had made at Beachy Head had shown them, in his view, to be accurate. The assessors paid particular attention to Lewis's knowledge of the ship's speed, and the first mate, Henry Summerfield, was closely questioned about this. He told the court that he had checked the speed at the log between 8 p.m. and midnight, written it on a scrap of paper, and then mislaid it. He thought the speed at that time had been about 5 knots, but it had then decreased to 2.5 to 3 by midnight. He had already made an earlier statement to the Receiver of Wreck that the speed was 7 knots, decreasing to 5, but when challenged on this he couldn't be sure which was correct.

The shallow site of the Liverpool wreck, covered with a thick layer of kelp

The assessors concluded that Lewis had set the correct course until the morning of the 25th, had kept a good lookout, and had taken proper soundings, but they were critical of the lack of knowledge concerning the ship's speed at various points. They were also of the view that insufficient allowance had been made for the dangerous current down the Alderney Race as it ran at full speed on the high spring tide, pulling the slow-moving vessel to the south. They found that 'the serious damage to the ship was not caused by the wrongful act or default of the master, but he failed in not sufficiently taking into account the dangerous indraught in this part of the English Channel.' They did, however, allow him to keep his certificate.

An attempt to get the ship off the rocks was made by the Whitstable Salvage Company, but this failed and with most of the cargo retrieved, the ship's owners sold her to a Guernsey syndicate for £250. The members retrieved more cargo and fittings, and took them to Guernsey where they were stored at the Piette sawmill, and later auctioned various lots, the total realised coming to around £10,000. This appears a good return, but once the cost of hiring salvage vessels, transportation and storage was taken into account, the profits made were not great, and some of the syndicate members came to regret the venture. The ship's steel spars were also taken to Guernsey. Details of the cargo are known because Eric Sharp researched the letters written by the syndicate's agent, Mr Robilliard, and published a summary in the *Guernsey Evening Press* in 1978. Marble from the *Liverpool* went into the stairs at the town hospital in St Peter Port, and many mantlepieces and counter tops in the island came from the same source. The ship's nameplate ended up in the Castel home of Mr Ozanne, a syndicate member.

In September 1902 the ship was still in one piece, though by now stripped out. Divers reported that she would probably not survive the winter, and by January 1903, eleven months after striking, she had broken. Attempts were still being made in 1904 by the syndicate to raise some of the remaining steel girders, but by this time the various sections of the hull were scattered and were being absorbed into the seabed.

Today a single bottle of Lucca olive oil from the *Liverpool* can be seen in the Alderney Museum, together with a bottle of 'pure currie powder' with a Crosse and Blackwell label; a second, smaller bottle without a label contains similar powder. In 1955 some tins recognisable as containing sardines were found in the rocks not far from the spot where the ship struck. It was not possible to say that they definitely came from the *Liverpool*. Clearly visible on the bottom are barrel-shaped blocks of cement – all that remains of the cargo which solidified under water.

The *Hilda* (1905)

The most terrible of all the early twentieth-century steamer wrecks was the loss of the London and South Western Railway's (LSWR) *Hilda* off St Malo on 18 November 1905. Weather and sea conditions were so severe that the normal descriptive terms could barely do them justice, and of the 137 people on board only six survived. Neither human nor mechanical error in the ship could be proved, and neither was involved. The ship was simply overwhelmed by tempest and blizzard, and battered into pieces on the rocks.

Built in 1882 in Glasgow, the *Hilda* predated the *Lydia, Frederica* and *Stella* by eight years and was slightly shorter in overall length. In 1905, after modifications, she was 235 feet long, 848 tons gross, (registered 373 tons), single-screw, with a speed of 12 knots. She ran on the Southampton route to the islands until 1890, when she was replaced by the faster *Stella*, and she then became the regular Southampton boat to St Malo.

Capt Gregory of the Hilda

On the evening of Friday, 17 November, the *Hilda* was due out of Southampton at 8.15 p.m., scheduled to arrive in St Malo at 9 a.m. the following morning. The master was Captain William Gregory, aged fifty-six, a family man with three grown-up children, who had been with the LSWR for thirty-six years. For twenty-five of those years he had been working on the St Malo run. On board were twenty-four saloon passengers, eighty-five Breton onion sellers returning home after a season in England, and a crew of twenty-eight, including two stewardesses. Ten tons of cargo had been loaded. The Breton men had been in England since July where they had been working in small groups of ten to a dozen; many were brothers or cousins, and some of them were boys of thirteen, fourteen or fifteen. The majority came from the Roscoff area. Some had substantial sums of money on them, their takings for the season.

Because there was dense fog over the docks and out in Southampton Water, Gregory delayed departure for nearly two hours, until 10 p.m.. They proceeded slowly down the Solent, but there had been no reduction in the fog by Yarmouth, and Gregory decided to

The Hilda discharging at St Peter Port, Guernsey

anchor for the night off Hurst Castle. There had been severe storms in the Channel earlier in the week, in which the American liner *St Louis* had taken a battering coming from Cherbourg, and the sea was still moderate to rough. At 6 a.m. with the fog clearing, they moved ahead past the Needles and out into the Channel and began the crossing, aiming to go east of Alderney down the Race. The weather was bright and clear throughout the morning, with a stiff easterly wind. The sea was lumpy, but nothing worse than ordinary rough weather. After the Race the route was to the east of Sark and west of Jersey, and by 2 p.m., when they were rounding Grosnez Point, the wind was increasing and the sea was much rougher. A deep depression had been moving from the Bay of Biscay across France towards Paris the previous day. This weather system was creating strong easterly winds over the south of the Bay of St Malo, and the *Hilda* was moving into these. By 4 p.m. and sunset the wind was severe gale, gusting storm force, and the ship was riding a massive sea. A little after 5 p.m. in increasing gloom the first St Malo light was sighted, the flash of the Grand Jardin lighthouse, pointer to the entrance of the harbour passage. Soon afterwards the light on Cap Frehel was also seen.

Saint-Malo — Naufrage du " HILDA " (19 novembre 1905)
L'avant du navire battu par les vagues

The Hilda fast on the rocks approaching St Malo

The way into St Malo is difficult, requiring ships to thread a careful path for several miles between substantial reefs and past the island of Cezembre. At one point the access passage is no more than a quarter of a mile wide. In 1905 the recommended approach was to keep the Grand Jardin light on with the green Balue light set up on the hill behind St Malo, until the Rochebonne light to the east was open south of Cezembre. One then passed just west of the Jardin to get two green lights together (Balue and Les Bas Sablons) for the two and a half miles down to the harbour bar. On board the *Hilda* was Pilot John Courtman from Jersey, an LSWR employee, who had permission from the Pilotage Board of St Malo to work in their waters.

At 6.30 p.m. the *Hilda* was aimed SE down the Petite Port Channel under a mile from the Grand Jardin light with all the other leading lights visible. The wind was still increasing. As she approached the Jardin a blizzard descended on the ship out of the inky sky, and visibility was reduced to a few yards – the snow was so thick that the men on the bridge could not see to the end of the ship. There was no fog siren on the Jardin lighthouse and with all the lights obliterated and rocks all round him, Gregory immediately ordered a turn to starboard to stand away, putting the engine to Slow. The ship headed back out to sea, and Gregory began a series of east-west sweeps against the main force of wind and tide. The state of the sea made it impossible to anchor. It continued to snow heavily in the gale, but from time to time lights were glimpsed. Each time Gregory took bearings and checked his chart. What happened next is unclear, because the only crew member to survive, AB James Grinter from Southampton (he was also the only British national to survive), went off duty at 8.30 p.m., turning in for a few hours' sleep. When he went below they were still on a holding course. The next thing he knew was the crash as the ship went onto the rock some time between 10 and 11 p.m.

Clearly at around 9.30 to 9.45 Gregory had decided to go in for another attempt. He may have been influenced by the fact that after 11.30 p.m. a falling tide would prevent him from getting inside St Malo harbour. The ship had now been twenty-four hours at sea, for the last six hours in gale to storm conditions, and his engineers and firemen would have been exhausted. The prospect of another night pitching and rolling in freezing conditions, with the screw racing on every crest, would have been something he wished to avoid. He had not left the open bridge once since the commencement of the crossing at 6 a.m. His reputation for caution and prudence was referred to by many people at the inquiry, and it was said that he would not have gone in if he had not been able to see all the leading lights. It is therefore likely that the snow thinned sufficiently for him to get a sustained view. Unfortunately the St Malo harbourmaster, Monsieur Leconbrun, later confirmed that a complete whiteout occurred again between 10 and 11 p.m. It is possible that Gregory tried to get in with only the Jardin light visible, a dangerous strategy, or that he went in confidently with all the lights clear only to see them vanish for the second time. The only other suggestion that was made at the inquiry concerned the possible failure of the ship's steering gear, but there was no tangible evidence to support this. Whatever the circumstances, the ship failed to pass down the narrow Petite Port Channel and struck a large rock on its western edge, one of the Pierres des Portes, a group north-west of the lighthouse and a short distance from it across the entrance channel. Gale and tide were pushing the ship to the west. It was later estimated that the angle at which Gregory came in was two cables (one-fifth of a mile) too far to the west at that point, but that she could have got past had she been 50 yards farther east.

The high seas threw her up onto the rock head-on, where she was wedged to a point just forward of the bridge, and at once big waves began to fall over her. She was badly holed in three places, and a substantial point of rock had gone through her bow. Her middle and stern section was still in the water, suspended over a gully in the rock, and the tide was falling. The foremast, loosened and swaying from the impact, fell over the port side. Gregory ordered the boats out, at least ten rockets were fired and the distress whistle was blown. With one exception all the passengers had been below or inside to escape from the storm, and they now came on deck and were gathered by the stewards and stewardesses by the after hatch, the most sheltered part of the ship. Lifebelts were tied on them by the crew, a fact which was later confirmed by the sailors' reef knots found in the lifebelt tapes. Some of the French men gathered under the bridge, and at least one remained on the grounded forecastle where he had been throughout the crossing. The *Hilda* carried six boats – two lifeboats, two cutters and two smaller quarter

Saint-Malo — Naufrage du " HILDA " (Nuit du 18 au 19 novembre 1905)
L'arrière du navire battu par les lames

Saint-Malo — Naufrage du " HILDA " (Nuit du 18 au 19 novembre 1905)
Scaphandriers recherchant les cadavres

*Pictures of the Hilda
fast on the rocks
approaching
St Malo*

SAINT-MALO - Naufrage du " Hilda "
(19 Novembre 1905) – L'Avant du Navire à marée basse

SAINT-MALO - Shiproreck of the " Hilda "
(November 19th 1905) – The prow of the ship at low-water

boats. Crewmen went first to the starboard and then to the port lifeboat, but couldn't lower either of them because of the rocks under the ship. The starboard cutter was being lowered when a wave smashed it against the ship's side, causing serious damage. Finally an attempt was made to lower the port quarter boat, but at this moment, some fifteen minutes after striking, there was a terrible rending noise audible over the howling of wind and sea, and the whole stern crashed down into the gully like an opening hinge. Sea swept over the fallen section and all but a handful of the passengers and crew were carried away. The condition of the bodies washed up later showed that some had drowned while others were smashed on rocks; extensive bruising, lacerated hands and broken limbs were seen in many of the victims.

Seaman Grinter was swept off his feet, washed along the deck, and by good luck thrown against the portside rigging of the main (rear) mast. He climbed the rigging, accompanied by First Officer Albert Pearson and William Murdock, the cook. There were other people in the starboard rigging opposite them, but Grinter could not make out who they were. Waves were thundering over them, and the snow was still blinding. The whole stern section then heeled violently over to port, so far that the men on the mast were briefly dipped into the sea, but she then righted somewhat so that the mast lay at an angle of 50 degrees. Grinter climbed higher to the mainmast light (which, he recalled, remained lit all night) and secured himself as best he could. He had difficulty holding on because his hands were frozen. Every wave fell over him and with each wave the tilted deck below disappeared. Later that night, Murdock's strength gave out, and he fell into the sea. Grinter endured seven hours on the mast. He was forty-eight, with grown-up children, and his survival was remarkable. Just before dawn (7.25 a.m.) he saw the first officer's arms give way and he fell to the deck. He had frozen to death.

Four other men, all French, survived the night in the starboard rigging. These were Tanguy Laot, Paul Marie Le Pen, Olivier Caroff and Jean-Louis Mouster. Le Pen described to *Le Salut*, a St Malo and Dinard newspaper, the events at the striking:

'The snow was falling, and the sea was very rough. All of a sudden at about ten o'clock we heard a terrible noise under our feet. The steamer had driven on to the rocks. We quickly gathered by the bridge, and we could see the First Class passengers gathering at the stern. There were women and children (at least two only two years old). The waves were hitting us on the right and left, and were going above the masts. Suddenly the steamer snapped in two with a crack which I can still hear. The stern disappeared completely with its passengers.'

'Did they try to launch the boats?'

'I don't know. I couldn't see very well. I did see a seaman cut the ropes of one lifeboat and put it into the sea on his own. He got on board, but when he came back to pull alongside the *Hilda* a wave turned the boat upside down, and he was swept away.'

Le Pen described how he had climbed into the rigging and supported a fourteen-year-old boy on his shoulders for several hours until he died. Olivier Caroff told *Le Salut* that one of the stokers had been in the rigging close to him; in the early hours of the morning when they were both dying of the cold the crewman had suddenly said, 'Stay here and die in hours, or go quickly in the sea', '*et il piqua une tete dans la mer*' – he took a header into the water. A fifth Frenchman, Louis Rozec, was taken alive off the forecastle having spent the night hanging onto the guard rails. These, with Grinter, made up the six survivors.

No one knew about the disaster until the following morning, Sunday 19th. As *Le Salut* commented, 'While the townspeople slept, a frightful drama was taking place at the entrance to the roads'. The keepers on the Grand Jardin, Monsieur Hamon and Monsieur Beaumont, insisted that they had heard and seen nothing, and since the lighthouse was not linked to the land by telegraph and no boat could have been launched, there was nothing they could have done in any case. They later reported that the sea was so rough between 9 and 11 p.m. that waves were going over the top balcony around the light and had actually broken one of the glass panes, which they had boarded up with planks. The snow had been falling thickly in 'gros flacons', large flakes, and they had lost sight of all the other lights around them. Only a handful of people in the town reported seeing anything. Three Englishwomen and a child had gone down to the mole at about 10 p.m. to await the arrival of the boat. They saw some rockets out to sea, and thinking this was a signal that she would stay outside harbour for the night, returned home. Mrs Eveleen Grindle, whose husband, George, was a passenger on board, and who lived at St Enogat, just across the bay from St Malo, told *L'Administrateur de l'Inscription Maritime* that she and her children had gone to the top floor of their house to watch for the boat, and that they had seen six rockets.

The LSWR's passenger steamer *Ada* had been in St Malo overnight. She had been due out for Southampton on the Saturday evening at 9.30 p.m., but stayed put because of the atrocious weather. She left at 8.20 a.m. on the Sunday morning, and was immediately alerted by the sight of a waterlogged lifeboat and planks floating just off the harbour entrance. During the night the heavy seas had swept all the *Hilda*'s boats away. One was later washed up on a beach, which caused people to think at first that survivors had managed to escape in it, leading to false press reports. Fifteen minutes later Captain Albert Howe sighted the *Hilda*'s mast sticking up above the rock, and closing with it was able to see Grinter waving desperately. He signalled back, and at that point a French pilot cutter, the *Alouette*, came up. Howe asked the cutter for help, and it promptly made for the wreck. The sea was still very rough and the cutter crew had considerable difficulty getting the five survivors out of the rigging, particularly since they were frozen and barely conscious. Unable to bend their limbs, they had to be pulled out of the ropes by force. The *Ada* lowered one of her boats, and this took off Louis Rozec, the Frenchman on the forecastle, and transferred him to the cutter. The dead were left on the *Hilda* for the moment.

The few survivors left clinging to the rigging being rescued the next morning

The cutter then made for the harbour, followed by the *Ada*, and the six survivors were landed and taken immediately to the town hospital, where Grinter was to remain for a week. Their arrival on the quay was the first news that the town had about the disaster. Later in the morning another boat returned to take off the bodies. One was hanging upside down in the rigging, and all had frozen to death. An eyewitness described them as being *momifies*, as if mummified. At midday the local vessel *Ville de Paimpol* was the first to pick up bodies floating in the water, including the body of Pearson, the first officer. Captain Howe went at once to the LSWR's agent, Mr Hamon, who telegraphed to Southampton; '*Ada* put back. Reports *Hilda* total wreck on the Portes outside Jardin lighthouse. *Ada*'s boat saved five men and seaman Grinter. These are the only survivors.'

Howe and Hamon then went back out to the reef in a tug to survey the damage. There was very little left that looked like a ship.

The first bodies were washed up on the beach at St Cast, seven miles west of St Malo, on Sunday. By noon on Monday sixty-three bodies had been recovered along a ten-mile stretch of the coast, and by the end of Tuesday 22nd ninety had been found. All were wearing lifebelts. The bodies of a mother and child were found together, the mother clasping the child to her, and another dead child was washed up, aged about four. In the church at St Cast the bodies were laid on boards in rows under white sheets, and a team of carpenters came from St Malo to begin work on the many coffins. A special mortuary was set up at St Malo hospital, hung with black drapes and piled with wreaths. Families came from Roscoff, Cleder, and Plouescat just north-east of Brest to identify the dead Frenchmen. Six pairs of brothers had been lost, and the Pichon family had lost three sons, Francois, Leon and Guillaume. There were heartbreaking scenes at the mortuaries. One woman had to identify the bodies of her husband and her two brothers. Madame Kerbiriou found her two sons, aged thirteen and seventeen, dead; the seventeen-year-old, Jean, had been found with a rosary wrapped around his arm. Captain Gregory's body was washed up at St Cast, and he was brought to St Malo on the Monday by the torpedo boat *Lancier*, the body covered with a tricolour. On Tuesday the LSWR's *Ella* arrived from Southampton bringing scores of relatives to identify the British bodies.

Rough seas prevented divers from getting out to the wreck until Wednesday, when they were able to report that there were no bodies below decks. They described the inside of what was left of the hull as a chaos of twisted metal and shattered fittings. Flags were flying at half mast at St Malo, Dinard and St Cast, and also at St Brieuc, where some of the bodies were laid in the cathedral. Public subscriptions were opened at Brest, Roscoff, St Malo and Paris to match those opened in Southampton and by the Entente Cordiale Society of London. Postcards with photographs of the wreckage were printed later in the week and sold in St Malo, proceeds going to the relief fund. In one day 8,000 were sold. One of these postcards depicted the body of Captain Gregory, respectfully laid out, admittedly, but rather shocking for all that (these postcards can be seen today in the St Malo municipal archives). The absence of squeamishness was continued in Le Salut, which described a retrieved female body in graphic terms – disfigured face, hair and eyes gone, two gold teeth.

On Wednesday 22nd a funeral service was held at St Cast, attended by civic and clergy representatives from St Brieuc, Dinan, St Cast, St Servan, St Malo and by representatives of the French government. Other funerals, including funerals of British passengers, were held at Dinard, St Servan and St Malo on Wednesday, Thursday and Saturday. The bodies of the two recovered Jersey crewmen, Edward Patch and Emmanuel Chappel, were taken back to the island by the *Duke of Normandy* on Thursday for burial. The other Jerseymen, Sidney Marett, Walter Fontaine and John Courtman, were not recovered. On Saturday 25th the bodies of British nationals whose relatives had requested burial at home were brought by boat from St Cast to St Malo prior to shipment on board the

Walter Herbert Fontaine, lost on the Hilda

Ada. It was very rough, and some of the coffins were nearly lost overboard.

On the Saturday afternoon, a week after the discovery of the disaster, the coffins of twenty-five British nationals – twenty-one crew and four passengers – were taken from the chapel of rest at St Malo hospital to the harbour. The St Malo and Dinard newspaper *L'Union* described in detail the solemn procession which included local dignitaries, mayors and councillors from the whole region, a military guard of honour, clergy, citizens, schoolchildren and a band playing the funeral march. Gregory's coffin was covered with a Union Jack. All shops in the town were shut and a huge crowd watched in silence. The coffins and the wreaths were then carried on board the *Ada*, which left for Southampton on Sunday morning. Seaman Grinter travelled on the *Ada* with his dead mates. On Monday 27th a requiem mass was celebrated in St Malo cathedral by the Cardinal Archbishop of Rennes for all those lost in the wreck.

The *Southampton Observer* and *Southern Daily Echo* described the arrival of the *Ada* and the coffins at 8 a.m. on the Monday morning. The crossing had been very rough, and Captain Howe had gone round the east of the Isle of Wight to get into the Solent. A large crowd was at the dockside, and the twenty-five coffins, each with its small brass plate and wreath, were offloaded and carried into a shed on the quay and laid in a long row.

Saint-Cast — Naufrage du " HILDA "
(19 novembre 1905)
Les débris du navire rejetés par la mer

The shattered remains of the Hilda stand testament to the ferocity of the gale

SAINT-MALO — Les Survivants du " Hilda "
Naufrage le 19 Novembre 1905
ayant a bord 120 Passagers. G. F.

SAINT-MALO — Shipwreck of the " Hilda "
(November 19" 1905) - 120 Passengers on Board
The Survivors

The only survivors from the Hilda

Relatives were then allowed inside. The *Ada*'s flags were at half mast, and Grinter was met by the LSWR Docks Superintendant, who shook his hand in silence. At 2.30 p.m. the first inquests began in a temporary courtroom set up in a Southampton hotel, and the jury's first task was to go to the docks to view the coffins.

The following day, Tuesday 28th, funerals were held at St Denys, St Mark, Albion, St Matthew, St James and in Sholing. Captain Gregory's service was at St Denys (he lived in Tennyson Road) and by 11 a.m. the church was filled to overflowing, with the mayor and other town officials attending. His coffin, draped with the red ensign, was then interred at Southampton Cemetery. That day, also memorable for its continual, torrential rain, four victims of the wreck were buried in the cemetery and other funerals followed on the Wednesday and Thursday. Shops were closed in town, and Southampton was in official mourning.

The disaster also left British dead in cemeteries all along the Brittany coast – at St Cast, St Servan, St Brieuc, Chatelaudren, and Dinard. Mary Miles, an English governess in her early twenties, was buried in error at St Cast when her family had requested her return to England, and it was necessary to exhume her.

Bodies continued to come up on the beaches in the weeks that followed. On 1 December a door, some blankets, a mattress, pieces of timber and some lifebelts were washed up at St Malo. On the 8th Captain Gregory's overcoat with his wallet in the pocket was also washed up, and some items were found on the Chausey Islands. On

Wednesday, 3 January, a body was washed up on Jersey, the initials in the clothing indicating that he was one of the Breton onion men.

The inquiry opened at Caxton Hall, London on Thursday, 1 February 1906, under Mr Robert Marsham, with Captain Ronaldson, Commander Caborne and Rear-Admiral Churchill as assessors, and continued on the 2nd and 8th. Since there were few surviving witnesses, they had very little to work with. Grinter provided most information, and two of the French survivors, Louis Rozec and Jean Louis Mouster, attended and spoke through an interpreter. Depositions were received from a St Malo pilot, Pierre Valloir, from the St Malo harbourmaster, and from Monsieur Auguste, master of the *Perle of Cancale*, who had been off St Malo at 5.30 on the Saturday afternoon and seen a steamer heading in. He waited for her to go ahead, lost sight of her, and then made his own way into the harbour, but nothing had arrived ahead of him. Another local captain had previously reported to the *Salut* that he had heard cries of distress at about 11 p.m. Captain Briand had been en route from St Malo to Granville in the *Gand*, and passing Cezembre was sure that he had heard the cries through the howling of the wind. He put about and went towards the spot, but the snow was too thick to see anything, and he went on.

Louis Rozec as an eye-witness could add little to Grinter's account. He had been laid low with seasickness the whole way across and had felt so ill at the point of striking that he had not been able to summon up the strength to go and look for a lifebelt. He had simply stayed where he had been since the Needles, lying on the foredeck. Mouster described how he had climbed into the starboard rigging and somehow managed to survive the cold.

Representatives of the LSWR confirmed that the *Hilda*'s compasses had been recently checked, and been found to be accurate. The ship had also passed all recent tests for seaworthiness. They also submitted a company circular, written 12 June 1899, and issued to all masters after the *Stella* disaster, which emphasised that passenger safety had to be paramount, that racing would mean instant dismissal, and that no risk of any kind should be taken.

Not surprisingly, counsel for the relatives of lost passengers wished to lay the blame on the captain. Mr Maurice Hill, for the late Colonel Follett, submitted that the position of the striking indicated that the ship came in at entirely the wrong angle and could not have had the Jardin light on with the Balue. The disaster therefore arose because the master tried to get in without having all lights visible. Mr D. Stephens, for the late Mr and Mrs Wellesley, was also of the opinion that the ship was not navigated properly, whether by master, pilot or someone else. Mr Butler Aspinall KC, for the LSWR disagreed, pointing out that no negligence could possibly be proved and that it was impossible to gauge the state of visibility from one minute to the next during the fatal two or three hours leading up to the striking. Several regular British travellers on the route testified that they always chose to travel with Gregory because of his reputation for care. He had been with the company since 1869, and had been a master since 1880. It was estimated that he had brought ships into St Malo on at least a thousand previous occasions without mishap.

The assessors agreed. They pointed out that Gregory had delayed departure at Southampton, anchored overnight in the Solent, turned back when his first attempt at St Malo became dangerous, consulted his charts, taken bearings at every opportunity and remained on the bridge throughout. No rashness or negligence of any kind could be perceived and no blame could be attached to anyone on board. The findings were: the ship's three compasses were in good order; the vessel was seaworthy; correct charts, both British and French, had been on board; the correct number of boats and lifejackets had been carried; the master had exercised care and caution, and no blame of any sort could be attached to him; but the precise reason for the stranding could not be ascertained.

On 20 November, *The Times* had first reported the disaster with the words, 'Recalls the lamentable loss of the same company's steamer *Stella*'. One of the drowned on the *Hilda* was stewardess Mary Hubbard, aged 48, whose husband, Edward, a fireman, had drowned on the *Stella* six years earlier. In the days immediately following the disaster a strange coincidence was noted; 17 November, the day the ship had sailed, had been the feast day of both Saint Hilda and Saint Gregory, and the previous Wednesday (the 15th) had been Saint Malo's day.

The Hilda lying alongside in happier times

The *Roebuck* (1911)

July 1911 was one of the hottest for decades. Heatwave and drought covered the country from the beginning of the month and in the islands the day temperatures continued unchanged in the seventies and eighties until the 26th, when Jersey had its first rain. The few dull mornings were caused by sea mists creeping in overnight, and on the morning of Wednesday 19th there was a particularly dense mist over the south coast of the island.

The Roebuck stuck fast at high water

The *Roebuck* left St Helier at 8.30 a.m. for Guernsey and Weymouth. There were 260 passengers on board and 44 crew, and she carried 20 tons of cargo. Many of the passengers were holidaymakers returning home, others were on a day out to the Guernsey races, and there was also a theatre company from the mainland on board crossing to Guernsey to give a performance that night. The sea was like glass, but the mist was very thick. Bystanders on the quay saw how the ship disappeared into the murk a few yards off the pierhead.

The *Roebuck* had been built for the Great Western Railway Company (GWR) at Barrow in 1897 for the Channel Island service. She was 1281 tons gross, 280 feet long, twin-screwed, double-funnelled and capable of 19 knots. She had first come to the islands in July 1897 after trials at Milford, and she and her sister ship *Reindeer* (also 280 feet) were 45 feet longer than the GWR's earlier generation of steam twin-screw animals, *Antelope*, *Gazelle* and *Lynx*. The GWR used her specifically for the summer service.

On the bridge was the master, Captain John Le Feuvre, who ordered her immediately to a speed of 17 knots. At 8.44 the leading mark of the Ruaudiere Buoy was glimpsed on the port side, but visibility was at best a few hundred yards and the island was totally obscured in the mist. Level with Noirmont Point there was a momentary thinning and Le Feuvre and a number of passengers made out the headland. Le Feuvre later told the inquiry that he guessed it was about a cable's length away. One of the passengers, Mr Verhuist, who was standing forward under the bridge, later said that he thought they were very close in. The mist then thickened again, and all marks disappeared. Le Feuvre told the inquiry that he then ordered the helmsman to turn slightly to a bearing NW by W1/2W. Le Fret Point was not visible to aid him, and the ship was now opening St Brelade's Bay. They continued at 17 knots, but Le Feuvre now doubled the lookout, put the telegraph to Standby, and began to sound the fog whistle. The men on the bridge then saw swirling water a short distance away dead ahead, a sign that rocks were there. Le Feuvre ordered an immediate turn to port, but moments later there was a violent shock, a long scraping sound, and the ship heeled over to starboard and shuddered to a halt, wedged on a substantial rock. It was 8.56 a.m.

It is not clear whether Le Feuvre's last order to come about had time to have any effect. A fisherman attending to his crabpots nearby said that he saw the ship heading south-west at the time she struck, but there was a general feeling on board that she had run straight on without deviating in any way. The *Roebuck* was wedged firmly on the Kaines; her stern and bow were protruding either side, but 200 feet of her keel was resting on rock. She was seriously holed on both sides of the hull, and water was flooding into her. As the tide was high the filling bow was going down and the stern was rising. When the tide fell later the opposite effect was achieved – the bow stuck up in the air while the stern lay just under the water.

Falling tide begins to expose the wreck

Le Feuvre's turn at Noirmont to NW by W1/2W, on a bearing about 298 degrees, was the correct one. After coming down from the Ruaudiere Buoy he was aiming at a narrow gap between Noirmont Point and the Fours reef to the south about two cables wide. The usual course was then along the North West Passage. This required a turn at or just after Noirmont Point to NW (to around 290 degrees), followed by another turn to almost due west (on 275 degrees) one mile later on opening St Brelade's Bay. This bearing would then have carried him in a straight line out past the Corbière. For some inexplicable reason, the second turn to due west was not made, and the vessel continued on the 298 degree bearing until it hit the opposite side of the bay. If he was unusually close in, as passengers said, then he must have just missed the Portelet Ridge and Le Fret Point without seeing them as he headed north-west, but the damage was caused by steaming on for between two and three minutes after he should have made the second adjustment. Considering that Le Feuvre had been navigating that route for decades and must have known how many minutes it took to cover the required distances, it is very surprising that he should have allowed the ship to get right across the bay before realising something was wrong. Once it was established that no one had been killed or injured, the islanders began to enjoy themselves with circulated stories about Le Feuvre (everyone remembered his episode with the *Ibex*, fourteen years before) along the lines that he had turned due north and steamed like a madman hard for the beach. In fact, his calculations, though serious in the outcome, were inaccurate only in matters of yards and single minutes, although given the conditions at the time he should have been going at a much slower speed.

The impact was violent, and the ship tilted alarmingly before righting herself again. Many passengers had gone to the dining room when she sailed to have breakfast, and crockery was tipped to the floor and smashed, while some people sitting in chairs were thrown to the deck. Rockets were fired, and the whistle blown repeatedly in the distress call. Lifebelts were distributed and the boats were swung out, although some passengers later complained that it took the crew ten minutes to go to the first boat, and a further eight minutes before it was in the water. One passenger maintained that one boat could only be shifted from the davits by applying an iron bar, and another said that her boat leaked badly. Although the *Roebuck* was stuck fast and there was no danger of her sinking, the passengers could not see the shore in the fog, and thought they were in open water. The steep angle the ship was taking was evident to everyone, and Mr J. Thorpe, governor of the Monmouthshire prison at Usk, later told a reporter that everyone believed the vessel would go under at any minute. The *Roebuck* had six lifeboats and over 800 lifebelts. The Kaines are only 300 yards from the shore, south of Fliquet Bay, and once filled with women and children the first lifeboat went off and headed to Les Creux harbour, just south of St Brelade's church, where it landed its passengers. By good fortune one of the Jersey pilot boats had been anchored in a small bay nearby, and hearing the whistle came out at once to give aid. In the course of the

Some fine crystalware taken off at the time of stranding

The Roebuck firmly wedged on the Kaines

next hour all the passengers were landed safely.

The news of the disaster was spread by the help of 1911 technology – telephones and motor cars. Minutes after the striking the harbourmaster at St Helier received a 'telephonic' message telling him of the accident, and he was able to despatch a tug, *Duke of Normandy*, at once to the scene, where she began to take off the baggage. The *Jersey Evening Post* was also informed, and a reporter was at once sent to St Brelade's in a car, filing a detailed report which appeared in the paper the same afternoon. A procession of horse-drawn vans and carriages began to make its way to the bay to pick up the landed passengers and convey them back to St Helier, all at modest charge. The rest of the day was spent getting the luggage and cargo off – or such of it as had not been flooded. The manager of the Alhambra cinema also hurried to the scene, and took several reels of film of the ship from a small boat, no mean feat given the size of the cranked cameras at that time; this he showed that evening to queuing customers, 'a striking example,' the *Jersey Evening Post* said, 'of enterprise.'

Had the ship not been wedged she would have gone rapidly to the bottom. In one place her hull was gashed for a length of nearly 100 feet under the waterline, rendering the watertight bulkheads useless. Observers were worried that as the tide fell and her stern lost its support, she would break in two, but this did not happen, possibly because she was emptied of baggage and cargo rapidly, possibly because her cargo weight was comparatively light that morning. The other advantage was the glassy nature of the sea, not just on the first day but throughout the eight days she was stuck. Had the accident occurred in winter, heavy seas would have broken her up very quickly.

By midday the mist had burnt off, and the news had gone round the island. A large crowd began to make its way to St Brelade's to enjoy the spectacle, many walking along the rough track past Bouilly Port on the west side of the bay to get to the best viewing point. At low tide the ship presented an extraordinary sight, with her bow projecting up into the air. 'There she lies like a great stricken colossus,' the *Jersey Evening Post* wrote, moving into epic mode. During the ensuing week of heatwave thousands of islanders went to see her, on foot, by bicycle, in horse-drawn vehicles and in motor cars. They put on summer clothes and took picnics. On one day the Jersey Railway estimated that it had carried over 3,000 passengers to La Moye or Don Bridge stations and on one afternoon 1,000 people were counted at Beau Port and Le Fiquet. Small boats filled with sightseers circled the bay, and the small steamship *Courier* ran 'Roebuck excursions' from the harbour at St Helier where queues of hundreds formed, and in the crush to get on the boat a number of women were nearly pushed over the edge of the quay. The tea houses and cafes around St Brelade's Bay did a roaring trade, and *Lloyd's Weekly* produced a jumbo-size souvenir postcard with nine photographs of the wreck and associated individuals which it sold in large numbers. None of this could have given the GWR much cheer, and Captain Le Feuvre took refuge at home, no doubt preparing his statement for the Board of Trade assessors.

Efforts to pump out while still fast on the Kaines

Salvage plans were prepared immediately, and on the day after the accident, the 20th, a number of vessels were mobilised to begin the operation, including the local tug *Duke of Normandy*, a War Department tug *Sir Redvers Buller*, and a salvage company tug from Hamburg, the *Albatross*. These were later joined by the *Svitzer*, belonging to the Svitzer Salvage Company of Copenhagen. Working at low tide, divers assessed the damage below the waterline, and workmen began to patch the holes with timber and cement and build timber watertight bulkheads the length of the ship. After patching she was pumped out, but attempts to refloat her on the high tides of the 21st and 22nd failed. On the second day she lifted sufficiently to float, but a six-foot pinnacle of rock was discovered piercing her hull, with water gushing in around it, so she was allowed to settle again. Another unsuccessful attempt was made on the 23rd, and after that the tides were too low to allow further attempts until the 28th. On the 28th, with all cabin fittings stripped out, and with the *Svitzer* alongside pumping with compressed air, she was floated and pulled off stern-first by the *Albatross* on the evening high tide. A huge crowd, covering every vantage point from Ouaisne to La Moye, watched the operation, and there were loud cheers as she came away. The Lieutenant Governor, Sir Alexander Rochfort, and the Bailiff were also present. She was towed, largely submerged, at a brisk 4 knots and beached, stern-first, at 7.40 p.m. on the sand in front of the Martello tower west of Le Grouin Point, where the receding tide left her high and dry.

On Saturday 29th the crowd going to see her was even larger, and queues had to be organised to give everyone the opportunity to walk past and view close up the huge rent in her port side, in some places large enough to allow the workmen to walk through. Particularly impressive were the large pieces of the Kaines rock lying inside her. Workmen now began stripping the damaged plates off and reinforcing the hole patches, and a false floor was constructed at saloon deck level to try to keep the upper decks from being flooded. On 14 August an attempt was made to tow her to St Helier; the tugs got her out of the bay, but she began to fill and list. She was beached again, this time on Belcroute. After pumping out, she was successfully towed the same evening into St Helier harbour, where further repairs were made, and on 29 August she was taken to the Harland and Wolff yard at Southampton.

The Board of Trade Inquiry opened on 14 September at Caxton Hall in London. Mr Robert H.B. Marsham presided, as he had in the *Ibex* case of 1897. Perhaps fortunately for Le Feuvre, the other two assessors were new to him. Le Feuvre repeated what he had already told the press many times – the collision had taken him completely by surprise, and he could only explain the accident by supposing that there had been a very strong, freak tide pushing him north that morning. Asked why he had proceeded at 17 knots when he felt it necessary to blow the fog whistle, he replied 'that he was confident of his position.' The GWR barrister was also firmly of the opinion that there must have been an abnormal tide or current involved. Dr Stubbs, representing the Board of Trade, disagreed, and pointed out to the court that the master had run for two miles at full speed in close proximity to one of the most dangerous shorelines in the islands without seeing a single mark.

The inquiry was over in three days (there had been no loss of life) and the assessors found against Le Feuvre. A safe and proper alteration of course had not been made after Noirmont Point, insufficient allowance had been made for tide and current, and the ship's speed had been excessive for the conditions. In view of a long unblemished character, they decided to suspend his certificate for three rather than six months.

Roebuck was back on the island service in January 1912, where she continued without incident until the outbreak of war. She was then commandeered by the Royal Navy and renamed HMS *Roedean*. At Scapa Flow in 1915 she dragged her anchor and fell foul of a battleship, the *Imperieuse*. In the collision she was so badly damaged that she sank, and no efforts were made to raise her. In 1925 the GWR commissioned a

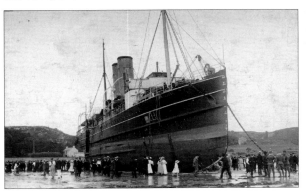

second, smaller *Roebuck* from Swan Hunter which served the islands between 1925 and 1965.

The Roebuck high and dry on the beach at St Brelade

The *Caesarea* (1923)

Visitors to the States of Jersey Maritime Museum in St Helier will see on the quay nearby a substantial bronze ship's propeller set up with a plaque. Closer inspection shows that the propeller comes from the *Caesarea*, sunk just outside the pierhead in 1923.

TRSS Caesarea at her launch in 1910

Three passenger ships with the name *Caesarea* have served the Channel Islands. The first was a single-screw London and South Western Railway (LSWR) ship, launched in 1867, and travelling to the islands until 1884, and the third and most recent, best remembered for her blue and white Sealink colours, maintained the Weymouth service between 1960 and 1978. The second *Caesarea*, which concerns us here, was built by Cammell Laird for the LSWR and launched in 1910. She made her maiden voyage to the islands in September of that year, and with an interlude of six years between 1914 and 1920 when she was requisitioned for war and post-war service, continued to run between Southampton and the islands until 1923.

On the morning of 7 July 1923, under the command of Captain E.T. Smith, *Caesarea* was leaving Jersey for Guernsey and Southampton when she struck a rock off Noirmont Point in thick fog. Captain Smith tried to get back into St Helier, but the disabled ship struck a second rock and shortly afterwards went to the bottom in shallow water. All the passengers were brought safely ashore, but the vessel remained grounded and partially submerged for a fortnight. This mishap ended her career in the islands. After recovery and a tow to Southampton, she was repaired and sold to a company on the Isle of Man where she was renamed *Manx Maid*. She continued in service until 1950 when she was broken up.

The *Caesarea* was 1499 tons gross at launch (later modified to 1504 tons) and 284 feet long. She and her sister ship *Sarnia* were built to replace the *Lydia* and *Frederica*, and were the first turbine-driven passenger vessels on the Channel Island run. The *Caesarea* was powered with three direct-drive steam turbines linked to three propellers, the outer two being right-handed for forward propulsion, with the central propeller for reverse. To go astern, steam had to be diverted from the forward-drive turbines, giving a slightly longer delay in changing drive direction compared to the conventional cylinder engines. In 1977 Sam Smith, Captain Smith's son, wrote to the *Jersey Evening Post* about the *Caesarea,* which he had known well as a boy, recalling some of her less endearing features. 'She was known as a crank ship, given to immoderate rolling, and at times shaking like a fury.' Vibration was sometimes a problem with the early turbine vessels, and she was certainly costly to run because the LSWR (and after January 1923, the Southern Railway) used her only during the summer months. Saturday, 7 July 1923 was Wimbledon finals day. The country was bathed in sunshine and temperatures were to go into the 80s over the weekend. Early that Saturday morning the south coast of Jersey was enveloped in thick sea mist, and conditions were similar to those of 19 July twelve years earlier, when the *Roebuck* made her contact with the Kaines.

The Caesarea underway in calm conditions

The *Caesarea* left Albert Pier at 7.15 a.m. with 373 passengers, 61 crew, and a cargo of mostly vegetables and flowers. The mist had reduced visibility to a few hundred yards. At 7.45 the Southern Railway's *Alberta* crept in from Southampton and began to land her passengers. As this was happening four long blasts of a ship's siren were heard to the west across the bay. At first it was assumed that this was another ship waiting to come in, but then rumours began to circulate on the quays that it was the *Caesarea* in some kind of trouble. More whistle blasts were heard and then the *Caesarea* was seen coming slowly in around the Elizabeth Castle breakwater, stern down, lifeboats lowered and attached, trailing in the water. The *Alberta* at once put down her boats, which went out to give aid. As the *Caesarea* approached the harbour entrance her stern went under, and shortly afterwards the whole ship subsided quietly onto the bottom. Fortunately the tide was a low neap and although most of the hull was covered, the upper deck remained above the surface. The passengers, including a good many children and some babes in arms, were taken off in boats and landed in relays at the pier. The sea was dead calm, and the mood was light-hearted with much calling out and some singing. For the rest of the morning small boats went back and forth, and the mail and as much freight as possible was brought ashore.

In his account Captain Smith described how the *Caesarea* had passed the *Alberta* to port in the fog as the *Alberta* crossed St Aubin's Bay on her way in. He had been aiming the *Caesarea* into the narrow gap between Noirmont Point and the Fours reef, but somehow the *Caesarea* was slightly at the wrong angle and too close to the southern side of the channel, and she ran over the northern edge of the Grand Four ledge. It is not clear whether any change to the course had been made since passing the Ruaudiere Rock buoy in the middle of St Aubin's Bay, but it would have needed an unadjusted error of only three or four degrees at the buoy to put him on a collision course, and at striking the vessel was only one hundred yards south of the recommended line. The impact tore a long gash in her port side and the port propeller jammed fast in a deep cleft of rock, and was pulled straight out of the hull along with the propeller shaft. Some passengers heard a grinding noise and felt a bump, but the impact was sufficiently subdued to leave many unaware that anything had happened. The damage was serious, however, and water was coming fast up the shaft tunnel and through the side into the stokehold and engine room.

The *Caesarea* still had steam on, and Smith decided to turn back and try and make it into the harbour. He blew the distress call and lowered the boats to water level, but there was no need at this stage to abandon the ship. He tried to contact the *Alberta* by radio, but failed. He did, however, manage to raise the GWR cargo boat *Reindeer* which was coming up, having left St Helier fifteen minutes behind him. Captain Mulhall on *Reindeer* came ahead slowly, then saw the *Caesarea* at a distance of about 200 yards, and turned to accompany her. Mulhall knew that the GWR's cargo ship *Gazelle* was anchored in St Brelade's Bay, waiting to come in. He radioed her, and she then came and escorted the *Caesarea* back towards the harbour while *Reindeer* continued on to Guernsey.

Miss Waddell, a Jersey guider taking a party of guides to camp on the mainland, later

The Caesarea heavily flooded lying just outside St Helier harbour

The Caesarea underway in calm conditions

told a reporter that she had seen the Ruaudiere buoy on the way out, but that Noirmont Point had been obscured. She had heard a grating sound and felt the ship shudder. They had then stopped, turned slowly and started back. Some passengers were unaware of what was happening, and when Elizabeth Castle came into view again she had heard one woman express surprise that they were in Guernsey so soon.

As the *Caesarea* moved slowly back towards St Helier she was filling by the stern, and further power was lost when her dynamos failed. The loss of one of the outside forward drive propellers was making her hard to steer, and the tide was beginning to run, adding to Smith's problems. After managing to get across St Aubin's Bay, he tried to pass between the Castle breakwater and the Oyster Rock before turning north-east for the harbour (the line the *Caledonia* had failed to make). Struggling with an unwieldy vessel that might go to the bottom at any minute, he tried to negotiate the narrow passage, but the combination of slow speed, erratic steering and strong tidal push was too much for him, and the *Caesarea* swung away and struck the Oyster with a force that badly holed her on the other, starboard side. This second impact flooded her boilers and brought the reality of the situation home to all the passengers, who could see that the ship was at an awkward angle, stern down. Smith was still determined to make the last half mile to the harbour, and he kept the ship going at a crawling speed. He very nearly succeeded. Three hundred yards from the pierhead, when it looked as if she might get in, the *Caesarea* dropped gently onto a sandbank in the Small Road, taking a tilt to starboard. Here she would remain for two weeks, the increasingly high tides covering her except for bridge, masts and funnel.

Landed safely, most of the passengers re-embarked on the *Alberta* which took them and the recovered mail to Guernsey and Southampton at 10.15 a.m. Forty-seven of the passengers decided they had had enough excitement for the moment, and stayed on the island. As the *Alberta* passed out through the pierheads the *Caesarea* passengers on board roared in a chorus, 'Are we downhearted?' to which the answering chorus from the crowd on the quay was, 'No!' Captain Smith remained on the *Caesarea* for the rest of the morning supervising the recovery of baggage until he was driven off by the tide. Many islanders were impressed by the action

Pumping out operations in the Small Roads

of Chief Steward Sanger, who left all his belongings on board, but came ashore clutching the ship's cash box. A diver came immediately from Guernsey, and he reported a long tear in the hull on the port side, an even larger hole in the starboard side, and one missing propeller and bracket.

It was decided initially to try to pull the vessel a ship's length nearer to the harbour. This would put her on flat sand, lift her slightly so that she would not be almost covered at every high tide, and clear the harbour road which she was partially blocking. On Monday 10 July two independent salvage tugs, the *Dandy* and the *Trover*, arrived to offer their assistance, but the Southern Railway brought in their own boat, the *Gundreda*, a converted yacht chartered from the All Seas Marine and Salvage Company. There was some local talk about the inadequacy of the *Gundreda*'s equipment, and it was later said that the Southern Railway's decision to use her delayed the recovery of the ship. Timber was taken out to the wreck, and with the aid of divers attempts were made to plug the holes. Cables were also attached to the hull, and she was partly pulled off her starboard side to give better access to the damage.

It was hoped to partially float and haul her forward on Saturday 14th or Sunday 15th, but the *Gundreda*'s pumps were suffering constant blockage from the liquified cargo of tomatoes, and divers had to keep unblocking them. Hundreds of people came to the harbour to watch the proceedings, and small boats with sightseers circled her throughout the day. As with the *Roebuck*, twelve years previously, the island cinema filmed her and showed the footage at the evening performances. Messrs Quenouillere and Son, photographers, had an eye-catching newspaper advertisement printed, 'SS *Caesarea*; An enlarged photograph of the wreck; place your orders early as there is a big demand.'

On Monday 16th intense pumping raised her stern, but she remained grounded forward. The tide was moving towards spring, and on that day it came in so quickly that the salvage men had to evacuate her in a hurry, leaving two pumps behind. This rendered them temporarily unusable. Many of her fittings were removed to try and lighten her, and hundreds of empty barrels were then borrowed from the St Helier Constable's Office, and packed into the below-deck spaces. On Wednesday 18th, with four pumps working and with low water at 5 p.m., she floated. With *Gundreda* hauling and the States tug *Duke of Normandy* lashed alongside, an attempt was made to move her forward. This failed when a hawser snapped and fouled the *Duke of Normandy's* propeller. A second attempt was then made by laying the *Caesarea's* anchors out ahead of her, feeding steam into her windlasses from the *Gundreda*, and trying to get her to pull herself forward. This worked sufficiently well to move her stern ahead of her previous bow position, and she was then dropped in four fathoms on the flat bottom, leaving her high and dry on the lowest springs.

Work continued on her in her new position, and on the evening of 20 July with a big crowd watching, she was part pushed, part pulled by lines attached to her bow from the Albert Pier, into the harbour and grounded just after midnight in London Bay. Appropriately, conditions that night were foggy. After more patching she was towed to dry dock in Southampton on 3 August. She did not return to the islands.

Pumping out operations in the Small Roads

In the summer of 1973 Tony Titterington began a systematic search for the *Caesarea's* lost propeller in the Noirmont area. Tony had started diving around Jersey in 1949, using oxygen re-breather sets from German submarines and then one of the first aqualung kits brought to the island. During the 1950s he was at university on the mainland, and then working in Weymouth where he joined the Weymouth and Portland Sub-Aqua Club. He was back in Jersey in 1959, where he joined the family hotel business at St Brelade, and he now began serious wreck diving. Over the next thirty years he discovered and purchased the rights to a number of major wrecks around the Jersey coast, and many of the artefacts recovered from them can be seen in the Jersey Maritime Museum. A superb example of wreck restoration is the German '88' gun which he recovered and rebuilt; originally carried on a submarine, it had been transferred to an armed trawler which was sunk off the south of the island by the Allies. His diving records are meticulously kept as part of a substantial library of charts, plans, photographs and maritime journals.

Local knowledge had put the *Caesarea*'s point of striking at or near the Fours reef. Tony began to search the area with a magnetometer and got a very strong signal at the Grand Four. A part-time crew member, George Clyde, dived but could not find anything. Tony returned to the area later, and his diving log records the following:

Friday June 29th 1973
Dived with Derek Horsfall on the Petit Four, then after a search round there we moved to the Grand Four and located a large propeller between the two main heads. The 'A' bracket with some of the shaft which was wedged between the large head and the smaller head was suspended over a small gully... the propeller was suspended from a narrow crack in the large south head and went to a smaller head to the west. This is probably the prop of the *Caesarea* lost in 1923.

Caesarea's propeller standing outside the Jersey Maritime Museum

The badly mangled propeller was jammed by the tips into the rock cleft, and the shaft and part of the 'A' bracket were sticking out horizontally, unsupported. Because they had been concentrating on the seabed, the divers had not at first seen the metalwork suspended above them. The large tapered nut holding the propeller to the shaft was still in place. Ten feet to the south was another section of shaft on the bottom, about nine feet long, and it was clear that the propeller had jammed hard into the cleft as the ship passed over, and been extracted from the hull like a well-pulled tooth and its root.

The head of the Jersey States Public Works Department then asked if the propeller could go to Elizabeth Castle as part of a new Jersey Maritime Museum, and permission to raise it was obtained from the

British Rail Board. The lift was clearly a very heavy proposition, made more difficult by the way the metal was wedged. In 1974 a Royal Navy clearance diving team from Plymouth under Lieutenant Bob Pillings was over in Jersey, working on the Arnold Maersk, a freighter which had sunk south of the island in 1943 when delivering bombs to the occupying force, and discovered by Tony in 1968. They offered to help with the *Caesarea*'s propeller. They were using a substantial 300-ton vessel with a five-ton vertical lift capacity. Lines were fastened to the propeller and shaft, but neither could be budged. The navy then brought a heavy 3.5 inch diameter nylon hawser with a tenton breaking strain into play. This was fastened on at low water, and then at three-quarter flood the vessel went away at speed down the tide, intending to prise the load out with one jerk. There was a massive bang, and the hawser snapped, but the propeller was partially dislodged and could now be lifted.

The States Arts and History officer, Rob Gibson, then asked the harbour office if they would lift and tow the propeller into St Helier. After Jean Rivoallan, the States diver, had put chains around the propeller and bracket, it was lifted in stages by the *Duke of Normandy*'s winch, without the need for airbags, and towed in on Monday, 8 July 1974, fifty-one years and two days since the ship had struck. Cleaning confirmed the *Caesarea*'s name on the propeller, which was first set up at Elizabeth Castle, and is now on the quay at St Helier harbour.

Still visible, the name Caesarea stamped onto a blade of the recovered propeller

The *Princess Ena* (1935)

Holidaymakers looking south from St Helier harbour and the Esplanade on Bank Holiday Saturday, 3 August 1935, would have seen a column of smoke on the horizon rising into the cloudless sky. The smoke column was visible until sunset, and its height and unchanging density indicated a ferocious consumption of something somewhere.

The Princess Ena moored alongside

In fact a savage fire was raging through the LSWR's passenger steamer *Princess Ena*, by now abandoned, ten miles south of the island, and being watched helplessly by her master and other officers from another vessel standing close by. By early morning on the Sunday the ship was a floating pyre, her superstructure a mass of twisted metal, the paint scorched off her sides, and the huge column of smoke pouring straight up hundreds of feet into the air. Her decks had collapsed, smoke was billowing through the buckled plates of the hull, and she was listing heavily to starboard in the flat sea. At 1 p.m. her stern went under, and shortly afterwards her gutted hull and the fire burning throughout it disappeared under the water. A *Jersey Evening Post* reporter, present at the scene, wrote:

> Suddenly, as we watched, the stern slipped under, the whole ship shivered, then slowly began to slide backwards, she gathered speed – there came a crash as though her stern had hit the bottom, she lurched forward, it seemed as though her back had broken, black smoke gushed from her funnel; up, stark against the sky rose her bow…then with a gurgling sound that, too, disappeared. The top of the foremast was visible for a second, then it was gone, a swirl of water, a tank and some small objects shot up to the surface, and that was the end…

The violent destruction of this twenty-nine-year-old ship after an accidental fire near the radio room which went on to burn for twenty-four hours and consume the whole vessel, was at least unaccompanied by loss of life. The *Princess Ena* had arrived at Jersey from Southampton on the morning of Saturday 3 August, with just under 600 passengers, including 300 Scouts, Cubs and members of the Boys' Brigade, going to the island for their summer camp. She then left at Saturday lunchtime for St Malo with only her crew of forty-three on board, and the fire was discovered less than an hour later. Everyone was taken off safely, but the rapidity with which the blaze gained a hold and the fact that it was impossible to get into the radio room to send an SOS indicate the scale of the tragedy that might have occurred if the fire had broken out before the hundreds of passengers had been disembarked.

After the loss of the *Hilda* in November 1905, the London and South Western Railway (LSWR) ordered a replacement ship for the St Malo run from the Gourlay Brothers of Dundee, which was built in the extraordinary time of four months. This was the *Princess Ena*, launched on 25 May 1906 and in service in July. At 1203 tons gross and with a length of 250

Princess Ena departing from St Malo

feet she was longer and larger than the *Hilda,* and of comparable length to the *Lydia, Frederica* and *Stella.* Like these she was twinscrewed, but slightly slower with a top speed of 16 knots compared with their nineteen. She also looked different from these three, all built sixteen years earlier, with a much taller funnel set well aft. The LSWR used her mainly on the St Malo run, but in summer she regularly called in at Jersey on the way down and was well known there.

During her twenty-nine years of service, first under the LSWR and then after January 1923 as part of the Southern Railway fleet, the *Princess Ena* had a number of adventures. On 20 May 1908, on her way to St Malo in thick fog and heading to pass round the north-west tip of Jersey, she veered too far south-east and ran onto the Paternosters north of the island. The lifeboats were put out with all the passengers, but as the tide rose she floated off, and everyone returned on board. She then made a slow journey around the island to St Helier with a flooded forward hold, and after temporary patching returned to Southampton for repairs.

On 10 September 1909, she went aground for a short time near the Needles, without much damage, and on 14 August 1923, passing south away from Jersey for St Malo, she struck a reef on the north-west edge of the Minquiers at 5.45 a.m., again in fog. Fifty-nine of the 217 passengers were put into boats, the others remaining on board, but again she refloated at about 7 a.m. This time the lifeboats had drifted away with the tide and could not be found in the fog. Fortunately the occupants had the good sense to secure themselves to the North-West Minquiers buoy, and they were found there some hours later by the Southern Railway's cargo-carrier *Bertha,* which had come out from St Malo in answer to the *Princess Ena*'s SOS (the *Bertha*, appropriately, was also a product of the Gourlay Company's yard). The *Princess Ena* had meanwhile given up the search and gone on to St Malo under her own steam, leaking badly and with a damaged propeller, arriving there at 9 a.m. Eventually the passengers were reunited in St Malo, and taken back to Southampton on the SR's relief ship, the *Hantonia.*

During the 1914–18 war the *Princess Ena* was requisitioned and fitted out as a Q-ship, based at Falmouth. She was then converted into a troop carrier, taking men to the Dardanelles in 1915, and operating in the northern Aegean between Lemnos and Salonica. She returned to her cross-Channel routine in 1920.

Princess Ena engulfed by fire

The weather over the weekend of 3–5 August 1935 was hot and sunny. The *Princess Ena* left Southampton on the Friday night and arrived at St Helier at 10.40 next morning. The master was Captain Percy Lewis of Totton, the first officer was H. Breuilly of Jersey, and nothing untoward was reported in the running of the ship during the crossing. After Jersey the *Princess Ena* was scheduled to travel to St Malo, from where she was to maintain the St Malo to Jersey service for the remainder of the summer. Because her crew would not be seeing the English mainland again for a while, they were carrying more than the usual number of personal possessions and clothes with them.

She left St Helier at midday and proceeded SSW to skirt the Minquiers plateau before turning SSE for St Malo. The Minquiers, a treacherous area of continuous reefs fourteen miles long, lie ten miles due south of Jersey, fifteen miles north of St Malo. Some time shortly before 1 p.m., smoke was seen creeping out from under the door of the radio room, which was situated on the main deck just aft of the funnel, and immediate investigation showed a fire on the port side, immediately below. The crew attacked the blaze with buckets and five fire hoses, but it spread rapidly into the second-class cabins and they were unable to contain it. Several crew members later reported a frightening rapidity in the spread of the flames. By 4 p.m., with most of the upper deck and superstructure on fire, the order was given first to let go an anchor to stop the vessel from drifting, and then to abandon ship. All forty-three crew, including the master, got away safely in three boats. No one was seriously injured, although many were blackened with soot and some were suffering from inhaled fumes. Stewardess Jean Shepherd, the only woman crew member, had been trapped below deck and lost her way in the choking smoke. She had been helped by a deckhand, who in turn was overcome, and they were both rescued by the first officer. All of the crew's belongings had to be left behind, and most went into the boats in singlets or shirtsleeves. Third Engineer L. Miller did have the presence of mind to grab his camera from his cabin, and he was able to photograph the ship from the lifeboat as they pulled away.

On Jersey the alarm was raised just before 3 p.m. by the lighthouse keeper at the Corbière, who could see the column of smoke, and shortly afterwards the States tug *Duke of Normandy* put out to give aid. The tug picked up the crew, leaving the lifeboats to drift, and remained close by the burning ship. When there was an apparent reduction in the flames Captain Lewis and other officers tried to get back on board, but the lull was short-lived and they were driven back.

As rumours of what was happening began to circulate around the island, two *Jersey Evening Post* reporters tried to charter a boat at the harbour to take them out to the ship. Unable to find anyone willing to make the trip, they then persuaded Jersey Airlines (founded two years previously, and using West Park beach as their runway – tide permitting) to fly them across. They were able to take some very dramatic photographs of the burning ship from the air which appeared in the paper the same day. They were joined on the flight by the Jersey correspondent of the *Guernsey Evening Press*, and his account appeared in the paper on Monday 5th:

> The long trail of smoke from the ill-fated ship grew bigger and bigger as we approached and then the awe-inspiring picture of the vessel lying helpless on the calm water with the flames hungrily devouring her met our gaze. As we dropped down to within 150 feet and circled it could be seen that the *Princess Ena* was a raging furnace from bridge to stern, with huge balls of flame eating up her innermost and vital parts. The paintwork on the port and starboard sides had vanished with the heat and had given place to long white patches …

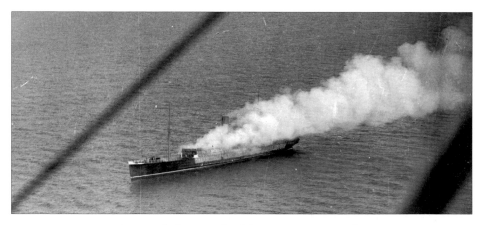

An aerial photograph of the Princess Ena on fire

Later that evening the GWR's *St Julien*, on her way direct from Weymouth to Jersey with 1,005 passengers, altered course to go to the scene. She took most of the *Princess Ena*'s crew back to St Helier, and shortly afterwards the *Duke of Normandy* also turned back to harbour. Once in St Helier, Captain Lewis made his report, and then returned to his ship at about 8.15 p.m. on the *Ringwood,* a Southern Railway cargo vessel, with some of his officers and a few crewmen. Here they remained all night, close by. At dawn a French tug, the *Cherbourgeoise* from St Malo, turned up, and thinking the burning ship was abandoned, some of the tug's crew actually managed to get on board her, trying without success to put the fires out. The tugmen then put a tricolour on her bow as a salvage claim. Lewis on the *Ringwood* ordered them off, and despite language difficulties there were some lively exchanges. The tug remained nearby.

On the Sunday morning senior officials of the Southern Railway came to the scene, brought over from Southampton on the *Isle of Sark* and then out to the ship on the *Duke of Normandy.* The officials included Reg Biddle, Assistant Marine and Docks Manager

St Julien picking up crew members from the Princess Ena

Left: Princess Ena's bell being recovered by French divers

at Southampton, senior Southern Railway engineers, W. Le Brun, the SR's agent in Jersey, F. Allix, the Jersey harbourmaster, some of the *Princess Ena's* own engineers and three reporters. On arrival they discovered the *Cherbourgeoise* lying close to the *Ringwood*, and Biddle used a megaphone to request its withdrawal. He was also apparently not understood, and Le Brun then informed the tug crew in French that the ship was not abandoned, pointing to a scorched red ensign still just visible at her stern, lying across the rail where it had fallen after the jack staff had burnt through. The tug backed off a little, but remained at the scene until the end came. The company officials then transferred across to the *Ringwood* in a small boat, and a preliminary inquiry took place with Captain Lewis and the first officer. The findings of this inquiry were later passed to the three reporters, the gist being that the cause of the fire was unknown, and that the behaviour of the crew was considered to have been exemplary in very dangerous circumstances.

After burning for exactly twenty-four hours, at 1 p.m. Sunday lunch time, the *Princess Ena*'s stern went under, and water began to flow through her open portholes. Captain Lewis and crew members stood watching from the deck of the *Ringwood*, and as she went they bared their heads. The bow rose, and she slid under in a huge cloud of steam and smoke. Ironically, the last thing visible as she went under was the French flag at the bow.

Tony Titterington began looking for the remains of the *Princess Ena* in the late 1960s, and in 1970 he purchased her from the British Railways Board. In that year he exchanged correspondence with Third Engineer Miller, who was able to describe the ship's layout for him, and the two then met in Jersey. The cause of the fire had never been established officially, but Miller told him off the record that the rumours at the time among the crew pointed to a number of scouts thought to have been smoking in a lifebelt locker. Some of the kapok belts might have caught, smouldered for a long time, then flared up. Whatever the cause, the fire spread through a bulkhead, first into a coal bunker, and then into the paint store, which went up in minutes, thus explaining the sudden increase in the ferocity of the flames.

The depth at which the ship lay (over 150 feet) presented Tony with a major challenge, and the positions given for her point of sinking in 1935 – one by the Jersey harbourmaster, another putting her three miles from the North-West Minquiers buoy – did not agree. A further difficulty arose from the fact that during the Second World War the buoy had been repositioned half a mile from its original spot, and these variables meant that despite the fact that an Admiralty chart gave a position for a wreck site that might have been her, he was confronted by an area over a mile and a quarter wide where she might lie. At this time there was no satellite navigation aid, and searching by elimination was difficult, because at nine to ten miles south of Jersey he had few marks to keep a check on his changing position, even though the western edge of the Minquiers plateau was visible a few miles away. On clear days he was able to take bearings on the radio mast at Les Platons on the highest part of Jersey and on a particular rock formation on the island's south coast, and also use a sextant to check the angle made by the Corbière Lighthouse and the power station tower at La Collette (some six miles apart), but in poor visibility this was not possible. Sixteen years of searching, on and off, brought no result.

Princess Ena's crew returning to the wreck aboard the Duke of Normandy

Captain and crew members landed in St Helier

Crew members at St Helier harbour

In July 1984 he used a Decca navigation aid out over the site for the first time, together with a metal detector, and on the 23rd, after four days of searching, had a promising strike. With him was Alan Gay of the police diving team. His diving log records the following:

Tuesday 24th July 1984. Dived on the wreck located yesterday. It was in 48 metres and due to the high wind gusting 7 we had to miss the morning low water slack, and dived on the high water. I dived with Gary Parrott tended by Carole at 3.30pm. The visibility was the best I have ever seen and clear at 60 to 70 foot in a horizontal direction, as we could see the wreck and the boat at the same time when we were half-way down. Found the wreck to be lying roughly bows to the SSE or SE and the stern to the NNW or NW. The bows are lying over on the port side with the deck at approximately 75 degrees to the vertical. Everything from abaft the foc'sle is broken up. Could not see the bell, but found the davit over the companionway where it should have been. I think it has fallen into the gravel. Third Class women's WC jammed in plating next to the break in the foc'sle…The stern is very broken up and in gravel. Did not really have time to do anything other than a quick check of the layout along the port side. Did ten minutes and started up.

The damage to the stern indicated that the vessel had hit the bottom stern-end first, and the hull configuration confirmed that this was the *Princess Ena*. It was forty-nine years since she had gone below the surface.

On later visits, each limited to ten or eleven minutes per day maximum with decompression stops, he found large numbers of scattered portholes, and lanterns in what must have been the lamp room in the forecastle. He also found what appeared to be a bevelled metal strip like a ruler, was unable to guess its function, noticed two holes in it, and realised it was the 'I' from the ship's name letters which had become detached from the bow and sunk to the seabed. At this moment the tide was beginning to run fast, he had problems releasing the line grapnel before ascending, and he had to jettison the letter in the sand between the forecastle and the boilers. When he returned, the whole area had silted over, and nothing was visible. The lanterns, which he had taken out and put in a line on the deck, had also gone and remained unfound on all subsequent visits.

When John Ovenden dived on the ship in the early nineties, he found that the bow was still intact leaning over on its port side but that sections of the side plates of the hull had fallen away onto the seabed. Many portholes down the sides still retained their glass, but in some cases the brass had melted, indicating the ferocity of the fire. Near the engines he found the two telegraphs with their large white dials and 'Liverpool' and 'All Stop' still clearly visible on them.

The SS *Schokland* (1943)

The sinking of the *Schokland* a mile off the south coast of Jersey on the night of 4–5 January 1943 was a major disaster, but since great efforts were made by the German Occupying Force to conceal the event, there was little publicity at the time. The *Schokland* was a merchant steamer, commandeered by the Germans from the Dutch and used for carrying cargo between France, principally St Malo, and the Channel Islands. She was also used to carry passengers when circumstances required, including military personnel travelling back to Germany via France. She was 225 feet in length, 1113 tons gross, and had been built in Holland by A. Vijk and Zonen (and Son) in 1915.

Schokland in her peacetime colours

She was registered at Rotterdam. Her three-cylinder triple expansion steam engine gave her a top speed of ten knots. She was schooner-rigged with a single, very tall funnel, and was long and low in the water. The Germans had added 20mm anti-aircraft guns at her bow and stern, the stern gun raised on a high metal platform reached by vertical ladders, and a photograph exists of her taken in the Old Harbour, St Peter Port with the gun crew up in their nest. She was not elegant, and had been one of many mass-produced ships to come rapidly off the production line without an individual maker's nameplate, but after nearly thirty years of good service in the North Sea and the Channel she was still sturdy and dependable despite a battered appearance. A curious feature of her recent history had concerned repairs made to her at Rotterdam in April 1941 after collision with a Swedish steamship at Cuxhaven. The report on her seaworthiness was made in Rotterdam by a Lloyd's surveyor, writing in English, a year after Holland had been occupied. Her owners were then given as the Scheepvaart and Steenkolen company. Her sinking off Jersey was not due to the efforts of the Allies, but to the incompetence of her relief master who managed to run her fair and square onto a rock in a calm sea on a clear night.

Left: Rudolph Reuter, a survivor from the Schokland
Right: Reuter and John Ovenden meeting in 1999

In his Occupation diary (kept in secret and published after the war in 1945) Leslie Sinel, a reporter on the *Jersey Evening Post*, records the loss of the ship. He gets her name slightly wrong, assumes that she struck the Grande Grune, and is somewhat awry on casualty figures, but his account is very detailed given that any talk about the ship would have been extremely dangerous for a civilian, particularly in view of the fact that the Germans had not ruled out sabotage as the possible cause of the wreck:

> January 5th 1943. In the small hours distress signals are sent out by a German ship (the *Schottland*, 1,500 tons) which had struck the rocks known as the Grande Grune, about a mile to the south-west of Noirmont Point. The ship had left here with the *Holland* the previous evening and had been waiting for an escort before proceeding to France, via the western passage; she had a Dutch skipper, and there were 370 passengers, the majority being soldiers going on leave. Boats going to the wreck were not very successful at rescue work, for only 40 were saved, 330 being lost. Many were in the water for several hours, including the Guernsey Censor (who was rescued), and all day today bodies have been washed up at various points along the south coast. A number of wooden spars has also been washed up, many of them being seized by inhabitants before they were seen by the German authorities.

 *The captain's nameplate recovered from the Schokland*

January 6th. More bodies are being washed up, and wreaths and coffins have been ordered by the Germans; many of the dead have been taken to the General Hospital, and most of the burials are to take place at St Brelade's cemetery, where already there are scores of soldiers.

January 8th. More bodies are being washed up and burials carried out.

January 11th. More bodies from the wreck are being washed up and it is learned that a raft with four German soldiers on it has been found at the Minquiers, with the occupants all fairly well after a severe buffeting.

Ralph Mollet, who worked in the Bailiff's office during the occupation, also kept a secret diary (published after the war with the title *Jersey Under the Swastika*) and he refers to the vessel as the 'Scoland' – another indication that the German authorities kept a tight clamp on all information concerning her loss.

At the time many islanders entertained the sabotage theory, more in hope than anything else. Sinel's diary was reprinted several times after 1945 and in one of the later editions he added a footnote to his account:

About a year after Liberation, a Spaniard called to inform me that his comrade – also a Spaniard, who was working on the quays under the Todts – had made a bomb, and placed it in the hold of the *Schokland*. He said the fuse was set to go off at 1.30 a.m., and he helped to steal the dynamite for this purpose.

This claim, as we shall see, was inaccurate.

The *Schokland* had been unloading a general cargo in St Helier on 4 January, when she was ordered at short notice to proceed directly to St Malo to fetch something, return to St Helier and then complete the unloading. There was a large contingent of German troops going on leave waiting for a troop transporter to take them to St Malo; this had been delayed, and they were told they could travel down on the *Schokland* if they wished to. A large number accordingly clambered on board, finding what space they could between the cement, rolls of wire and other cargo, impatient to be on their way home, some of them after years away from Germany. When she sailed with another freighter, the *Holland*, at 6.30 p.m. she had 284 troop passengers on board in addition to her crew of twenty-six. The two vessels moved out into St Aubin's Bay and anchored, awaiting a boat from Guernsey and the two VP (*Vorpostenboot*) armed picket ships which were to escort them to St Malo. The night was clear, and the sea calm, although it was very cold. Research by W. M. Ginns of the Channel Islands Occupation Society at the Convoy Office at St Malo has shown that the *Schokland*'s master that night was a relief who had been flown into Jersey only that afternoon, a Dutchman who had no previous knowledge of Channel Island waters.

The escort ships arrived south of the island at 11.30 p.m. and signalled for the two cargo vessels to move out to join them at a point south of St Brelade's Bay beyond the inshore reefs. Lighthouses, normally blacked out, were briefly lit to help the ships effect the rendezvous. As the *Holland* and the *Schokland* approached, the VP boats realised that the *Schokland* was turning to the south too soon, putting her on-line for several dangerous hazards. Flares were fired to warn her, but at that point she struck, with severe damage below the waterline. She sent an immediate distress call, and fired rockets. Two boats came out from St Helier to join the *Holland* and render assistance, and at some risk to themselves the VP boats moved in to give aid, but within half an hour, at about 1.30 a.m., she sank. She went down by the stern, and it was later reported that a number of men had been trapped in one of the stern holds. There was time to launch one of the two lifeboats, but most of the passengers and crew had gone into the bitterly cold water, not all in lifejackets. Of the 310 people on board only 170 were taken out of the water and landed alive that night. Four more survivors were picked up in the succeeding days, some having drifted on makeshift rafts miles from the island, and twelve further bodies were picked up or washed up on the beaches. The final toll was 174 surviving, twenty-seven bodies found, and 109 missing – a total loss of 136.

The *Holland* and the VP boats worked for several hours to pick up those in the water, but confusion surrounded other rescue attempts. Four harbour protection boats and a tug were hurriedly mobilised to go to the scene, but for some reason they went one and a half miles south-east to the Demie de Pas light instead of two and a half miles south-west, so that their search attempts were fruitless. This misdirection or misunderstanding certainly contributed to the number of lives lost.

On board the *Schokland* was the young Rudolph Reuter, aged twenty-two, a private in the occupying force tank division (French tanks had been taken to Jersey in 1942). He survived the wreck and the war, and in the 1960s returned to Jersey on holiday, when he recounted his experiences to a local reporter, Pauline Boddie. We interviewed him again in the summer of 1999, and from his two accounts have put together this story of his survival.

He had been taking his first leave home after over a year on the island and was not impressed with the ship, which was crowded, uncomfortable and full of timber and bags of cement for the trip to St Malo. There was a bitterly cold wind blowing, and he looked for a sheltered corner to sit in, going first to a spot near the gun crew's quarters:

All the soldiers were singing and everyone was happy to be going on leave; there were some French girls on board too, although I didn't know that until later. It was too cold on deck, and I felt warm air coming up from the engine room, and no one noticed me as I went down the stairs. A Dutch sailor said that he hadn't seen me, and he let me sit down there. I dozed against the warm boiler.

St Brelade's cemetery, where twenty-seven of the Schokland casualties were buried

Suddenly there was a loud crash, and the lights went out. There was another, smaller impact, and the lights returned. He then saw water running in along the large pipes along the engine room bulkhead, first a small flow, then a cascade. Water was rushing across the floor at high pressure and he could see a hole opening up in the rusty plates in her side:

> It was getting bigger and bigger, so I told the engineer and he promptly sent me upstairs. I took my pistol from my luggage and a piece of sausage, and as I reached the top of the steps I looked down and saw the engineer putting out the boiler fire.

As he came on deck distress rockets were being fired, and he saw one lifeboat already in the water with some men and eight to ten women in it. There was a desperate attempt being made by a group to release the second lifeboat, but this was not successful. No one seemed to be in charge or giving orders and there was a good deal of panic. Men were jumping off the deck into the water, some stripping their clothes off first, some holding suitcases, one man clutching a goose under his coat with its head protruding:

> I thought about trying to cut the ropes to release the boat, but I wouldn't have had time, the ship was sinking so quickly. Men were jumping overboard with their luggage, while others were trying to swim across to the *Holland* and other boats which had let down ropes and ladders. But there were too many on each rope, and they couldn't all be pulled up. Many must have drowned then.

Reuter found a life-raft on the deck, but it was under a heavy pile of wire which he could not move. He got hold of a piece of timber, and went into the water with it. The *Schokland* was now going under. He then saw an empty life-raft floating nearby, surrounded by pieces of planking, and he clambered onto it. It was seaworthy but damaged, so that he was sitting in water. He tried to paddle towards one of the other ships, which picked him out in its searchlight, but the crew shouted down that as he was not in immediate danger they would give priority to those in the water and pick him up later. What the rescuers had underestimated was the speed of the rising tide, which now pulled him and all the wreckage surrounding him away towards St Helier. He was swept around to the east of the island passing Gorey and St Catherine's breakwater and on towards the north-east.

After about an hour he had managed to pick a floating oar out of the water, and he attempted to move the raft with it, but the tide was too strong:

I thought of trying to row ashore despite the mines and barbed wire that I
guessed would be there, and I rowed until my hands were skinned to the bone
in parts, but it was no use. I even put my coat up on an oar as a sail, but it made
no difference.

As the coast began to recede he nearly gave way to the desperate temptation of abandoning the raft and trying to swim ashore, a course which with tide, cold water and mines would certainly have proved fatal.

By daylight he was already leaving the island behind and heading in the direction of Les Ecrehous, which lie five miles north-east of Jersey. He had drifted some fifteen miles altogether, east and then north around the coast, and he was now convinced that he would drift for days until he died. There was a cold, hard wind and he was still wet through. As a desperate measure he fired six shots from his pistol, hoping that he might be heard by someone. The last round he kept for himself in the event of not being rescued. He then saw a rocket go up on the coast, but it is not clear whether this was in response to his signals. As it happened, a tug was out that day searching for bodies along the north coast of the island, and two hours after he had fired the shots Reuter saw this tug coming towards him. The Germans on board were accompanied by one of the St Helier harbour pilots, Silva Le Riche, who had been given the unenviable task of negotiating the tug around the offshore mines without being told where they had been laid. They had already picked up a number of *Schokland* bodies. Reuter saw the tug coming towards him, but was then distraught to see it turn away. In fact it had seen him but was avoiding mines, and it blew the letter 'V' for *verstehen* (understand) in Morse on its siren to show that he was recognised. It then turned back towards him and picked him up. It was late afternoon and he had been on the sea for sixteen hours in the bitter cold without water or food. He recalls Silva Le Riche telling him that in all his professional career he had never known of a case where someone had survived exposure on the sea for that length of time in winter. Back on Jersey he was to spend the next eight weeks in hospital recovering from his ordeal.

His account clears up one mystery surrounding the ship, the truth of the claim that there had been women on the *Schokland* that night. The German authorities did not list any women among the drowned, saved or missing, but there were strong rumours at the time that on board had been a number of prostitutes from the forces' brothel at the Victor Hugo hotel. Another version of the story suggests that there might have been some German nurses travelling on the ship. Certainly pilot Le Riche and lifeboatman Larbalestier, the two Jerseymen who helped recover bodies from the water next day, both said that there had been women on board.

Twenty-seven of the dead were duly buried with full honours in the military cemetery at St Brelade's church. The pillars at the heads of the graves were surmounted by large iron crosses with swastikas at their centre and postcard photographs exist of these graves taken just after the war. The headstones were later removed.

The discovery of the *Schokland* in 1964 was Tony Titterington's first major Jersey wreck find, and he is now the owner of the ship with the right to all fittings. At the time, many islanders still remembered her sinking, and her mast tops were

Compressed air cylinder lying in the stern hold

A soldier's helmet together with his possessions

Schokland's main cargo of cement stacked in her hold

Above: Live ammunition still stacked in racks after fifty years submerged on the bottom
Left: Still discernible, this ladder may have led the way to safety for some of the survivors

visible at the lowest tides until 1948. Her (approximate) position was shown on Admiralty charts.

His diving log reads as follows:

Wednesday 1st July 1964. Dived on SS *Schokland.* It was found by taking transit marks and buoying the position, then doing a circular search by echo sounder. It was located within half an hour. I dived tended by John Faiers. Vessel is lying on a flat stony bottom in an upright position with bows to the west and stern to the east. Its condition is fairly good. The upper bridge has gone as this section seems to have been made of wood but all the metal-plated sections of the upper works are still intact. The forward hold is cement bags still stacked in rows. Number Two hold, just forward of the bridge, has a cargo of steel girders. The

Tony Titterington with the builders' plate

aft hold has wooden beams and these are tucked under the engines with rolls of tarred felt or similar material going towards the stern. All the area between these is covered with soft mud to the upper webs of the hatch side walks [the webs are stiffening plates under the upper deck, indicating that the depth of mud in the holds was about 17 feet]. German equipment showed in the mud. A mast lies across the stern hold from the engine room to the poop. I found the ship's bell in a cleft between the bridge and the forward hold. All ship's lamps are lying around the area. The light broke up on moving and the glass fell out. The prop is iron.

Monday 6th July 1964. Dived on *Schokland*. Checked around the bows and found a hole under the stem and a gash approximately 6 to 8 feet up the port bow. Found two anchors on deck by the winch, also glass and the masthead lamp lost on the first dive. Caught a lobster, lost glass again on ascent. Got another cylinder, 40 cubic foot, and dived again on the port side. Found the glass on the port side opposite the bridge, also the ship's telegraph.

The anchors Tony had found were spares bolted to the deck. The two main anchors were still stowed in their hawser pipes, indicating that no attempt had been made to release them at the time of the striking.

The ship is in twenty metres of water, and Tony dived on her two or three times a week for over a month. In the course of these visits he found rows of plates in the galley racks, rifles in what had been the marines' quarters, helmets, more crockery marked with the eagle and swastika, and 20mm ammunition and ammunition boxes up on the forepeak. He also noted a number of signs indicating that German naval divers had probably worked on the ship soon after she went down. Over her stern hold there had been a row of substantial iron beams laid; a number of these had been unbolted and removed, some dropped in the gangways, one put on the seabed leaning against the hull. This suggested that divers had been into the hold to remove part of its contents. The stern gun had also been lifted off its main mount.

From his examination of the ship and the holes at her bow and along the sides, Tony is certain that she was not sabotaged but sank as a result of a collision with a rock. There was no bomb, as the Germans quickly ascertained themselves. The obvious question – did the Dutch master deliberately run her onto the rock – can also be answered in the negative. He was unfamiliar with the area, there were German officers on the bridge alongside him all the time, and the chances of deliberately hitting the rock she did hit in the dark were extremely small. Hence his exoneration at the military inquiry that followed. From the ship's position on the bottom it is clear that she was not attempting to pass out along the Sillette or Middle Passages, but was going west behind the other vessel in the convoy to round the Passage Rock before they turned SSW for St Malo.

At that point the tide was rising, pushing everything to the east. As the ship ahead drifted across on the turn, the *Schokland* turned a little too quickly after her and hit the South West Heads, where she shed some of her plates. The damage was substantial, water began to flood into her immediately, and she passed on only a few hundred yards before stopping.

Years later, revisiting the *Schokland*, Tony found her builder's nameplate with the ship's job number lying in front of the boilers where it had fallen down from the bridge. This bore the name of A.Vuijk, scheepsbouwmeesters, Capelle A/D Ijsel, Holland.

In 1990 John Ovenden dived on the *Schokland* for the first time. He recorded his impressions in his diving log:

> As we descended I saw the eerie shape appearing out of the darkness. An
> amazing sight, almost intact apart from the superstructure. Came down by
> the bridge section where you could see the remains of cabins with cupboards
> intact, timber floors, brass portholes, and a shiny white bath looking as it must
> have the night she sank. Just forward of the bridge is a hold stacked with steel
> girders. The forward hold has cement bags in neat piles. The stern is full of silt
> but you could see helmets, boxes of ammunition, wine bottles, even a rifle.
> Went round the stern straight into the largest propeller and rudder I'd ever
> seen.

Rudolph Reuter's account describing women on board has been supported by the finding of earrings in the vessel (by Tony) and of a woman's chain-work purse with a roll of film in it (by John Ovenden). It is possible that these were being taken back home either as presents or souvenirs by soldiers, and there were other signs of loot in the shape of steelware with 'Sandringham Hotel' stamped on it, but the finds substantiate the claims about female passengers made at the time.

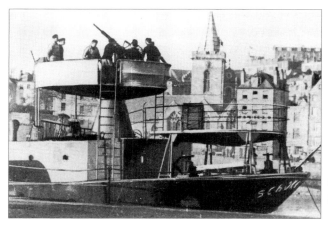

*Schokland alongside in
St Peter Port harbour*

HMS *Charybdis* (1943) and HMS *Limbourne* (1943)

The naval disaster that had most impact on the civilian population of the Channel Islands during the Second World War was the sinking of the cruiser *Charybdis* and the destroyer *Limbourne* off the Brittany coast on the night of 22–23 October 1943, about fifty miles from the islands. Over five hundred British seamen were lost from the two ships, with fifty-nine bodies washed up on Jersey, Guernsey and Sark. The loss of the ships was one of the worst disasters the Royal Navy suffered in the English Channel during the war. In Guernsey the burial of the dead saw a massive silent demonstration by thousands of islanders who went to the Foulon cemetery to witness the funerals.

Until this disaster *Charybdis* had had a distinguished war. Built by Cammell Laird, Birkenhead, and commissioned November 1941, she had joined the fleet in March 1942. She was a Dido class cruiser of 5700 tons displacement, 512 feet long with a top speed of 33 knots and a complement of 580. Nicknamed the 'Blue Devil' by the Germans because of her dazzle pattern, she had come unscathed through one of the most destructive convoy operations of the war – Operation Pedestal, the mission to escort merchant ships to beleaguered Malta in the summer of 1942. The convoy had involved two battleships, three aircraft

The launching of HMS Charybdis at Birkenhead

Above left: A diver approaching a quadruple pom-pom gun on HMS Limbourne

Above right: A diver examining a searchlight on Charybdis

Right: Captain George Voelcker in command of HMS Charybdis

*Charybdis under attack
during Operation Pedestal.
Photo taken by Dennis Nicholls*

carriers, eight cruisers, and twenty-eight destroyers all escorting the fourteen merchant vessels. For the three days and nights – 11, 12 and 13 August – the convoy was under continuous attack from Italian and German submarines, E-Boats, Stukas and torpedo bombers as it travelled from Gibraltar. Many of the escorting warships were sunk, 350 men were killed, and only five of the merchant vessels got through, but enough cargo was delivered to the island to save it. By holding Malta as a British base, it was later possible to cut off important supplies to Rommel in the North African desert. Surrounded by burning and sinking ships, *Charybdis* suffered no casualties, although her gunners were repeatedly at action stations for twelve hours at a time, and once back at Gibraltar – where she was given the honour of leading the fleet in – her gun barrels had to be replaced because they were worn out.

In 1943 she escorted Winston Churchill on board the *Queen Mary* across the Atlantic for talks with President Roosevelt in America, and she also carried troops for the North African landings. In September 1943 she carried General Eisenhower to the beachhead at Salerno in southern Italy for the Allied invasion. She also transported some of the unfortunate 8th Army Salerno mutineers from North Africa. These men, many wounded and all exhausted after the long desert campaign, were lied to by their officers and told that they were rejoining their units. They were carried by three cruisers, one being *Charybdis*, to the beaches, and once landed 191 men mutinied. The savage reprisals taken against them by their own superiors was one of the most shameful events of the war, and *Charybdis* crew members are on record as finding the duplicity practised on the men outrageous.

Birkenhead's 'warships week' committee, led by the mayor, decided to adopt *Charybdis* in 1942, no mere token gesture, since this meant the need for local people and businesses to collect £1,000,000 to 'purchase' the ship as a contribution to the war effort. A plaque bearing the borough's coat of arms was subsequently presented and fixed on the quarter-deck, and her activities were thereafter reported in the *Liverpool Echo* in as much detail as government censorship would permit. Noel Coward, carried on *Charybdis* as a passenger from Plymouth to Gibraltar when he was working on publicity material for the Royal Navy, described her in his diary as a very happy ship.

In 1943 German merchant vessels were regularly running at night under warship protection from Brest to Cherbourg via St Malo, keeping close to the Brittany and Normandy coasts. To counter these movements, a small task force of British ships, despatched from Plymouth, would regularly carry out a sweep of the north Brittany coast to intercept the enemy convoys. The operation went under the code name 'Tunnel'.

On 19 October the German merchant ship *Munsterland* was reported to be at Brest, en route for Cherbourg. She had come from Japan, and was carrying a cargo of tungsten, chromium and rubber for the manufacture of armaments in Germany. This cargo was vital to Germany's war effort, and the ship had been identified as a prime target by the Allies. For some reason – possibly because of fear of sabotage by the Resistance as it passed along the French rail system – the Germans had decided to move the cargo by sea. The RAF attacked Brest in an attempt to sink the ship but the raid failed. Air reconnaissance on the 20th over Cherbourg showed that she had not yet arrived there, and the Commander-in-Chief Plymouth accordingly ordered a sweep for the night of the 22nd–23rd. Force 28 duly sailed from Plymouth at 1900 hours on the 22nd hoping to intercept the *Munsterland* and her escort moving east along the Brittany coast.

In order to give Force 28 extra power and increase its chances of destroying the convoy, an innovation in the form of a heavyweight was added, namely HMS *Charybdis*, under the command of Captain George Voelcker RN, a former submariner who had taken the ship successfully through 'Pedestal'. *Charybdis* was just back from the Mediterranean and was due for a spell in dry dock. The ship's company was looking forward to leave, and the men were surprised that they had to take her out again for a Channel exercise. Many were due at shore barracks, but because of accommodation problems they had been ordered to stay on the ship another twenty-four hours, and this actually put her above normal complement on the night of the 22nd–23rd. With *Charybdis* were two Fleet destroyers, *Grenville* and *Rocket*, and four Hunt class destroyers, *Limbourne*, *Talybont*, *Wensleydale* and *Stevenstone*. Some of the destroyer captains expressed concerns at the inappropriateness of adding a cruiser to the group, particularly one that had never been on the Tunnel exercise before, but these misgivings were ignored by the operation planners at Plymouth. There was also unease at the decision to adopt a line-ahead formation, where previously the destroyers had moved line abreast in order to reduce any damage to the group as a whole from torpedoes fired on their beam.

Maintaining radio silence and blacked out, the group crossed the Channel in single line ahead keeping out of range of the German heavy guns on Guernsey. It was a cold night, and to the men just back from the Med it seemed bitter. At 0030 (half past midnight), having arrived just north of Les Sept Iles, seven miles off the Brittany coast to the south-west of Jersey, they turned west and began their sweep at 13 knots. Unknown to them the *Munsterland*, escorted by six M-class minesweepers and five T (torpedo) boats, was closing from the west, and also unknown to them, German coastal radar was already alerted to their presence.

The Elbing class boat T23 that torpedoed HMS Charybdis

The escorting German torpedo boats, T22, T23, T25, T26 and T27 of the Fourth *Torpedobooteflotille* had left Brest at 1800 hours the same evening and caught up with the *Munsterland* and the minesweepers at 2145 as they proceeded east. These T-Boats were double-funnelled and of small destroyer size, 334 feet in length, 1294 tons displacement, capable of 33 knots, and in addition to guns and mines carried six torpedoes each. All had been built between 1941 and 1942 by

Schichau, and were referred to collectively as Elbing class vessels. Guided by the shore communications, and shortly afterwards picking up the echo of *Charybdis* on their own radar, they adjusted their course slightly to the north and moved away from the minesweepers and the *Munsterland* to come within striking distance of the approaching British group. Their initial intention was to attack from the north, but they then altered course to starboard to come south of the British line.

Some of the British destroyers carried 'Headache' radio, which allowed them to intercept German signals, and at 0045 *Wensleydale* picked up some messages apparently passing between the enemy in the area. At 0103 an unintelligible enemy signal was also overheard by *Limbourne* and the information 'three units close' was passed to *Charybdis* at the head of the line. The British group was having difficulty with radio tuning, and *Charybdis* asked for a repeat. At 0130 *Limbourne* picked up more radio signals, indicating at least five and probably six enemy units close by, and at the same moment *Charybdis* got a radar echo at a range of 14,000 yards (just under eight miles) due west. For reasons which are not clear, neither ship exchanged this information with the other nor with the rest of Force 28, and the radar on the destroyers was being masked by *Charybdis* directly ahead of them. *Charybdis* thus knew where the 'something' was, but not what it was; *Limbourne* knew what it was, but not where. At 0135 *Charybdis* signalled her radar contact, now at a range of 8,000 yards (four and a half miles), to the other ships.

HMS Limbourne

The signals *Limbourne* had picked up at 0130 were the German T-Boats being ordered to alter course by *Korvettenkapitan* Franz Kohlauf to put them in attack position south of the British line, and at 0138 *Leutnant* Paul of T23 got a sighting of *Charybdis* (the moon had risen at 0125). At 0143 *Charybdis* radioed for the British group to turn slightly to starboard and increase speed to 18 knots. Unfortunately because of the radio problems this signal was picked up only by *Stevenstone*. *Charybdis* went forward alone on the new heading, drawing away and leaving herself isolated. She had still had no visual sighting of the enemy, but the T-Boats could see her and were moving in at 27 knots. Seeing the cruiser coming straight for them, they were now in a state of considerable anxiety. Kohlauf's log on T24 reads:

Leutnant Paul, commander of T23,
addressing some of his crew

0142; Saw a major enemy vessel making straight for us at 15 [sic] knots. The situation critical. When the enemy opened fire he would surely hit one or several vessels in the flotilla, and I didn't believe anything hit could escape. Surprisingly the enemy was observing complete radio silence. Behind him were two destroyers. Torpedoes made ready.

Between 0143 and 0144 two things happened. Paul on T23 made a tight turn and fired six torpedoes at *Charybdis* in a fan formation, and the cruiser turned slightly again and fired starshell (magnesium flares) to illuminate the enemy and bring her guns to bear. Both sides estimated the same distance between them – the Germans around 3,500 metres, the British 4,000 yards (just over two miles). The British were also maintaining hydrophone and echo sounder silence and were not aware of what was happening until, in the light of the starshell, torpedo tracks could be seen approaching *Charybdis* on the port side. Gerald Evans, a wireman, was standing at one of the port searchlights waiting for the order to open the shutters and light up any target, when he saw four white tracks rushing towards the ship through the water. Captain Voelcker ordered an immediate hard turn to port, but less than a minute later there was a colossal explosion

The torpedo impact into the port side of the Charybdis hurled many of the crew off thier feet

as *Charybdis* was hit. To AB Submarine Detector Dennis Nicholls, who was on the port afterbridge, the explosion seemed to be directly beneath him, and John Eskdale, who was at a high point of the ship at 'Y' gun turret, describes a huge wave being thrown up by the explosion that swept men near him over the side. Suffering massive damage, and with a dynamo room and 'B' boiler room flooded, *Charybdis* slowed and then stopped, already listing 10 degrees. About ten minutes later, at 0154 or 0155 she was hit again by a torpedo from T27. The time between first radar contact at eight miles and destruction had been less than twenty minutes.

The senior surviving officer on board *Charybdis* was Commander E. Oddie. In his official report he wrote:

> When the range had closed to 4000 yards we fired three starshells from 'B' mounting. I was on the bridge at the time, which I judged to be 0145. Simultaneously two torpedo tracks were reported approaching the ship from the port side, and the captain ordered hard-a-port. The ship was hit by one torpedo on the port side, probably underneath the torpedo tube.
>
> I left the bridge and proceeded to the upper deck to take charge there. On my arrival the ship had a list of about 20 degrees, increasing slowly. As I proceeded aft the ship was hit again on the port side. The approximate time of the hit was 0155. It did a lot of damage which was apparent on deck. The after director was displaced and the deck was blown up aft. The list increased rapidly and soon put the deck under water on the port side.

Reports differ as to whether *Charybdis* was first hit by one torpedo or by two almost simultaneously. On board some thought she had been hit by only one, but the T-Boats believed they had hit her with two together. Paul's log on T23 reads as follows:

> 0142; Sighted a cruiser and two destroyers on her line. Gave the order to fire torpedoes. Distance 3000-3500 metres. 0143; The situation of my ship and of the flotilla was very vulnerable. I expected at any moment to see the flames from the cruiser's guns and for her to hit us. We waited as the torpedoes went. The tension on board

Lookouts on the German T23

was high. 0145; I saw the smoke of two explosions, almost simultaneous, on the large target aft of the bridge, level with the second funnel. Straight afterwards I felt three detonations which were like those of mines going off. Two seemed to come together, the third a moment later. I was certain we had hit the cruiser with two torpedoes, and the following destroyer with another.

R. G. 'Rattler' Morgan, in charge of the *Asdic*, had been making his way to the top bridge just before *Charybdis* was struck:

I had ascended three ladders when one of the ship's guns started to open up, firing star-shell fused to burst behind the ships to show them outlined. Seconds later my senses were numbed and shocked by the most awful explosion imaginable coming from some point amidships. The whole ship seemed to rear up out of the water like some stricken animal, settling back a little later with a list over to port. The shock of the explosion had thrown me off my feet. The lights had gone out when the dynamos were shattered. I started to make my way down below decks again, this time via the outer ladders. When I got about half-way down, I was almost flung the remainder of the way by the shock of

*Jim Duckworth,
Chief Petty Officer*

a second explosion – as near as I could judge in approximately the same position as the first.

A few moments later the First Lieutenant's voice was heard informing the men that the Captain wished no one to leave the ship yet as our accompanying destroyers had made off – presumably in an effort to bring the enemy ships into action. By this time the ship had increased her list to 45 degrees and we found some difficulty in maintaining our grips on the starboard guard rails where we had congregated, ready to slide down the sloping ship's side and into the water when the cry 'abandon ship' came. We could clearly hear the overstrained bulkheads down between decks bursting under the enormous pressure of water.

Most of the men around me had now shifted their positions to the outside of the guard rails, relieving themselves of the strain of holding onto the inside. I could dimly make out the form of someone slashing with his knife at the ropes which held in position one of the Carley rafts. At last the two fateful words 'abandon ship' came. A last check on my lifebelt, a hasty look around, a small cheerio to my left hand neighbour, and then I was sliding on my beam ends down the ship's side. I hit the water seat first.

When the first torpedo struck, David 'Rocky' Royle was down in the ship in the radar room. On the screen he watched the enemy closing from 8,000 yards to 6,000, to 4,000 and then heard in his earphones the order for 'B' gun to fire:

> Suddenly there was a terrific explosion. I left my seat, hit the deckhead, and fell back across the table. All the lights had failed. Water was rushing in somewhere. The ship was now listing over to port, so that in the inky blackness one could not tell if one was standing on the deck or on the dividing bulkhead.

He and his shipmates groped their way out in the pitch dark, and climbed a ladder. The escape hatch at the top wouldn't open, and it took time for them to force it. They ascended a second ladder, now lying almost level, and emerged on the deck to find the sea lapping over the port side.

The torpedo explosions had killed men and started fires, and some were badly injured by scalding steam. Chief Petty Officer Jim Duckworth tried to fight his way through to rescue a man in the sick bay, but he was driven back by the flames. The situation inside the ship was made worse by the loss of all power and lights, and she was filling rapidly from the holes in her side. It was not possible to launch lifeboats because of the angle of the list, and because there was no power for the electric cranes.

Stoker Roger Roberts, down below in the engine room with two colleagues, was frantically pumping oil and water between port and starboard tanks to try and reduce the ship's list. He was aware that the after hatches above them were closed, and that if the ship went down they had no chance of escaping. They worked until the list was so bad that their efforts became pointless, and then began to make their way forward walking on the wall. Luckily a hatch was opened for them by someone above and they were able to get out and over the side.

Eric Brookes had been down in the magazine, and he also describes a desperate struggle to get out of the ship. He and four others climbed ladders until they were blocked by a jammed hatch. They forced it part open, and then Eric, the smallest, squeezed through, and by pulling while his mates pushed, managed to free it. He recalls fires, dense choking smoke, and a strong smell of cordite and explosive. He went into the water where sheets of oil were burning fiercely and managed to swim around the flames.

As *Charybdis* had moved away, Commander W. J. Phipps on *Limbourne* had not picked up the signal to alter course and increase speed. He still did not know where the enemy was, and for a brief moment as *Charybdis* made her attacking turn ahead of him thought she was the enemy. He immediately fired rocket flares, some of which burst prematurely, lighting up both *Charybdis* and *Limbourne* 'like a ballet dancer' in the words of AB Len Bates of *Charybdis*. *Charybdis* was already clear to the enemy, but the flares helped them home in on *Limbourne*, and at 0151, about four minutes after *Charybdis* had been hit for the first time, T22 put a torpedo into her. There was no warning. Neil Wood, a radar operator, heard the port Oerlikon (anti-aircraft) gunner yell, 'Torpedo on the port quarter' and almost at the same moment there was 'an almighty bang'. *Limbourne* was hit forward, and the forward magazine blew up, taking her entire bow off as far as the bridge. T23's log records:

> 0151; We saw a flash to port accompanied by an
> explosion. It was like an ammunition dump going
> up with tracer flying through the air. The explosion was
> different from that seen on the cruiser. Two vessels were
> burning at 210-220 (degrees) about 1000 metres apart.

Fortunately *Limbourne*'s remaining bulkheads held, and although listing badly she was not in immediate danger of sinking. It was exactly one year since her commissioning, on 24 October 1942. Neil Wood recalls how, trapped in the radar room where the door had jammed, he heard the cry to abandon ship. At the last minute his shouts and hammering were heard and someone forced the door from the outside to let him out.

Such was the good organisation of the German group that they were able to pass south along the British line firing twenty-four torpedoes in ten minutes. It was amazing good fortune

Neil Wood,
radar operator

that only two of the British ships were hit, and several torpedoes appear to have passed under the hulls of other destroyers. The T-Boats then turned away and, under cover of a heavy rain storm which closed down visibility, moved rapidly back to the *Munsterland*, which reached Lazardrieux later that morning unscathed. Force 28 still did not know what ships had attacked them, and had not seen them. The Germans had not needed to fire a single gun, and had therefore not given their positions away.

Among the British ships there was considerable confusion. After the war Roger Hill, in command of *Grenville*, described the attack in his memoir *Destroyer Captain* (1975). 'The next ten minutes,' he wrote, 'were hair-raising. The force was in complete confusion.' At first it was thought that *Charybdis* and *Rocket* had been hit. *Stevenstone* had picked up the signal to alter course and accelerate, and had done so, but the rest of the group was unsure whether to follow suit and there were near collisions between several ships. Torpedoes were fired towards the south in retaliation, but at nothing in particular. At 0231, having received no orders from *Charybdis* or *Limbourne*, Hill took command as senior officer, and ordered the remainder of Force 28 to move north and regroup. At about the same time, *Charybdis* was disappearing below the water.

The fear now was that German ships would wait by any stricken vessels and attack anything trying to rescue the crews, and it was believed that the attack had been made by E-Boats – small, very fast vessels capable of over 40 knots which carried a reload of torpedoes. Consequently the British group headed north, intending to return and search for survivors only at daybreak. In fact the T-Boats did not carry additional torpedoes, and having made their attack they quickly left the area having been informed by the shore radar stations that another British force might be moving towards them, which was not the case. The effect of this was to remove all seaworthy ships capable of rescue, with the result that some of the men from the British ships were in the water until 0630 – over four hours – and many did not survive this ordeal. Not only was the sea bitterly cold, but the furnace oil that poured out of *Charybdis* covered a wide area, smothering and poisoning many of those struggling to stay afloat.

R. G. Morgan's account continues:

My brain did not register any conscious shock of cold as I took that first plunge – I was so keyed up that I just did not think about it. The one thought that kept pulsing in my brain was to get away from the ship as quickly as possible. So I struck out and did not relax my efforts until I was completely exhausted. Floating about slowly regaining some of my strength and gasping for breath as wave after wave broke over my head I happened to glance over my shoulder and caught a glimpse of a dark mass behind me. With a shock I realised it was the ship; in spite of my frantic efforts I had not travelled more than ten yards. I felt hopelessly discouraged, as I had hoped to be well clear by this time. I made no further attempt to get away, indeed I don't think I could have mustered sufficient energy to do so. After a while I took another glance at the ship and to my utter amazement I saw that her forward part was standing almost perpendicularly out of the water to a height of what must have been well over a hundred feet. I had the terrifying impression of the whole mass being about to topple over towards me.

Other survivors spoke of this impression that the ship was standing almost vertically in the water with over a hundred feet of her bow projecting. Given that she was in about 80 metres of water (260 feet), and given that her length was over 500 feet, her stern was almost certainly already on the bottom, and she was upright at an angle, probably with nearer 150 feet projecting. Others described men jumping down this awful height and dying as a result, either from the impact with the water or from having others land on top of them.

Morgan:

I found that I had plenty of companions in my vicinity – most of the lads were conserving what remaining strength they had and endeavouring to avoid swallowing too much of the nauseous mixture of crude oil fuel and salt water. After a while I received a terrific thump in my right side and to my immense relief I discovered that I had come into collision with a large plank or log of wood, a heaven-sent gift of which I took immediate advantage by firmly clasping my arm around it. There must have been about thirty men clinging on. Peering through the darkness I once again made out the huge hulk of the ship with her bows still pointed skyward as the tide carried us away. That was the last we saw of *Charybdis*.

The whole of my body now felt deathly cold, and nothing I did to try to alleviate the excruciating pain seemed to have any effect. The sea was still fairly boisterous and the waves still broke over our heads. Every now and then I had violent fits of vomiting, each bout leaving me weaker. Every one of our party was by this time well nigh physically exhausted. Time and again one of the chaps would heave his stomach across the log to gain a few seconds rest, with the inevitable result that it was completely submerged and adding to the acute discomfort of the remainder of the party. Every time this happened loud curses rent the night air.

Seamen from HMS Charybdis pitched into the dark, oil-filled and cold October waters (artist's impression)

As the long night dragged by he saw despairing men close to him give up the struggle, deliberately deflating their lifebelts, throwing up their arms and letting themselves sink below the surface.

HMS Wensleydale

Talking to survivors today it is clear that this is one of the recollections that gives them most distress when they come to retell their experiences. The thought occurred to Morgan to do the same, but something told him to stick it out for a little longer each time. When the moon broke through the clouds he could see bodies floating close by rolling sluggishly in the waves, upturned faces glistening. He could no longer feel any sensation in his legs:

> We endeavoured to console ourselves with the prospect of the coming daylight which now could not be so far away. We might possibly catch a sight of land, or a ship might come up, or a plane fly overhead. We did not stop to think that if we did sight any of these it was an even chance we should find ourselves in the hands of the enemy. Even if we had thought about it I don't think it would have worried us; getting out of the hellish water was our only desire. The sky over on the horizon ahead of us was showing some indication of greyish light when to my ears came a rushing sound, not unlike that of a strong wind, and which appeared to be increasing every moment.
>
> Then it struck me – it was a ship; my God, yes, a ship. The noise we were hearing was coming from her boiler uptakes, a destroyer most like, and ten to one a British destroyer. Would it find us? Would they see the tiny red light attached to my lifebelt? In my excitement I tried to detach the lamp intending

Dennis Nicholls, on the right, with his friend Cliff Murray

Steve Keeling, the ship's diver

All lost except Tubby King (seen here with Jago the cat). Arthur 'Flash' Pearse, on left, tragically killed by HMS Stevenstone's screws

to wave it above my head, but the muscles of my fingers were too cramped to respond, and I had to abandon the idea. We could now distinguish practically the complete outline of the ship, a destroyer, which was becoming more distinct as she nosed her way towards us. Thank God; we could make out the dim figures on her decks as they stood by to pick us up.

At last a line was thrown. How good it was to feel the sensation of being pulled through the water towards the ship. I could make out the scramble net dangling in the water. I lost no time in getting a firm grip on it with my hands, succeeded in getting a foothold in the mesh, and commenced to climb. At least, I made an attempt at it. With dismay I realised that the effort was utterly beyond me. Surely we were not to fail now? A few seconds later I felt strong hands grabbing my shoulders. A couple of the lads had climbed down the net to assist me and after a tussle I found myself being pushed through the guard rails like a sack of soggy potatoes. I then passed out. [He was aboard HMS *Rocket*.]

Eric Brookes, swimming away from the ship, had found a floating rope. He wound it round his arm, felt it go taut, and knew it must be attached to something. He part swam, part pulled, and found himself by a Carley float, where he was pulled in by the four on board. Here he remained until the *Wensleydale* picked them up the following morning. During the night, one of his companions, unable to endure the cold and desolation any longer, stepped into the water deliberately.

Bill Hustler, in charge of the Number 4 port Oerlikon guns on *Charybdis* had already had a ship sunk under him, the *Kandahar*, off Malta. As the ship was going down, Dennis Nicholls found him and said, 'You've done this before, Bill, so I'm going with you.' Together they slid down the ship's side into the sea, and managed to swim to a Carley which had about sixty men in it or clinging to it. The Carleys were large oval rubber tubes with a net base, designed to take about twenty men, and they became very unstable when overcrowded. During the night the sea became very rough, and many men were lost as the float tipped over on the downward slopes of the waves. By the time Dennis was rescued there were only seventeen of them still alive. Bill also survived. The oil covering them was so thick that they could not recognise their mates, and some of them were so far gone by the time they were rescued that they did not know whether they had been pulled aboard British or German ships. Once on board, many of the survivors had to be cut out of their clothes and scraped to begin the removal of the oil. Steve Keeling, the ship's diver, had been with Jim Duckworth on one of the anti-aircraft guns when the ship was struck. In the confusion the two men went different ways. After a time Steve went over the side with the help of a rope, and after swimming about on his own found, first, part of a wooden ladder, and then a larger piece of floating timber; hanging onto the other end of this was Jim. They survived the night together and were

Gerald Evans being hoisted to safety by Ernie Mosely.
They were to meet again some fifty-one years later

Left: Ernie Mosely

Right: Gerald Evans

picked up by the *Wensleydale*.

Gerald Evans also managed to get to a Carley which had a crowd of men hanging on to it. Every time the float tipped over men were lost, so that by the time he was rescued there were only four of them left. He managed to swim to the *Wensleydale* and grasp the scrambling net, but was too weak to climb up. Ernie Mosely on the destroyer threw a heaving line down to him, but this was blown away from him by the wind, so Ernie attached a bucket to the end of the line as a weight, and lowered this down. With one foot supported in the bucket Gerald was able to pull his way up to the deck. The two were not to meet again until fifty-one years later in 1994 at a Charybdis and Limbourne Association reunion in Birmingham.

Even at this late stage there were tragic losses of life. Arthur 'Flash' Pearse, having survived the night and seeing *Stevenstone* approaching, swam towards her while she was still under way, and was killed by her screws. Captain Voelcker was seen in the water on a small piece of timber as he approached a float. Because it was severely overcrowded he refused to grab hold of it, and swam away shouting encouragement to his men. He was not seen alive again.

Lawrence Edwards had been off-duty and asleep when action stations was sounded, and he had had no time to dress before going to his post as a gun layer. He was a founder member of the ship, having been with her since her trials in November 1941, and had survived Operation Pedestal. Not long afterwards he found himself going over the side in his shorts and vest, but he had the presence of mind to cut a number of Carley floats free first and push them into the water, an action that undoubtedly saved lives. True to the merciless indifference of the events taking place he was then unable to find room on a float himself, but he managed to survive the night by swimming, kept up only by his lifebelt, and was picked up next morning.

Perhaps the easiest time was had by AB Bill Nightingale, who did everything wrong. In the event of sinking, crews had instructions to go to the high side of the ship; Bill

Left: Laurence Edwards; Centre: Telegraphist Victor Dodds, lost on HMS Charybdis; Right: Maurice Page, who survived the sinking of HMS Limbourne

went to the dipping port side, where he found himself completely alone. Instructions were to remove all heavy clothing; Bill was wearing duffel coat, oilskins and sea boots. He saw a Carley float tied to the guard rail, got in, and cast off. He pulled another man in, and together they remained in the float until rescued at dawn. Bill was landed at Plymouth in immaculate condition, having suffered nothing worse than a bit of damp around the lower legs.

The family of leading mechanic, later petty officer Sydney Leleux still have his combined diary and sketch book which went into the water with him. The pages are stained, and sixty years on the paper still smells of oil. Sydney was fortunate to be one of the survivors (he continued in the navy and died in 1988). He had joined *Charybdis* at Gibraltar only a month before, his previous ships including *King George V,* when he had been present at the sinking of *Bismarck* in 1941. His personal log is illustrated by fine ink sketches, and his survival allowed him to record the events of the 23rd immediately while events were still clear in his mind. It is interesting that his account confirms the German belief that they had first hit *Charybdis* with two torpedoes, striking almost simultaneously.

> 23rd October 1943. While on an offensive operation we were hit by three torpedoes – two amidships and then one astern – at 0045. They had been fired by E-boats which had been detected at 15000 yards and allowed to close to 4000 yards; all we fired was three starshells. The concussion was not so heavy

Left: Captain Goodfellow of HMS Wensleydale, who picked up some of the last remaining survivors; Right: Royal Marine John Eskdale

as I should have expected, just a heavy jar which caused a few loose articles to fall down, then all the lights died and the ship started to list: when the second hit came the list immediately doubled, and it was obvious we were done for, so I slipped my fountain pen and sketch book inside my overalls, blew up my lifebelt, and with the others made my way on deck…By this time the list was about 30 degrees and as word was passed round that two destroyers were coming alongside we all slid down the ship's side into the sea which soon became a mass of dark heads and bodies bobbing in the faint phosphorescence with here and there a larger dark patch to show a float or raft. I saw a man with a bundle of planks, so joined him, and though I may have lost him I never lost those three planks all the time I was in the water. After a few moments I turned to look at the ship, and saw to my amazement and horror that she was vertical, her bows towering above me.

The next five hours were a hell of darkness and cold, drifting in constantly reforming and dwindling groups with our planks to keep us together. At one time I held to a man who was calling for 'Mother', and it comforted him, but I lost him; once an unconscious man drifted past, moaning softly; once a man got his arm entangled in the tapes of my lifebelt, and it terrified me so that I fought frantically to free myself. Oil fuel and salt water burnt our eyes, and we shouted at intervals for help. Lights were occasionally visible, but too far away to be reached, and at last hope almost died; then a shout went up, 'Look, destroyers.' Sure enough, two shapes, one ghostly white in the faint starlight and the other a black silhouette, had appeared, and the group disintegrated as we made for it. With my last strength I left the wood and swam to the ship, where came the worst moments of the night – thrown a rope, my hands were too greasy to get any grip on it, so I swam to the netting on the starboard quarter but was too weak to climb it. In the end four men came over the rail and jointly hauled me aboard, rolling me over the rail like an old sack.

Having moved north, the remainder of Force 28 had then returned to the site of the attack, arriving at 0345 to find the *Charybdis* gone and the crippled *Limbourne* drifting towards the French coast six miles away. Roger Hill radioed the situation to Plymouth and the instructions were for the Fleets to sweep to the west in case of an enemy presence while the Hunts picked up survivors. The Commander-in-Chief Plymouth also ordered all the ships to be out of the area by 0600 at the very latest. While *Grenville* and *Rocket* swept to the west, *Wensleydale* and *Stevenstone* began to pick up men from the water, while *Talybont* took *Limbourne* in tow. In the torpedo strike *Limbourne* had lost her radio and consequently had not known where the rest of the group was. She had recovered steam and actually managed to get under way, but could only be moved in a circle. The towing cable then parted, and at 0500 when *Grenville* and *Rocket* returned to the area having seen nothing, it was decided to get all the men off *Limbourne* and sink her to prevent her falling into the enemy's hands. *Grenville* and *Rocket* now joined in the rescue of survivors until 0630, despite orders from Plymouth to clear the area.

This decision to disobey orders and stay on taking men out of the water saved Rocky Royle. He and John Eskdale were the last two to be picked up, just before 0630. At this point, with day breaking and the French coast clearly visible, the destroyers had no choice but to turn for home, although they knew they were leaving men in the water. Back in hospital at Plymouth, Royle described how, after being in the sea for a while, he had clearly seen an Elbing destroyer pass close by at speed – so close, in fact, that he had nearly been pulled into her screws. He was told by a naval intelligence officer that no Elbings had been involved that night, but the German records made available after the war proved him correct.

Talybont and then *Grenville* torpedoed the *Limbourne*, eventually sinking her at 0640. Force 28, with 107 survivors taken out of the water then returned to Plymouth. As they turned for home Hill radioed for air cover, and four Beaufighters eventually appeared near the English coast, but there were no incidents on the way back. Losses were devastating; 462 had been lost from *Charybdis*, including the captain, and 42 from *Limbourne*, either in the initial explosions or in the sea. Waiting for the returning ships were rows of three kinds of vehicle – coaches for the fit survivors and walking wounded, ambulances for the seriously wounded, and mortuary vans. Looking around him, John Eskdale could see only fourteen of his Royal Marine comrades out of sixty-five.

When the news of her loss was made public, Birkenhead went into semi-official mourning, and The *Liverpool Echo* reported at some length, including the words: 'She won a place in our hearts that no other ship will fill for a long time to come…this town's sorrow is that of a proud mother who has lost a favourite son.'

The *Munsterland* continued to make a slow passage up-Channel, going into harbour during the days. She was delayed at Lazardrieux after fouling a propeller on an anti-submarine net, and survived a massive Allied air attack at Cherbourg. She was eventually sunk on January 20th 1944 by the longrange guns at Wanstone and South Foreland while trying to pass through the Straits of Dover. *Korvettenkapitan* Kohlauf, who had led the successful German T-Boat attack, was killed in April 1944 off the Brittany coast on board T29 in an engagement with two Canadian destroyers, *Athabaskan* and *Haida*.

So many criticisms were later raised about the organisation of the 'Tunnel' operation that it became a Training School example of how not to do something. The Director of Training was scathing in his summing-up: 'A mixed force with no collective training, no knowledge of what enemy forces were at sea, and with accepted disadvantage of light,

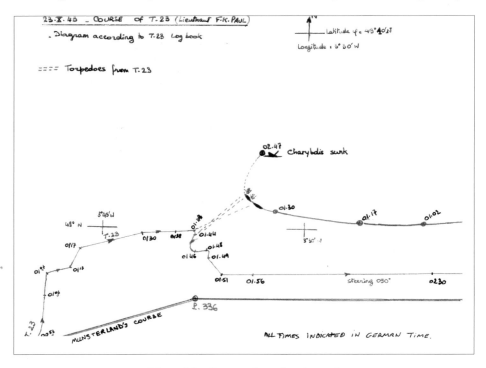

Plan of the German line ahead attack

was about to encounter a highly-trained striking force which almost certainly knew the numbers, position, course and speed of our own force.' Charles Cruickshank in his history of the war in the Channel Islands is critical of the fact that Operation Tunnel was carried out by whatever ships happened to be available on the day, and the fact that Force 28 had no collective training. Captain S. W. Roskill in his official *History of the War at Sea* wrote: 'The squadron was ill-fitted to act as a substitute for a properly organised and well trained night striking force.' The report on the action made by Lieutenant E. Baines in command of *Talybont* included the comments: 'Communications on the whole failed. No manoeuvring signals received at all. Conclusion: Force far too unwieldy', and Roger Hill summed it all up in his personal memoir as 'the classic balzup of the war'.

Not only had the ships not worked together before, but only *Grenville* had been on a previous Tunnel operation. Many of the officers in the group were newly trained, and the captain of *Limbourne*, Commander Phipps, though very experienced, had joined the ship only two days previously. He also missed part of the briefing because he had been held up taking on fuel, and like the other captains was told very little when he did arrive. The idea of putting a cruiser in with the group looked impressive on paper, but the control systems and 4.5 inch guns on *Charybdis* were best suited to anti-aircraft activities, not surface actions at night. For some time the ships carrying out Tunnel had always gone the same way, east to west, and the German convoys always went west to east, and in Bill Hustler's words, 'We knew this, and the Germans knew that we knew this.' Peter C. Smith, in his account of the engagement (*Hold the Narrow Sea*, 1984), calls the tactics of the patrols 'stereotyped', and suggests that 'Operation Tramlines' would have been a better code name.

It was well known that German radar along the coast of France was very effective, and even enemy tactics were not secret – escort warships would try to attack unobserved with torpedoes, and then turn rapidly away. Having done the operation before, Roger Hill was certain that one night the enemy would prepare a nasty surprise, but suggestions that the sweep be varied to go west-east were rejected, even though the position of the moon that night put the British at a disadvantage. This rejection was supposedly based on the fact that the Hunts were slower, at 28 knots, than *Charybdis*, *Grenville* and *Rocket* (all capable of 32–36 knots), and would not be able to keep up in a chase to the east after the enemy, but this only highlights the unhappily mixed nature of Force 28.

The formation required of the group, line astern, was open to serious question. Strung out in a line, the rearmost ships were too far back for rapid and effective control, and the difficulties in passing and receiving messages that night made this worse. It was said that instead of leading the group from the front, *Charybdis* would have been better placed at the centre with destroyers on each quarter, guiding them onto the target (this formation was subsequently adopted, with some success). There was an obvious problem with both radio communications and radar among the British, but it was also admitted that the Force had inadequate training in night actions based on radar. *Charybdis* did not carry the radio equipment that would have allowed her to intercept enemy signals and thus alert the group and take offensive action much earlier. Only Captain Voelcker was informed about the *Munsterland* and her possible escort – the other captains were not told, and thinking they were on a routine sweep were not sure what to expect. Roger Hill in his book maintained that he later heard unofficially that the German order to fire torpedoes had been picked up back in Plymouth, but had not been passed to *Charybdis*. Given that *Charybdis* knew nothing about the torpedoes until she saw their approaching tracks, that half minute might have been crucial in allowing her to take evasive action.

In his action report Franz Kohlauf expressed surprise at the huge success his flotilla had achieved. 'If the cruiser had opened fire on us without delaying, we would have been done for. The enemy had all the advantages. He saw us first, was at a state of alert, we were not in a good position to fire torpedoes, and we had the horizon light behind us. I can only suppose there were poor communications between the operation centre and the gunners. Possibly the night op with destroyers was a bit cumbersome...' What the T-Boats did not know was that they had not been seen and the action turned, literally, on one minute when T24 had time to get its torpedoes away before *Charybdis* could light her up and open fire.

Three weeks later, the first bodies were washed up on the islands. The first to come ashore in Guernsey were those of John Maidment and Royal Marine Clifford Roberts (both at Rocquaine) and Alfred Young (at Cobo) on 13 November, and for the next three days more bodies came ashore at Perelle, Grandes Rocques, Rousse Tower and Fort Doyle. In all, thirty-eight were to be washed up in Jersey, twenty in Guernsey, and one on Sark, while over a hundred bodies were found on French beaches. Not all of these bodies were identified. Berlin claimed that men had been found alive on the French coast, and for some nights Lord Haw Haw read out lists of the 'captured' over the radio, but these names were fictitious.

In Jersey the German authorities refused to permit a public burial service, since there had previously been civilian disturbances at the burial of two Allied airmen in June 1943. The first Jersey bodies were accordingly buried in a common grave at Mont-a-l'Abbe cemetery on 17 November at a ceremony held at nine o'clock in the morning. A few weeks later these bodies were transferred to the new war cemetery in Howard Davis Park, consecrated 26 November). A firing party was provided, and the Dean, Bailiff, Attorney-General and Constable of St Helier were present, together with representatives from the Red Cross and the Navy League. The following day, the 18th, many islanders visited the grave. Further bodies were washed up on succeeding days. In all, what were believed to be thirty-eight men from the two ships were eventually laid to final rest in Howard Davis Park, although only twelve were identified (they lie in graves 24–33, 39 and 42).

Funeral service held at Foulon cemetery

In Guernsey the Occupying authorities agreed to allow a burial service attended by the public, and this was held at the Foulon cemetery, St Peter Port, also on Wednesday 17 November at 3 p.m. Nineteen men were buried. The resulting silent demonstration by thousands of islanders who attended the service took the Germans completely by surprise. The civilian population walked to the cemetery from all over the island to pay their respects, and over seven hundred wreaths and small sprays were placed by the graves (the final total was over nine hundred). Those unable to find garden flowers took wild flowers. Three years into the Occupation the spirit of the islanders was not crushed, and the act of collective remembrance was a clear signal of defiance and a reminder to the occupying force that it had no right to be in the island and would never be accepted.

The burials were carried out in a formal, decent manner by representatives of the Anglican, Non-Conformist and Roman Catholic churches. The Germans provided a firing party, and two of the coffins were draped with Union Jacks. J. C. (Jack) Sauvaray of Guernsey kept a secret diary throughout the Occupation, which was published in 1990. His entry for 17 November 1943 was as follows:

> After the N gales last week there have up to now been 19 bodies washed up on our N coast from the cruiser *Charybdis*. One was brought from Sark. They were buried this afternoon at the Foulon cemetery, each in a separate grave. The public was invited. I was not going but after dinner the sun burst through so beautifully through the cold clouds that I suddenly decided to go.

Ministers of the Church of England, the Roman Catholic Church and the Free Churches all took part in the service. The Bailiff and other island officials were there. The German funeral party consisted of naval and military forces who gave full naval honours.

In spite of the thousands present there was dead silence. This was broken by the Marines (Germans) about 80, who fired three volleys. (No bugles). Then came the laying of the wreaths, first the Bailiff for the island, then two Germans. The Harbour Commandant, Dr Greff [Greeff], said that the men they were burying had fallen in battle near the Channel Islands when the cruiser *Charybdis* and the destroyer were sunk. We honour them as soldiers and we commit them to their graves. They did their duty for their country. Dr Kratzer also placed a wreath.

When the service was over I managed to get through the crowd and pass the graves (two coffins covered with Union Jacks remained on the ground) and the display of flowers, over 700 wreaths, one a huge anchor, about 9 feet.

So many islanders attended that the whole hill at the Foulon (the cemetery is laid out among trees on a gentle rise) was covered with mourners and some had to stand outside the wall. Estimates at the time put the number there as between four and five thousand, and with the civilian population of the island at that time numbering about 23,000 this represented attendance by over twenty per cent of the islanders. People were still filing silently past the graves to pay their respects as dusk was falling. Frank Falla, who worked on the *Guernsey Evening Press* throughout the Occupation, recalls in his book *The Silent War* that the paper wanted to print all the inscriptions on all the floral tributes left at the Foulon. The German censor then went through the list and crossed out every reference to 'British', 'Royal' or 'King and Country'. Despite this, on the following day the paper carried four long columns in small

Remembrance service held anually at the Foulon cemetery Guernsey. Gerald Evans placing the wreath.

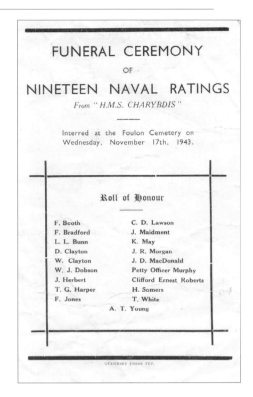

FUNERAL CEREMONY

OF

NINETEEN NAVAL RATINGS

From " H.M.S. CHARYBDIS "

Interred at the Foulon Cemetery on
Wednesday, November 17th, 1943.

Roll of Honour

F. Booth	C. D. Lawson
F. Bradford	J. Maidment
L. L. Bunn	K. May
D. Clayton	J. R. Morgan
W. Clayton	J. D. MacDonald
W. J. Dobson	Petty Officer Murphy
J. Herbert	Clifford Ernest Roberts
T. G. Harper	H. Somers
F. Jones	T. White
A. T. Young	

GUERNSEY PRESS TYP.

Left: Steve Keeling visiting the wreck site in 2001
Right: Booklet printed for the funeral service, so sought after by the islanders

print of the names of those who had donated wreaths. They came from individuals and from businesses – from the town shops, banks, the Fire Brigade, the bus companies, the Post Office, bakeries, vineries, and from church congregations and schools. The paper also had to submit all photographs taken of the event, and several were rejected by the censor, one on the grounds that the rifles of the German firing party were being held at odd angles. Frank Falla also wrote a memorial booklet to describe and celebrate the funerals under his initials 'F. W. F', and the German authorities ordered that this be limited to 2,000 copies. The booklet was eagerly sought after by islanders, and the Press surreptitiously printed another 3,000 copies.

One of the local undertaker's employees was William de Carteret. After the coffins had been lowered, the two Union Jacks were put on the ground beside the graves. Later that day he took one of the flags, stuffed it under his jumper, and cycled home to Amherst with it. He put it in a biscuit tin, and hid it up the chimney. The Germans took the theft extremely seriously and began immediate searches for the missing flag, actually going

*Above: The sidescan sonar which produced
the image of HMS Charybdis
Right: Sidescan sonar image*

to de Carteret's house. Luckily for him, they did not
find it. Under normal occupation conditions this act
of defiance would have meant a prison sentence on
the island, but the mass turnout for the funerals had
greatly angered the authorities, and if de Carteret
had been caught he would have faced deportation to a concentration camp. When he
died in 1973 his widow presented the flag to St John's Church, St Peter Port, where it
hangs today.

Two further bodies were washed up in Guernsey, that of Joseph Kane, found at
Chouet and buried on 6 December, and that of an unidentified seaman. Both were
buried at the Foulon with full honours but no members of the public were permitted to
attend. The unidentified man lies under a stone engraved 'Known Unto God'.

Since 1945 an annual memorial service has been held at the Foulon graves attended
by island dignitaries and Royal Navy and Royal Marine representatives, and since 1975
this service has been enhanced by the presence of members of the Charybdis and
Limbourne Association, made up of survivors. The service, now held every October,
is almost as significant in the island as the November Remembrance Day parade. The
graves continue today to be immaculately tended by the War Graves Commission, and
can be seen in two rows just to the left of the Route Isabelle entrance to the cemetery. It
is only after reading five or six of the names on the gravestones that a truly horrifying
fact becomes clear; some of the dead are aged 17, 18, and 19.

In addition to the fifty-nine men buried in the Channel Islands, over a hundred from
both ships were buried in France, many of the bodies coming ashore at St Cast. At least
forty-nine were buried at Dinard, including Captain Voelcker, forty-seven at St Brieuc,

and others at the Ile de Brehat, Bayeux, Anneville-sur-Mer, St Charles de Percey and the Isle de Bas. Three men made it to Plymouth on the rescue ships, but later died, and are buried at the Weston Mill naval cemetery. One of the lost seamen from *Charybdis* was the 22-year-old father of former MP and television presenter Robert Kilroy-Silk.

Steve Keeling, HMS Charybdis's diver

With the interest in wreck diving which developed in the 1970s there were a number of searches for the *Charybdis*, but as there was some disagreement about her last position, and because of the depth of the water in the area, no sustained search was made. She was then found in 1993 as a result of the persistence of a French diver, Alain Launay, and his team from Archisub, a diving company based at Brest. Alain had begun diving regularly off the north Brittany coast, and in his research on local wrecks he discovered accounts of the loss of the *Charybdis* and the *Limbourne*. The size of the ships, their importance, and the tragic nature of their loss made him determined to find them. Using Perros-Guirec as his base, and travelling out every day over a period of months in his cabin cruiser *Isis*, he began by searching a rectangle twenty miles by ten miles due north of the Sept Iles using a magnetometer, an X16 echosounder, and charts which had marked but not named wrecks. At the same time he was researching the German war records, and

SHIPWRECKS OF THE CHANNEL ISLANDS

Ron Frankel, the British Vice-Consul at Dinard, introduced him to Philip Lockwood, a Royal Navy attaché, whose father had been lost on *Charybdis*, and who was able to help him with information.

Alain and his team reduced the search area to a block five miles by five miles, and having located wrecks of appropriate size in that block with the echo sounder, began to check them with a searchlight ROV. After three weeks one in particular caught their attention as seeming to have all the characteristics they were looking for. When the ROV was put down it showed a very large hull lying on the bottom, and then Alain saw on the monitor a set of four anti-aircraft guns apparently in their original position. He was also able to see a tripod-based mast lying alongside, and realised the significance of this from the information Philip Lockwood had given him about *Charybdis*. This was in early April 1993.

Further exploration with the ROV confirmed that they were looking at a very large warship, surprisingly clear of weed and other marine growth. Substantial damage on one side was visible, compatible with a torpedo strike. In addition to the anti-aircraft guns, in position and pointing upwards, they detected another, larger gun lying on its side. Part of the bridge was still in place, and lying close to the hull were pieces of what might have been a funnel.

In May one of Alain's team, Michel Cloatre, attempted to dive on this wreck, but was prevented from doing so by the strong current. At over 250 feet this is a dangerous and difficult dive. On 14 August Michel and Joel Guizien dived successfully, staying twelve minutes. The ship lay on sand and gravel in 82 metres of water, and was upright with a slight lean to port. At that depth it was dark but their lights gave them a visibility range of about 12 metres. There were many fish around, and a good many snagged fishing nets. Joel discovered a number of unspent 40mm cannon shells, and also a larger empty shell case at the stern. These were brought to the surface, and were then sent to the UK where it was confirmed that the arrow markings, barrel gauge and type of cordite used showed that the shells were from a Dido class cruiser. It was now clear that *Charybdis* had been found, and Alain began to edit the high quality film footage they had obtained into a video about the ship and its discovery.

It was now possible for Alain and his team to mark the fiftieth anniversary of the sinking of the ships with a ceremony at Perros-Guirec, due south of the site. Members of the Charybdis and Limbourne Association duly attended on 23 October 1993, and a service in the parish church was followed by the presentation of one of the shell cases to the Association in the Town Hall (a shell case presented to survivor Eric Brookes can be seen in the Guernsey Maritime Museum). A memorial tablet was then unveiled on a hillside nearby overlooking the sea. The tablet is placed on a low granite block and is inscribed 'In Memory of Her Majesty's ships *Charybdis* and *Limbourne* 23rd October 1943 sunk with the loss of over 500 lives off the shores of Perros-Guirec. RIP'. As a final gesture of remembrance, Alain and his divers went down to place a glass plaque on the hull of the wreck inscribed: 'Les Allies Francais; A Ceux du HMS *Charybdis*; In Memoriam.'

In July 1999 John Ovenden and Paul Haslam went out from Jersey to locate *Charybdis*. They knew she had been dived on by a French team, but had not met Alain Launay at that date. They had an approximate position for the ship, and also had the advantage of side-scan sonar which gives a quarter-mile footprint on the sea bottom, provides images of objects from above and partly from the side, and on high frequencies can pick up extremely small targets at depth. A scanning 'fish' is towed behind the boat at a depth of 15 metres, and this is connected to an onboard monitor by a steel-cased fibre optic cable. A traverse pattern is first worked out and fed into a computer, and this ensures that the boat steers an exact course to cover the plotted area on the seabed. After half an hour they made a contact, the monitor showing the shadow of a substantial vessel, slightly bent in the centre, and leaning over to port. The data provided by the scanner on the object's length proved to be within a few feet of the known length of *Charybdis*. Two masts were visible lying to one side, and the large bridge could also be seen.

In June 2001 two further visits were made to the site. John Ovenden and Paul Haslam took Steve Keeling (formerly the ship's diver) out, and after they had obtained new sidescan images of the wreck, Steve laid a small wreath of flowers in memory of his lost shipmates. It was the first time he had been in those waters since the disaster. In the same month a British diving team led by Keith Morris visited the site and dived on the ship over a period of five days. With the team was underwater photographer Leigh Bishop. Leigh has an international reputation and his work includes the filming of the remains of the *Lusitania*, *Britannic* and the *Egypt*. From his own dives, and pooling the observations of the other team members, he has provided us with this account of the vessel's current appearance close-to:

The wreck lies across the tide north to south with her bow at the far northern end and she is completely over to her port side on a gravel seabed. The bow tip appears intact and her starboard admiralty anchor can clearly be seen still housed within its hawser. From here and only a few meters aft of the anchor the wreck shows obvious damage, mainly located at the starboard hull forward of the bridge. Swimming towards the stern across this wreckage becomes confusing at first and guides the diver to deeper and broken open sections of the wreck where a variety of internal fittings are visible. For example, complete and intact toilets can be seen although broken free of their original fixings. All manner of electrical fittings can be seen including switchboxes and fuse boards with heavy electrical cable. Again within the same area are numerous heavy-duty portholes complete with deadlights which all appear securely fixed shut

This porthole on HMS Charybdis still has its deadlight securely fastened

A 4.5 inch gun looming out of the darkness at 83 metres below the surface

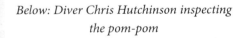

Below: Diver Chris Hutchinson inspecting the pom-pom

Left: One of Charybdis's screws resting on the seabed

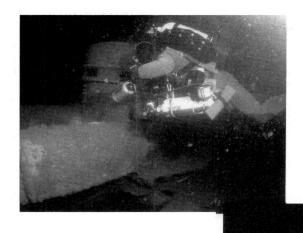

Two views of the twin torpedo tubes mounted on the deck of HMS Limbourne

Below: The bell from HMS Talybont seen for the first time in more than fifty years

179

and bolted at their dogs.

Swimming along the seabed from the anchor one is immediately met by the remains of sections of safety rail. As one swims aft the rail disappears in the seabed wreckage. One is then confronted by the first guns, what would have been the foredeck double 4.5-inch gun turret. The turret itself has fallen from its mount due to its own weight, and rests on the seabed. Both gun barrels now point out towards the port seabed but project above it. The bridge still remains fairly intact although it leans over level with the gravel bottom, and there is no room to swim underneath it. At the very front several sections of plate appear to have fallen free, perhaps from corrosion, although the main superstructure has worn well. The starboard side of the bridge does however appear slumped perhaps due to its own weight. Continuing along the port side the diver is then confronted with a large spotting light approximately 4–5 feet in diameter which has almost certainly fallen from its mounting which lies directly behind and is attached to the main wreckage. Running out across the port seabed here and disappearing into the darkness lies the main mast framework with a small ladder running the length of it.

Above here at least two watertight doors become apparent. Above again is what looks to be a small launch craft prop and shaft (?). To its immediate right the diver is confronted by a large number of shell cases. Further on towards the stern there appears to be a pom-pom gun lying to the port seabed. A short swim aft of midships the wreck becomes broken, possibly as a result of seabed impact? However, having said this, neither stern nor bow show any signs of impact. This central break is clearly visible in John Ovenden's sidescan, and taking into consideration the fact that neither end shows impact damage it may be that the ship's back broke as a result of an attack on a weak point in its structure. The stern mast can be seen lying out across the seabed to port. Neither funnel was seen, these quite possibly having collapsed and dispersed not long after sinking because of their thin construction.

The *Limbourne* was discovered in the early summer of 2002. After calculations based on the ship's reported last position, the time spent trying to tow her, and tide tables for October 1943, indicating the direction and speed of drift at the time, a likely area was searched by John Ovenden and Paul Haslam and a significant trace registered on the sidescan sonar. A combined diving team from the mainland returned to the site on 3 June and quickly confirmed that a substantial vessel lying in two pieces in 80 metres of water was the *Limbourne*. Two boats made up the expedition, *Deep Seeker* (skipper Paul Haslam, with John Ovenden on board) and the catamaran *Skin Deep* (skipper Ian Taylor). The divers were expedition leader Keith Morris, Leigh Bishop (photographer),

Chris Hutchinson (videographer), Mark Bullen, Julian Guest, Toby Herbert, Andy Hetherton, Guy Middleton, Steve Parker, Tim Back and Roy Smith. Accompanying the expedition were Steve Keeling and *Limbourne* survivor Neil Wood.

The first group of divers went down in very rough conditions on the 3rd, and further dives were made on the 4th and 5th.

The split hull of the *Limbourne* lies in complete disarray, no doubt partly as a result of what she suffered in the last hours afloat, partly from marine decomposition. Individual sections of the ship are identifiable in the devastation. The transom stern is complete with one propeller still present. The engines are exposed and the twin barrels of one gun turret are lying on the seabed. Close to where one of the quadruple anti-aircraft guns is lying, neat stacks of ammunition are visible, left after steel boxes which held them in position have disintegrated. The torpedo room, with some of its instruments and dials still recognisable, lies intact with two torpedoes projecting from it. The bridge has collaped onto the seabed with the telegraph still identifiable. Nearby lay conclusive proof of the wreck's identity, as described by Leigh Bishop:

> dropping down off the main hulk there is a scattered debris field and I am soon confronted by a bridge telegraph. A quick glance over my shoulder gives a comforting feeling that I'm alone on this part of the wreck as high intensity lights glimmer in the faint distance. From the corner of my eye I catch what I have in fact searched for. After fifty-nine years I am privileged to be the first to set eyes on the ship's bell. From the side of the bell and through almost sixty years of marine growth I can just about make out the words HMS *Limbourne* 1942.

With the dicovery of the ship the *Charybdis* and *Limbourne* story is complete. It it particulary fitting that confirmation of *Limbourne*'s resting place should have been witnessed by Neil Wood, one of the very few surviving crew members who were on board the ship the night she was lost.*

---

* While we were researching this section, a small memento was discovered by chance and purchased. HMS *Talybont* survived the war and was scrapped in 1961. In the summer of 2000 the ship's original brass badge was found under a pile of odds and ends in a marine antiques shop in the UK. Metalwork and enamel have now been restored to their original bright condition.

USS PT 509 (1944)

Most schoolboys used to know about MTBs – motor torpedo boats – small, very fast craft functioning like powerboats to make glamorous raids on enemy ships and bases in the Second World War. The small torpedo boat was pioneered by the Italians during the First World War, and Britain and Germany developed designs in the 20s and 30s leading to the British MTB and the German *Schnellboote* or E-Boat. The vessels in the torpedo boat class were usually wooden-hulled, with a very shallow draught, and highly powered. Their torpedoes were carried and fired at deck level. In 1937 the United States Navy held a public competition for the design of a torpedo boat, and the Patrol Torpedo Boat, or PT boat, was born.

These 40–45 knot American craft featured in four major Second World War theatres, the Pacific, the Aleutians, the Mediterranean and at the D-Day landings. PT boats were used at Guadalcanal and New Guinea in the fight against the Japanese Navy, and played an important role at the landings on the Philippines. At the Normandy landings PT squadrons guarded the flanks of the beachhead and fought German E-Boats attempting to attack the invasion fleet lying offshore. Other routine tasks included deliberately drawing the fire of enemy shore batteries so that these could be pinpointed exactly. It was not accidental that PT crews tended to be young and individualistic. Age brings caution and caution was inappropriate for this unorthodox force. PT boaters often offended established navy views, but it was their recklessness that made them so dangerous to the enemy. The effectiveness of the boats, usually confronting much larger and more heavily armed opponents, was dependent on speed and daring.

President John F. Kennedy commanded a PT boat – PT 109 – as a young lieutenant in the Pacific, and was lucky to survive when it was cut in half by the Japanese destroyer *Amagiri* in the Solomons in August 1943. The Japanese were running convoys to their base at Vila on Kolombangara Island (adjacent to New Georgia) along New Georgia Sound. The PT squadron was based at Lumberi, and was out on night patrol in the

Right: Photo by Russ Schuster of the devastation that awaited the arrival of RON 34 squadron at Cherbourg

straits looking for the convoys. In the darkness PT 109 was taken by surprise and saw the destroyer only moments before being hit. Two of the crew were killed instantly, and one man sustained serious burns when the boat's fuel tanks exploded. The eleven survivors swam for five hours to an uninhabited island, Kennedy pulling the wounded man by holding a strap from his lifejacket in his teeth. They then swam a considerable distance to two further islands before being picked up days later. Kennedy was decorated for this feat, and a full-size model of PT 109 featured at his presidential inauguration in January 1961. He also kept a small replica of the boat in the Oval Office of the White House.

Although the PT boats were fast and carried guns, torpedoes and depth charges, they were very vulnerable. Their wooden hulls were full of gasolene, and any direct hit would cause them to disintegrate or explode. At speed they left long, highly visible wakes, and their engines were liable to overheat. Given the usual association of the PTs with the Pacific or the Normandy landings, it is interesting to discover a fierce engagement between American PT boats and German ships taking place less than a mile off the south-west coast of Jersey in the early hours of 9 August 1944.

At that date the Allies were fighting their way down the Cotentin peninsula towards St Malo. Leslie Sinel in his war diary describes a state of panic among the occupying force in Jersey in the first ten days of August. The noise of the guns in France could not only be heard in the island, but their vibration could be felt, columns of smoke could be seen on the French mainland, and he describes a frenzy of shipping movements at St Helier harbour. Ralph Mollet in his diary records all troops being put on permanent alert, all beaches closed to civilians, and the appropriation of the telephone system by the military. German hospital ships were bringing hundreds of wounded across from the French mainland to be treated in Jersey, and there were rumours that the Germans might be about to pull out of the islands. These rumours were optimistic, since new guns

*Lt Harry Crist and Ensign Buell Heminway,
bottom right, with the crew of the 507 boat
off Utah beach in June 1944*

USS Maloy

were being set up in the Rozel area, facing the French coast, and existing batteries were being strengthened. German cargo convoys were being run at night between the islands and to the Brittany coast, in a desperate attempt to maintain supply lines.

At the beginning of August, American PT boats from the 30th and 34th squadrons of the US Eleventh Amphibious Force were withdrawn from the Normandy landing area. Some went to Portsmouth, and eighteen were based at Cherbourg to operate in the Bay of St Malo. Command responsibility for the Channel Islands passed to Cherbourg from Plymouth, and Lieutenant Commander Peter Scott RNVR (son of the Antarctic explorer, and later founder of the Slimbridge Wildfowl Trust) went to Cherbourg to liaise with the Americans and work out the daily details for the CI operations. He was also required, in the directive of Admiral Wilkes's Chief of Staff, 'to go out and do it'. Information on enemy movements was passed on from the Allied radar stations at Cherbourg and Granville, and by this point in the war the enigma code was cracked and enemy signals were being intercepted and decoded.

In his account of the naval war in the Channel, *The Battle of the Narrow Seas,* published in 1945, Scott describes the nature of the PT patrols, their mission being to intercept and destroy German Leutnant ships travelling between the islands, and between the islands and France:

'Our routine was to meet in Cherbourg at four in the afternoon with the plans for the night; then set off at five in the PT boats for a rendezvous with the destroyers amongst the islands. At daybreak we returned to Cherbourg and after a belated breakfast planned the operations for the next night. The signals had to be made out, then briefing, and then away once more into the islands for our nightly vigil.'

The most regularly used destroyers on these sorties were USS *Borum* (DE-790) and USS *Maloy* (DE-791). Both ships had been at the forefront of the troop landings at Omaha Beach on D-Day, and *Maloy* was later to escort the first Allied convoy into St Peter Port harbour at liberation in May 1945. The destroyers would stay out for a week at a time, steaming round the clock off the islands at alert condition 'B' with the crews getting little sleep. On the nights the PTs were in action, they would rendezvous with one of the destroyers off the islands. The overall commander would then go on board the destroyer, which used its longer radar range to direct the PTs to their targets. Scott's

German convoy underway in the waters between Jersey and Guernsey

The Robert Müller 8 alongside in Jersey harbour

task was to travel out with the PT boats, then go aboard the destroyer and act as vector controller to the PTs during the ensuing patrol.

On the evening of Tuesday 8 August, a group of PT boats from RON (Squadron) 34 left Cherbourg at 1700. They had reliable prior intelligence that a German convoy would be moving from Guernsey to Jersey that night, and their mission was to take up position with the USS *Maloy* and patrol to the west of Jersey, intercepting and destroying any enemy ships. On this particular day the *Maloy* was also at Cherbourg, and she accompanied them on the way out. The PT boats were divided into two sections – 'Tunny' group, PTs 503 (Lt James Doherty, group leader), 500 (Lt Douglas Kennedy) and 507 (Ensign Buell Heminway), and 'Barracuda' group, 509 (Lt Harry Crist, group leader, who had previously served on PTs in the Pacific), 506 (Lt Robert Brettell) and 508 (Lt Calvin Whorton). PT 503 had entered service in December 1943, and all the others in January 1944. All had been involved with the Normandy landings, indeed 500 and 509, together with 498, had nearly invaded France singlehanded. D-Day had initially been fixed for 5 June, and early in the morning the three PTs and their minesweepers set out for the Normandy coast; because radio silence could not be broken there was no way to call them back, but fortunately they were headed off by a patrolling US destroyer, which told them that because of the bad weather the invasion had been postponed until the 6th. All the call signs on the night of the 8th–9th were fishy. PT 500 was 'Kipper', 503 'Herring', 507 'Haddock', 506 'Crab', 508 'Crayfish' and 509 'Lobster' (the crew's permanent nickname for 509 was in fact the 'Sassy Sue').

Above: M4626
Right: Ltn Christian Cremer, Commander of the M4626

The group took a wide anticlockwise sweep around Guernsey passing ten miles north-west of the Casquets, and twelve miles west of the Hanois. The guns on the islands were known to be extremely accurate at nine miles and the Frie Baton battery on Guernsey had an even longer range. At 1945 a thrown screw caused PT 506 to turn back for Cherbourg. The group's surveillance position was established west of Jersey at 2210 on a bearing 290 degrees from the Corbière, about eight miles from the point, and the PT crews put on their flak and lifejackets. *Maloy* ('Sturgeon') began a patrol on a north-south line six miles long, turning at the northern end of the line on the hour, and at the southern end on the half hour. Grouped at the northern end of the line were PTs 503, 500 and 507, and PTs 509 and 508 were positioned at the southern end. On board *Maloy* was overall commander Lt Herbert J. Sherertz, accompanied by Peter Scott. The PT boats were 51-ton 80-footers, built by Elco of Bayonne, New Jersey, each powered by three 1350 hp Packard V12 engines. Each carried two 50-calibre guns, one 40mm stern gun, one 37mm bow gun, two Mark 13 torpedoes on roll-off deck racks, and six 600-pound depth charges. The sea was smooth but there was a dense fog moving in from the north-west and visibility was less than 200 yards and deteriorating.

In Guernsey a substantial convoy was preparing to sail for Jersey. This was made up of two freighters, the *Lena* and the *Robert Müller 8*, carrying five or six 15cm K18 field guns intended to reinforce La Coupe Point on the north-east of the island. One of these guns can be seen today at Noirmont Point, where it was set up after the war. The need to strengthen the Jersey defences was clearly considered an urgent priority, indicating that an Allied attack from the Cotentin Peninsula was anticipated. The freighters were accompanied by an exceptionally heavy escort of five M-class armed trawlers, and three VP boats. In addition to their crews, the trawlers were each transporting about sixty men down to Jersey – a total troop movement of nearly three hundred. The group was commanded by *Kapitanleutnant* Armin Zimmermann, who travelled on board M4626 (Zimmermann was later to play a part at the surrender of the islands, being sent by *Kommandant* Admiral Huffmeier to 'negotiate' with the liberating British ships). The convoy sailed at 0345, the freighters in the centre with the *Lena* being towed by M4621 because of her slow speed. As the group proceeded south the fog became so thick that at times visibility was no more than 25 yards, and Zimmermann had difficulty keeping the group together. There were several near collisions and the ships put their searchlights on in order to see each other. *Maloy*'s log shows that at 0450 she made the first radar contact, picking up a target on a bearing 32 degrees, heading 150 degrees at 14 knots, about twelve miles from the Corbière. 'Tunny' group at the northern end of the line was vectored in with muffled engines to make an attack, and at five miles the PTs picked up the enemy on their own radar. Visibility in the darkness and fog was a few yards. Beginning at 0535, using radar, and at ranges of 2,000-3,000 yards, starboard torpedoes set for between 10 and 15 feet depth were fired by 503 and 507, and both torpedoes by 500 who misunderstood the order. None of these hit a target, although Russell Schuster, who was the wheelman on board 503, has told us that he later heard that one torpedo had lodged in an enemy hull without exploding. 'Tunny' group then returned to the *Maloy*. The German ships were not equipped with radar but they were now picking up the sound of propellers on their hydrophones. They had not seen any torpedo tracks.

At 0545 'Barracuda' group, 509 and 508, were vectored in to intercept the convoy as it turned east around the Corbière. Crist led in 509, and at 0550 began an attack run due south of the point. Visibility was now about 100 yards. The two PTs crossed the convoy's bow without seeing it, circled, and came in from the shore side. Using radar, 509 fired one torpedo, but again without success. PT 508's radar was not functioning, so Whorton did not fire. The two PTs then circled to port at idling speed, returned to their original position, and this time 508 fired a torpedo guided from 509's radar which showed the enemy to be dead ahead, again without success.

Crist on 509 must then have decided to make a strafing run close up alongside the convoy running parallel with it on the shore side. It is not clear whether in the fog he came on top of the trawlers sooner than he expected. He took the boat in at speed (the only survivor, radarman John Page, said they went in at 1500 rpm), guns blazing. The crew on 508 heard the gunfire, and heard on their radio someone on 509 say 'We are in the middle of them'. Leutnant Hans Constabel, on board M4626, saw the PT come out of the fog, run alongside them and take out the crew of the trawler's 8.8cm gun. Within moments the Germans were returning a heavy and accurate fire.

Leutnant Hans Constabel, who leapt aboard PT 509 and helped to pull John Page aboard the M4626

The commander of M4626, Leutnant Cremer, also saw the PT, knew it carried torpedoes, and knew that it had only to turn slightly to fire them with devastating consequences for the trawler. He immediately turned M4626 hard to port, across 509's bow, with the deliberate intention of ramming it. At this moment a shell burst hit 509's wheelman, Lt John Pavlis, killing him outright. As Pavlis fell on the deck, the boat held its course and at near full speed ran straight into the port side of M4626, where it lodged, bow split open, wooden hull in flames, engines racing. The impact forced its bow up to the trawler's deck level, and the thrust of the engines kept it wedged against the hull. On board the trawler some crew members desperately tried to push the PT Boat off with boat hooks and iron bars. There were explosives on 509's deck, and a live torpedo unfired on the rack (Sherertz in his official report on the action, dated 12 September, wasn't sure about this, saying that 508 had fired one, and 509 'probably' two, but he was mistaken). Hans Constabel and another German crewman actually jumped onto 509's deck to push explosives into the sea. Other crew members were pouring small arms and machine gun fire down into the boat. All this time the trawler was still under way with the PT wedged into her.

John Page had been temporarily stunned. Regaining consciousness he detonated the radar set, and crawled into the cockpit in a hail of bullets. The flames drove him forward to the shattered bow, and despite having thirty-seven shrapnel wounds – one through a lung – and a broken right arm and leg, he was able to grab a line thrown to him from the trawler's deck, where he was pulled aboard. He had seen some of 509's crew jumping into the water and two dead – William Ausley, a gunner, with dreadful head injuries, and Pavlis, who was lying on the deck. Ensign James Mathes, who had been with him in the chartroom as the enemy opened fire, had disappeared below to destroy confidential gear; it is not clear whether he had been wounded. As Page got onto the trawler, 509's engines stopped, and the Germans managed to push it away. Some lines on the PT's deck had become entangled with the trawler, and it took a while to free them. The boat was then pushed off and it drifted into the fog. Page then heard, but did not see, a tremendous explosion accompanied by a blast of heat 'as if from an opened furnace door' which was 509 exploding and sinking.

When we interviewed Hans Constabel, now in his eighties, at his home in Bremerhaven* in November 2000, he recalled how he first became aware of 509's approach:

Hans Constabel and John Ovenden in Bremerhaven, 2000

> Suddenly there was a wave, a high swell, and our boat rocked. We could now hear some motors, and a short time later a loud engine. Our boat turned, leaning, then righted itself, and at that moment the Americans rammed us … A battle then ensued. At first shots were fired from both sides and then hand grenades were thrown from one side to the other. The PT boat then began burning and we knew we had to extinguish the fire as we were sure that any ammunition on board would cause both ships to be blown up. All this took about ten minutes. The fire was then extinguished. An American was brought on board, and we went over to rescue some of the others. As we were doing this, the propellers of the PT boat stopped. The boats separated and drifted apart. We then attempted to get back to our own ship. I nearly failed to make it as my feet became entangled in some ropes on the American boat. Luckily some of my comrades were able to free me.

He recalled how some of the contents of 509 had spilled out over the trawler's deck, including duffel bags and boxes of toilet paper.

Christian Cremer also agreed to speak to us at his home in Lage. Now aged 84 he retains clear memories of the events of the 8th–9th. The convoy, he told us, anticipated some kind of Allied activity that night, and was at a high state of alert all the way down. Although the German trawlers were not equipped with radar, they had hydrophones and FuMB (a straight-line radio detector) which were giving them a lot of generalised information after 0500. They did not see any torpedo tracks at any point. Asked if the convoy was primarily in attack or defensive mode, he insisted that the aim was to get

---

* Knowing nothing about the reason for their visit, the eight-floor hotel where John Ovenden and cameraman Adrian Walker stayed gave them rooms 507 and 509 – see illustration overleaf.

PT 509, with Ltn Crist in command, laying alongside M4626 under the command of Capt Cremer

Left: Commander and Mrs Cremer at their home in Lage, Germany

A fierce firefight erupted between the German troops and the PT crew

safely into harbour, firing only if fired on. Seeing instantly the danger to M4626 as the PT came at them out of the fog, he had turned the trawler onto a collision course; 'We took this course to prevent the Americans from releasing their torpedoes. These would have been aimed at my ship... not only did I want to avoid the torpedoes, I realised that the water nearer the coast was not so deep and that there would be less chance of us drowning.' He remembered clearly the sight of 509 wedged into their side, burst bow up over the low freeboard of the deck, engines racing, American flag fluttering.

The crew of PT 508

On 508 the radar began to work just in time to see 509's blip merge with the enemy's, and *Maloy* had also lost her. The loud explosion caused the other PTs to think that a torpedo had been fired successfully. Some distance away on 503 Russell Schuster, at the wheel, heard 508 trying unsuccessfully to raise 509 by radio. 'We heard the gunfire

Shelton 'Bos' Bosley in PT 507 aft twin 50cal gun turret

of this attack which surprised us, since the plan was to make a silent torpedo attack using the fog and darkness to cover the approach.' (Letter to the authors.)

PT 508's handwritten log records the events as follows: '0545 closing distance to targets, riding on starboard quarter of PT 509. Visibility 50 yards – dense fog had set in. PT 509 gave us target bearing and distance by radio, our radar still inoperative. 0550 made run on targets, following PT 509. Returned and proceeded to go in for second run.

Above: The crew of PT 503. Standing left to right: Boyd Brumm, Al Duquette, Donald Fisher, Kraemer, John Eastery, Ralph Allbee, Robert Biele, Elmer Albright, Foucher (kneeling), James Fox

Norman Hoyt at the controls of PT 503

PT 509 reported target dead ahead and ordered us to fire a torpedo. We released the port torpedo. 0555 generator and radar temporarily operational – radar showed four targets ahead on port and starboard bows, 200 yards distant. PT 509 opened fire on the targets and the enemy returned fire. We withheld our fire and turned hard to starboard as the enemy's fire was to our port and high. We made a complete circle and approached target positions again in search of PT 509. 0605 followed targets to within one mile of Jersey. On orders from USS *Maloy*, we proceeded to close her. We were unable to [word illegible] any trace of PT 509 up to this time. 0735 moored port side to USS *Maloy*.

The reason 508 had withheld fire was because PT 509 had been directly between her and the enemy.

The convoy had not stopped, but in the fog and confusion M4621 and the *Lena* had veered south from their proper course and had gone aground on the Grunes Vaudin. Efforts were being made to pull them off. It was now daylight and the fog was thinning, and at 0725 Sherertz took personal command of 503, and with 507 went to search for 509. As they made their search to the east they located two stationary ships ahead on their radar. Moving towards these, they passed into a clearing in the fog and saw an enemy vessel less than 200 yards ahead, stern-on. It is not clear which side opened fire first. John Aldridge, 507's bow gunner, immediately opened up with 37mm shells, hitting the ship's superstructure, and at the same moment the trawler's guns fired. The PTs were so close that the Americans could see the expressions on the faces of the German crew running for cover along the trawler's deck. Norman Hoyte, acting as Aldridge's loader, was packing shells in a sequence armour piercer, high explosive, tracer, and Aldridge yelled that he didn't want the tracer as he could see what he was firing at.

Shelton 'Bos' Bosley was on 507's aft 50cal gun, and he describes the attack as follows (letter to the authors):

We started our run with mufflers closed and at a speed of approximately ten knots. Daylight was breaking and the fog was lifting somewhat. On the way in I could hear our radioman O'Leary calling from the chart room to the bridge advising the distance to the targets. I remember he gave no distance in his last report but shouted that unless we stopped soon we were going to ram the object on the radar screen. As he said this we cleared the fog bank and there were our targets approximately one hundred yards in front of us. We came under heavy fire at once and both PTs turned hard to port. After the first two tracers went over my head, I opened fire instinctively and without hearing the command to do so…During the engagement I recall feeling a stinging sensation on the left side of my face that I later learnt were splinters that came from our boat as a result of being hit by several large caliber shells. As we withdrew, the order was given to lay smoke. Until Ensign Davies grabbed my shoulder and enquired if I was okay, I was assuming we were going in for a second attack and therefore had not secured my guns. Climbing from my turret I noticed several large holes just inches away in the port side of our day room.

Gunner, the 507 boat's mascot

Most of the hits we received were between the forward and after 50cal turrets, and considering the number, we were fortunate that Bob Hatmaker, our quartermaster, was the only one wounded. After the crew, our prime concern was for our mascot 'Gunner', a Newfoundland dog, who was in the shrapnel- and bullet-riddled day room. To our amazement he was shaken but not injured, lying under the port side bunk.

PT 503 had also opened up and fired its remaining torpedo, without result. Don Fisher was on 503's stern 40mm gun, and he describes a stream of shells and tracer coming in from the German vessel. Up at the front end of the boat Al Duquette was acting as loader to 'Sully' Sullivan on the bow gun, and in the excitement he jumped up onto an ammunition box to get a better view of what was happening; at that moment a large hole was blasted in the side of the boat's chartroom, and he threw himself down onto the deck. Lieutenant J. J. Daniel on board 507 was quoted a few days later in an American newspaper (there were reporters in Normandy); 'Gunners from both of our boats fired everything they had. Shells and machine-gun bullets whistled around us. We took a few hits but our gunners sprayed the enemy bridge and the decks.' The official engagement report stated that 503 had managed to fire 400 rounds of 50 calibre in the

Above left: Russ Schuster, exec officer of the 503 boat

Above right: Stan Allen, exec officer of the 500 boat

Below left: After the battle, 'Brumm' was painted on the port torpedo

Below right: Gunner Boyd Brumm, killed in action on PT 503

short time available, and 507 had fired 156 rounds. The two boats turned away to port, accelerating, and 503 was saved the trouble of making smoke when the liquid smoke tank on its fantail was hit and fumes poured through the boat. The crew thought the engine was on fire. One engineer was dead and Paul Peppell, the other engineer, was wounded, so Fisher and Bob Biele went into the engine compartment with extinguishers. They then realised that the smoke was coming down through a hole in the deck from the ruptured tank above. They cut through the straps securing the tank and jettisoned it. Of the fifteen crew on 503, only three had not been hurt – Schuster, executive officer and wheelman; Duquette and Sullivan.

In his action report, Buell Heminway, in command of 507, wrote: 'It is interesting to note the accuracy of the enemy gunfire – most fire covering turrets and cockpit with many near casualties. It should further be noted that he was aware of our position either by radar or ear due to mufflers of PT 503 being negligible. His guns were alert and trained in our direction and upon sight opened up immediately.' In fact 507 had had a narrow escape. During the attack three large shrapnel holes had been made in the aft section of their remaining (port) torpedo just inches away from its compressed air centre (communication from Dean Wilkinson of 507 to Bos Bosley).

PT 503's log reads: '0811 sighted target distance 100–200 yards. Fired port torpedo. Retreated to port and opened fire. Target returned fire within 30 seconds. A smoke screen was laid and zig zag course taken. 0837 came alongside USS *Maloy* to put casualties aboard.' Of the seven men transferred from 503 to the destroyer, Boyd Brumm (gunner) was already dead, and six were suffering from severe shrapnel wounds. Elmer 'Pop' Albright (mechanic) had been so badly wounded that he died later in the morning. On 507 Bob Hatmaker had a bad thigh wound. All the PTs now regrouped on *Maloy*, south of the Corbière, and at 0926 headed back to Cherbourg, where they arrived at 1400. On the way the *Maloy* requested a Sunderland Flying Boat from Plymouth to make a search south of Jersey for any sign of PT 509. Once back at Cherbourg, PT 503 began a ten-day programme of repairs.

The *Robert Müller 8* and five of the escort ships went into St Helier at 0810, while the remainder pulled the *Lena* and M4621 clear. Sinel records that at 0800 that morning Allied planes machine-gunned the German positions at Elizabeth Castle, but it is not possible to say whether this was connected to the convoy. Despite serious damage the grounded ships were also brought in. On board M4626 John Page, barely conscious, had been put below in a crew compartment with the German wounded and given basic first aid. He thought about fifteen were dead, but later records show that this was an overestimation. At 0930 M4626 went into St Helier harbour and he was put to lie on the quayside where two plainclothes Gestapo officers tried to question him. Seeing his critical state, they went away again. He was then taken to St Helier hospital, where first a British and then a German surgeon working skilfully in dirty conditions began a

Battle damage sustained by the M4626

*The point of impact between PT 509
and the M4626*

series of operations to remove the thirty-seven metal fragments from his body. He saw at least seventy wounded Germans in the hospital and thought they had come from the convoy, but it is clear that some of them were casualties of the fighting on the French mainland. Soon afterwards he was questioned again by the Gestapo, but refused to give any information other than name, rank and serial number. He remained in hospital being treated until January 1945, and was still on the island in a POW camp at the liberation in May.

Fourteen men were lost from PT 509 and two from 503. There are records of three of the dead from 509 being washed up on the island: Darril Bricker at St Ouen's Bay on 11 August, Richard Horsfield at Gorey on the 12th, and Rudolph Schaffroth on the 15th at Bouley Bay. The civilian police records show that Rudolph Schaffroth, who was from New Jersey, had driving licences, thirty-five photographs, ID cards, and British and French money on his person. All three men were buried with military honours at Howard Davis Park on 15 August (in 1946 the bodies of Bricker and Schaffroth were returned to the USA, and Richard Horsfield was transferred to a US military cemetery in France). A fourth body was seen by an Allied spotter plane on 10 August at St Ouen's Bay, and actually retrieved by the crew, who landed to pick it up. Leslie Sinel recorded this information in his diary. 'August 10th. An Allied seaplane came down in St Ouen's Bay to pick up survivors of yesterday's naval engagement, and the Germans fired on it as it took off with a heavy load.' On the following day, the 11th, he noted that 'the body of an American naval rating has been picked up at St Ouen's'. This must have been Darril Bricker.

The identity of the body recovered by the spotter plane is unclear. The August 1944 report of Squadron 34's activities, now declassified, says that it was that of Walter Wypick of 509, but the records held by the US Total Personnel Command show Wypick to be listed as never recovered (communication to Shelton Bosley, November 1992).

American casualties aboard a PT boat

Wreckage of PT 509 discovered drifting in the Channel

Above: Russ Schuster visiting Howard Davis cemetery, Jersey in 2001

Right: Rudolf Schaffroth

Crew of the 509 boat lost in action. Richard E. Horsfield standing third from the left

On 24 August a large piece of 509's wooden bow, showing numerous shrapnel and bullet holes, was found floating between the islands by USS *Borum*. Frederick Brooks was on board, and he noted the event in his personal diary (information courtesy of Bos Bosley):

> Night of August 23rd/24th. Another monotonous patrol between Jersey and Guernsey, broken by the discovery of the PT 509 which failed to return from night patrol. She had been shot in half, her bow section still afloat...We wonder

Darril A. Bricker with the 509 boat

> if she lost out in an engagement with an enemy mine layer. Judging by her riddled hulk it is doubtful if there were any survivors.

In fact Borum's log indicates that they saw the wreckage at 1515 in the afternoon. The Germans lost four killed and forty-one wounded, and three warships were put temporarily out of commission. The German dead – Hans Buchholz, Hermann Reinhardt, Heinz Hildebrandt, and Hermann Schwen – were buried in St Brelade's churchyard, but removed to the German military cemetery at Mont-des-Huisnes in France in 1962.

Of the fifteen crew who left Cherbourg at 1700 on 8 August in PT 509, only John Page survived. The bodies of five of the 509 men were recovered, but nine were never found. The grim tally is as follows:

Recovered and buried: William Ausley (buried in a private cemetery in North Carolina), Darril Bricker (Fort Snelling National Cemetery, South Minneapolis), Richard Horsfield (Normandy American Military Cemetery, St Laurent), Marvin Lossin (private cemetery, Michigan), Rudolph Schaffroth (Beverly National Cemetery, New Jersey).

Never found: Harry Crist, Charles Kornak, Kenneth Line, James Mathes, John Pavlis, Tony Reynolds, Alfred Ricci, Edward Thale, Walter Wypick.

PT 509 wrecksite

The Packard engines remain remarkably intact after more than fifty years on the seabed

'Bos' Bosley on one of the 509 boat's Packard engines, fifty-seven years after the sinking

The names of these men are inscribed on the memorial wall at the Brittany American Military Cemetery, near St James, north-west of Fougeres.* Boyd Brumm of PT 503 was buried at a private cemetery in Iowa, and Elmer Albright of 503 was buried at the Normandy Military Cemetery, St Laurent.

In assessing what went wrong, the density of the fog, PT 508's temperamental generator and the non-functioning radar, and the absence of 506 from the second attack group were all noted. The fire brought to bear on 509, 503 and 507 had been very accurate, and this may have been helped by the fact that the Americans were using tracer, making it easier to spot the source of their fire. Hans Constabel has told us that all the German gun crews were well trained and had seen plenty of previous action. A further problem may have lain in the fact that the US crews were unfamiliar with the water around Jersey and had begun operating there only a few days previously. Recent conversations with survivors show that in the darkness and fog some did not realise until much later how close they were to the island. Firing torpedoes using only a radar bearing is not a precise art, and it is possible that the speed of the tide in the area may have been underestimated by the crews and helped to put the torpedoes offline. Altogether seven were fired unsuccessfully in the course of the night's action, and although some damage was done to the convoy, it eventually reached its destination. In his action report, dated August 11th, the commander of *Maloy*, Frederick Kellogg, identified a number of lessons that had been learnt, including the need for more information on the enemy's course and speed to be given to the PTs so that torpedoes could be aimed more effectively, and the need for the PTs to keep more accurate navigational plots of their positions.

There were other engagements between PT boats and enemy shipping off the islands on 12 and 14 August, but on the 18th St Malo fell to the Allies, and with movement between the islands and the continent stopped, the PTs were withdrawn from the area. Their brief appearance around the islands must have brought home to the occupying forces the realisation that time was running out, and they must have thought that an Allied invasion to recapture the islands was imminent. Neither they nor the islanders could have imagined that the Allied advance would leave the islands behind, and that nine more months would have to elapse before they were liberated. 'There came a time when the enemy in the Channel Islands was held to be no longer dangerous. The destruction and loss of life attending an assault would not have been commensurate with the advantages to be gained by liberating this territory' wrote Peter Scott, echoing Churchill's belief. The PTs were later turned over for use by the navy of the USSR under the Lend-Lease scheme.

---

* It is not clear how many crew 509 was intended to carry on the night of the 8th–9th. Motorman Arthur Hanson of PT 505 was assigned to 509 for the exercise to replace an absent 509 crewman, but was delayed, got to the dock as 509 was pulling away, and missed her. With fifteen crew 509 was not below strength. Hanson has never been able to establish who he was supposed to be replacing. (Letter to 'Bos' Bosley, October 1995)

In all, thirteen Americans from the different services had received burial at Howard Davis Park in the course of the war, and their bodies were handed over to the American Military Authorities and taken from the island in June 1946, either to be returned home or buried at military cemeteries in France. The *Jersey Evening Post* described the formal ceremony of farewell on 15 June where island officials and many islanders gathered at the Victoria Pier to hand over the flag-draped coffins. There was a minute's silence. It was fitting, the paper commented, to pay a special tribute to these men 'who had come so far to liberate the suffering peoples of Europe', giving up their lives to help drive the illegal and repressive occupying force out of the islands.

After the war, Hans Constabel continued to serve with the German merchant fleet, later writing a personal memoir of his years at sea. In April 1950 his ship passed close to the Channel Islands, and he recalled the blacked out tension of the war time sorties:

Today, five years on, it is so different here. Peaceful ships are steering their courses, and lights are there to guide them. No one asks now whether a ship is Russsian, American, German or French – there are only people who need to be protected. May there never again be a time when a human life is considered of no more worth than a piece of paper.

A curious find came to light in January 1996. In a cupboard in St Helier Town Hall some American shoulder flashes and two sets of service dog tags were found in an envelope, clearly after being left there and forgotten for many years. One tag belonged to William Ausley of PT 509, last seen lying dead on the boat's deck by John Page. Gordon Young, the *Jersey Evening Post* reporter, stated at the time that Ausley had not been one of the Americans disinterred and transported home in 1946. It was usual for one of the individual's tags to be buried with him, and for the other to be returned to the relevant military authority. There was no record of Ausley's body being washed up on the island.

A trawl through London Air Ministry and German records together with documents from the Quartermaster General's Office in Washington has partially solved this puzzle. Ausley's body was washed up not on Jersey, but on Guernsey at Havelet Bay on 21 August, twelve days after the action. It was correctly identified by the German authorities, but buried at the Fort George military cemetery on 23 August under an incorrect name, A. W. Shreve (Ausley was William Shreve Ausley). The German report at the time describes the recovered body as being dressed in blue linen shirt, cotton zip jacket and pants, leather jacket and kapok lifebelt. One of the identity tags was put in the coffin. In June 1946 the body was disinterred and taken to Jersey, where the coffin joined those of the other Americans prior to their transfer to the US military cemetery at Blosville in France. Here the correct identification was made. Ausley was then later moved again to final rest in North Carolina in 1948. It is still not clear how the second tag got to Jersey, but it might have accompanied the disinterred coffin in 1946, and then remained on the island.

Some of the families of the missing PT crew had to wait until September 1945 before they were informed officially that loved ones were presumed dead. The parents of Alfred Ricci, gunner's mate on 509, did not receive a letter from the Secretary of the US Navy until 11 September 1945; this told them that Alfred would not be returning to his home at Johnston on Rhode Island. The letter concluded; 'I extend my deepest sympathy to you in your sorrow. It is hoped that you may find comfort in the knowledge that your son gave his life for his country, upholding the highest traditions of the Navy.' Alfred had been 21. In July 1981 his home town erected a plaque in his memory at a ceremony which included a naval guard of honour. In all, 531 PT boats were employed by the US Navy in World War Two. Of these, sixty-nine were lost with 331 men killed.

The sunk remains of PT 509 were found in 1981 by Tony Titterington, aided by members of the island police diving unit, which Tony trained. It was some time before they realised what the different pieces were adding up to. On 20 June they dived on the *Schokland*, and afterwards went a little way inshore and did a couple of drifts to the east looking for flatfish. A bronze rudder and bracket were located lying on the bottom in about eight metres of water. These could have belonged to any one of a large variety of vessel types, and they did not realise at this stage that they were looking at one of 509's three rudders. They then found some pieces of wood nearby which proved to be doublediagonal mahogany.

On 29 June, searching a short distance away, they found a six-foot length of copper pipe, and then close by a propeller on a stainless steel shaft sticking out of the sand. They now began to suspect that rudder, wood and propeller might come from the PT boat. Discovery of a lubricating pump with a partly burnt wooden handle confirmed a vessel that had been on fire, and when more wooden sections with steel bolts were uncovered, they were sure that this was 509. Shaft and prop were brought up, and when the two were separated the mark '509' was clearly visible stamped in the metal. This was the starboard propeller. They then found the three engines on a shale bed with a second propeller lying across them. The engines were Packards, and the second propeller was also marked '509' and 'center'. Final confirmation came from the 40mm ammunition found scattered around. The shell bases had 'US' stamped on them, and when one of the shells was dismantled, a small strip of paper was found inside among the charges. This read: '40mm AA ammo. Lot No. UB191 TEI 44 Powder Index No. SP DN4616 Powder Charge WT.296. 2 grams. Inspector BLL. Date assembled 2/44. Place assembled Elkton MD. Initial of foreman AHR'. The ammunition had been manufactured in the Elkton factory, Maryland, in February 1944.

A further development came in May 1982 when a spear fisherman found what he thought might be a torpedo lying on the bottom on the West Park (St Helier) side of St

Shelton Bosley with the dive team after visiting the wreckage of the 509 boat

The PT reunion Boston in 2000, where members of RON 34 were presented with a part from the remains of PT 509

Aubin's Bay to the west of the Elizabeth Castle pier. Tony was called to check the object, and he confirmed that it was a torpedo, lying one-third buried in the sand, its head pointing to the north. His measurements showed that it was 14 feet long, and about 18 inches in diameter. The external casing had become very thin from corrosion and there were some holes in the metal. Corrosion had also roughened the fin edges and eaten away the ends of the propeller blades. The forward section of the device was almost detached, and the forward filler (a substance which had become a yellowish-brown) was two-thirds gone. The thickness of seaweed on the casing and the levels of corrosion were at a similar level to those seen in other objects known to have been lost in the 40s and early 50s.

The object was potentially lethal, and the harbour office immediately marked it and set up a three-quarters of a mile exclusion zone around the hazard. A call was made to the Royal Navy, and two days later, on the 15th, the Plymouth Command Deep Diving Team blew it up. The disposal crew put a slow fuse on the charge, and there was added drama when the States tug nearly fouled a propeller moving away from the site, getting clear just in time. Jean Rivoallan, the States diver, was present, and he estimated that a plume of water a hundred feet high went up. Interviewed in 2000 he told us that the site was about 200 yards south-west of the Baleine buoy, which lies half a mile west of the castle pier. The explosion left a crater in the seabed six feet deep and twenty feet in diameter. Tony then dived on the site and recovered many of the fragments. Some of these bore the marks 'USN' and 'MK 13- 2A' showing that this was an American Mark 13 torpedo of the kind carried by the PT boats.

The following year, in August 1983, he made a further discovery at the site of the sunk 509. A heavily concreted mass attached to a large piece of granite lying about fifty yards from the engines was found to contain the deformed parts of another partly or fully detonated torpedo. Prop, fins and part of the engine were identifiable and markings on the metal matched those found on the West Park fragments. This was the unfired torpedo that was still on 509's deck when she was pushed away from the trawler, and the torpedo had clearly exploded in the air just before she went under. This was the explosion Page heard, and it explains why the crews on the other PTs thought a torpedo had been fired successfully. The West Park torpedo was quite certainly the one fired by PT 503 as she went in with 507 for the last attack on the two stranded German vessels. Its position and alignment indicated that it had been fired in a north-easterly direction, and that it then ran out of power or went onto the bottom after crossing the bay.

In July 2000 John Ovenden flew to Boston for the annual reunion of PT Boat Squadron 34. Here he met former crew members of PT 500, 503 and 507 who had been in action off Jersey on the night of 8–9 August 1944, and presented them with Squadron 34 replica plaques bearing the original Walt Disney-designed Sea Wolf emblem. He also presented a section of PT 509's engine, part of a propeller shaft box, recovered from the Jersey seabed in 1990, also mounted on a plaque. This bore the inscription 'PT 509 comes home' and the plaque now hangs alongside the Elco-class PT 617 preserved at the PT Boat Museum, Newberry Hall, Battleship Cove, Fall River, Massachusetts, sixty miles west of Cape Cod.

Two months later, in September, 'Bos' Bosley, now 77 and living in Baltimore, who had been on PT 507 that night, set foot on Jersey for the first time. He went out to the site of the 509's sinking with Paul Haslam and the authors, and on one of the best days of the summer was able to sit quietly, watch the unruffled sea over the wreck, and think about the events of fifty-six years before. What surprised him most was the close proximity of the Jersey shore and the fact that the PT boats had been operating little more than a stone's throw from one of the most heavily fortified batteries on the island. Had the fog that made their task so difficult that night lifted more rapidly, the outcome might have been far worse for the Americans.

Three days later, on Thursday 14 September, at low water slack, he returned to the site and dived with John Ovenden and Graham Holley, spending fifteen minutes on the wreck. Here he was able to see the PT's engines and one of her guns still in their original resting place on the bottom. As they made their way back to the harbour there was another reminder of the 1940s. It was the 60th anniversary of the Battle of Britain, and as they approached the breakwater the Red Arrows began their celebration display directly overhead.

MV *Heron* (1961)

Wholesale tomato prices in the third week of September 1961 were good, and island exporters were getting a healthy six shillings a tray at Covent Garden. Jersey was shipping much of her produce that summer on the *Heron*, a Dutch cargo vessel on charter to Channel Transporters of Portsmouth, with J. G. Renouf and Co acting as local agent. The *Heron* was registered at Groningen in the Netherlands. She had been built in 1956, was 497 tons gross, 188 feet long, and had a top speed of 10 knots. She carried her cargo in deck containers.

At 7.40 p.m. on Saturday 16 September, the *Heron* left St Helier for Portsmouth carrying just under 57,000 fourteen-pound trays of tomatoes, together with some sweetcorn and green peppers – about 320 tons in total, value around £7,200. Her master was 45-year-old Dutchman Harm Bartelds. It was a dirty night for September, raining heavily, and with a high swell although the wind was only Force Three.

The Jersey pilot came off at 1950 and the *Heron* proceeded west with Captain Bartelds, First Officer A. van der Zee, and a Spanish able seaman, Francisco Reboiros Dios, on the bridge. The *Heron* carried radio, echo sounder, radar and Sestrel-Owen automatic steering gear, fitted in February 1961. At 2025 they passed the Corbière one mile off, and turned onto a 10-degree course up the west of the island. At 2030 the first officer went below, leaving the master in charge on the bridge with Dios. At 2055 they passed the Grosnez light on the north-west tip of Jersey, and Bartelds now set the automatic steering to a course of 30 degrees magnetic to take him up to the Race.

Ten minutes prior to the *Heron*'s departure, another cargo ship, the *Cranborne* under Captain Bob Curtis, had also left St Helier with market produce. The two ships often kept company across the Channel. At the Corbière Curtis noted the *Heron* about half a mile directly behind him. At Grosnez, the distance between the two ships was about the same, but the *Heron* was now to the west of the *Cranborne*'s wake. After moving onto his own NNE course, Curtis noticed on his radar at 2105 that the *Heron* was not following the required 30-33 degree line behind him. Having passed the point she had veered almost due east, putting herself directly on line with the Paternosters, the large reef two miles off the north Jersey coast. He tried to raise the *Heron* by radio, but was unable to do so. He then used his Aldis lamp to flash 'U' in Morse ('you are standing into danger') for a good five minutes. Again getting no response, and seeing the other ship closing rapidly with the rocks, Curtis radioed Jersey Harbour to ask if the *Heron* had sent them any message indicating a problem. This was at 2122. The reply was in the negative. Curtis, very worried, now had the presence of mind to request that the lifeboat be put on standby. He then tried again to communicate with the *Heron* using his signal lamp. Three minutes later at 2125 he heard her send a mayday to Jersey Harbour: 'We have struck rocks and sinking fast. Get lifeboat.'

MV Heron leaving St Helier harbour, Jersey

The Pierres de Lecq or Paternosters run for nearly two miles east-west, and include extensive underwater ledges and five large rocks just covered at the highest tide. Great Rock and Sharp Rock are permanently above water. The reef has a bad reputation, and is well known to ships both leaving and approaching the island from the north-east. For reasons which are still not fully clear, the *Heron* failed to pass through the gap between the Desormes Buoy and the reef, and instead of leaving the rocks a mile and a half to starboard had gone straight for them. Captain Curtis later reported that despite the heavy rain, visibility was fair, and the lights on Jersey's Grosnez and Sorel Points were clearly visible. The *Heron* was in the red, danger sector of both lights for at least a mile before she struck.

In the *Heron's* engine room, Chief Engineer Henrik Krans had received a telegraph order to go full speed astern. He carried out the order, estimated that the reversed screw had turned for about half a minute, then felt a bump, heard a long grating sound, and the ship came to an abrupt stop. He maintained full reverse for two or three minutes, then got an order first to stop, then to go astern at half speed. He did this for about two minutes, then got the order to stop all. He started the auxiliary engine in case the pumps were needed, and as he did this he felt the ship begin to tilt. He immediately ran topside, and arriving on deck saw that the bow was almost under water. The ship was being pounded hard by waves, and her waterfilled compartments were pulling her under.

From striking to arriving on deck, Krans estimated just under ten minutes had passed.

There were two women on board that evening, the wife of Captain Bartelds (who was both master and part owner of the ship) and the wife of First Officer van der Zee. The first person Krans saw was Elske van der Zee standing by herself on the starboard side. She was weeping and apparently so agitated that her manner appeared demented. As Krans went towards her, the stern rose and the ship slipped again heeling over to port. This either threw Mrs van der Zee into the water or caused her to panic and jump over the side – different witnesses claimed both versions. The master had already ordered all crew to put on lifejackets, and he was working to release the two lifeboats. Both boats went into the sea, one upside down. Some crew were already in the water, but in the hope that the ship would not go completely under, Krans climbed up the sloping deck to the highest point at the stern rail. Here he found five others. They clung on for a few minutes until the *Heron* slid away underneath them. Captain Curtis of the *Cranborne* said later that the *Heron*'s lights disappeared at 2135 – which meant that she went below the surface ten minutes after striking. In the water, Krans found a floating oar and used it to make his way to the upturned boat, climbing on top of it. Three other men swam to the boat and climbed up with him, and using the oar they managed to paddle to the second, upright boat and get inside. Here two more joined them. The boat was half full of water because the bung was not secured, but they managed to bail it out, found a second oar, and tried to row against the fierce current. The six in the boat knew immediately who was missing – Elske van der Zee, her husband, Captain Bartelds and his wife, and Spanish able seaman Dominico Abelleira Caamano. There had been nine men and two women on board, all Dutch with the exception of the two Spaniards.

Three others were also accounted for. As the ship went under Captain Bartelds was thrown into the sea, where he found his wife. They grabbed a plank and part of a wooden ship's ladder, and were able to part lie across these. After a while they were joined by Dominico Caamano. There now began a ten-hour ordeal as they drifted through the night in the high swell under heavy rain.

In St Helier the RNLI maroons were sent up immediately the *Heron*'s distress call was received, and the lifeboat, *Elizabeth Rippon*, coxswain Ted Larbalestier, was launched eleven minutes later, passing through the pierhead at 2145. The *Cranborne* had been about five miles past the Paternosters when the mayday was heard. Captain Curtis signalled the *Heron*'s exact position to Jersey Harbour, and then turned around and headed back to the eastern side of the reef. He told the *Heron* on the radio what he was doing, and got the reply 'Thank you. Out.' Curtis went in as close as he dared, so close that he could see and hear the surf breaking on the rocks. He stopped his engines briefly to listen for shouting, but the reef was pulling him in, and he had to keep under way. He circled in this area and then at 2235 saw a boat with six people in it. He went close, picked them up, and radioed in to St Helier. By this time the *Elizabeth Rippon* was approaching Grosnez Point. It heard the message and told the *Cranborne* it would take the survivors. As the lifeboat turned east around the point it saw the *Cranborne* standing in towards Greve de Lecq where the water was calmer. It went alongside and took the survivors on board, and the *Cranborne* then went on her way to Portsmouth. The lifeboat then commenced a careful search north and east of the reef with its searchlight, finding nothing, until the Secretary of the RNLI radioed from St Helier to advise that the six survivors should be landed at Bonne Nuit Bay three miles along Jersey's north coast, where an ambulance would be waiting. The lifeboat then moved into the bay, and at 0100 in torrential rain, by the light of car headlamps, put the survivors ashore at the small jetty. They were driven to the general hospital in St Helier, and after an examination which found them shocked but unharmed, they were taken to the Jubilee Hotel.

MV Cranborne leaving St Helier harbour, Jersey

The lifeboat went back to its search, going as far north as the Blanchard Buoy to the east of Sark, calculating that this would be the limit of any tidal drift in the time elapsed. Still finding nothing, the boat then went west of Jersey. By this time two Jersey fishing boats had also joined the search, Mr G. Collenette's *Ann*, and the *Sea Mist* owned by Basil Le Brun. Just east of the reef the people on the *Ann* saw a trail of tomato trays, a tobacco tin and a woman's shoe floating on the water. There was also an oil slick not far from the Flat Rock, suggesting that the ship had struck on the southwest corner of the reef.

It was now getting light. Four miles west of Grosnez Point a French tanker *Port du Bouc* was heading south for St Malo. At about 0800 she saw two people on timbers in the water, changed course towards them, and found Captain and Mrs Bartelds, suffering from exposure but otherwise in fair condition considering they had been drifting all night. They reported that at some time in the early hours Dominico Caamano had slipped away and disappeared. The tanker radioed the news to St Helier, saying it would go on to St Malo, and the *Elizabeth Rippon*, hearing the message, moved towards the pick-up area. A substantial amount of floating debris was seen, and then two bodies, one that of a woman. After getting these on board, a capsized boat was sighted, and the lifeboat took it in tow. It then returned to St Helier, arriving at 1000 after twelve hours at sea. A small crowd on the quay watched in silence as the bodies were lifted ashore and put into an ambulance. The two drowned were identified later in the day as being Elske van der Zee and Dominico Caamano. Of the eleven on board, eight had been found alive, two had not survived, and First Officer van der Zee was still not accounted for. The second boat was found drifting off Grosnez Point the same day by a Guernsey fishing boat, the *Stormdrift*, and towed to St Peter Port.

An inquest on the two bodies was held at Jersey hospital on Tuesday 19 September under the acting Attorney General, Mr H. F. C. Ereaut (Sir Frank Ereaut, later Bailiff). Those giving evidence included Captain Curtis, Ted Larbalestier, Henrik Krans and Francisco Reboiras Dios, who spoke through an interpreter. At one point it was suggested that an explanation for the collision course might have been temporary disconnection of the automatic steering system when power was switched from one generator to another, but Henrik Krans told the court that at no time had the main generator been switched off. The resourcefulness and seamanship of Captain Curtis were singled out for special praise. Since the master's account of events had not yet been received from St Malo, where he was in hospital, the inquest was adjourned to await his statement.

This was duly received, translated from Dutch, and read to the court. It simply constituted the relevant entry from the ship's log book and shed little light on what had gone wrong:

18th September 1961. Started loading tomatoes at 8 o'clock and finished at 1930 with approximately 320 tons. Cleared the deck and left at 1940. Guided by pilot we went outside and put pilot off at 1950 hours. Guided by the shore we carried on and at 2055 passed the Corbière lighthouse. Course 10 degrees, wind WSW, raining, heavy swell. Passed 2055 hours the Grosnez lighthouse course 30 degrees. At 2120 a rock appeared straight ahead. Straight away we went in reverse at full speed. At the same time all the crew was warned to come on deck with lifebelts and the lifeboats were prepared. The helmsman was ordered to send out a mayday. After that there was a heavy collision and the ship rapidly made water. At 2130 the ship stood on end with some people on the rear and the others, who were next to the wheelhouse, were washed overboard.

An official inquiry into the loss was held in the Netherlands by the *Raad voor de Scheepvart* (National Shipping Council) in March 1962 under the Chief Inspector of Shipping. Captain Bartelds and Henrik Krans were questioned, and written statements were submitted by Captain Curtis and Francisco Reboiros Dios who had made his statement to the Consul at Coruna on his return to Spain.

Bartelds confirmed the courses in the log, and said that he had been on the bridge with Dios as lookout. Dios spoke only Spanish, and orders had to be given to him by hand signals. Bartelds told the assessors that after setting the 30-degree course at Grosnez Point at 2055, he had spent ten minutes fine-tuning the automatic steering equipment. The Paternosters were clear on the radar to starboard. Ten minutes after that (at about 2115) he had felt the need to go to the toilet. He told Dios 'to keep a good eye on the course' and follow the *Cranborne*, which was still directly ahead of them, and left the bridge. When he returned five minutes later, the *Cranborne*'s lights were no longer visible, and looking at the compass he saw that the *Heron* was heading almost due east. At the same moment he saw rocks dead ahead and on both sides, and immediately ordered 'full astern'. He signed to Dios to rouse up the crew with lifejackets, and at that point the ship struck. He went astern, she seemed to come free, but they were already sinking by the bow. At no time did he see any signals from the *Cranborne*.

An expert witness explained the functioning of the Sestrel-Owen steering gear. This operated with a light-sensitive cell under the compass rose, and with a light source above. While the compass pointed correctly, the cell was darkened, but if the pointer swung too far either side, the light fell full on the cell, triggering an electric current that brought the steering mechanism into play. The witness (B. van Wijk) confirmed that the system was reliable, but added that it was still necessary for the helmsman to check the compass regularly, particularly since there was no alarm if anything went wrong. Captain Bartelds had already expressed full confidence in the system, which he had been using for several months before the accident.

The statement of Francisco Reboiros Dios was then read out: he had been on the bridge from 2000 as lookout, but he did not know the courses steered because he had not looked at the compass. The captain had not left the bridge at any time, at no point had he been told to keep an eye on the course, he saw no signals from the *Cranborne*, and the *Heron*'s radar had not been switched on.

Recalled and asked about these contradictions, Captain Bartelds repeated the main points of his previous statement, conceded that he might have been away from the bridge for a little more than five minutes, and said that the radar had been on because he had been using it to take bearings. He also added that he had not seen the red sector of either of the main Jersey lights. He declared himself unable to explain why Dios's statement differed so substantially from his own.

The implication of his version of events was that all had been well until about 2115 when he went to the toilet. Up to that point the *Heron* had been following the correct 30-degree course for the Race, and had been doing so since 2055 when he set it. By the time he returned to the bridge, five or so minutes later, everything had gone haywire, and the ship had swung nearly 60 degrees off course, striking minutes later. The assessors were not satisfied with this account. Captain Curtis maintained that he had noticed an incorrect line at 2105, a good ten minutes before Bartelds said he left the bridge. At 10 knots, this meant that the *Heron* had travelled a mile and a half towards the rocks before Bartelds gave his instructions to Dios. The assessors were equally sceptical about these; Bartelds's claim that at the point he left the bridge the *Cranborne* was still directly ahead was at odds with Curtis's statement, and telling Dios to ensure they continued following behind the *Cranborne* made little sense, given that (in their view) she was by this time way out on the *Heron*'s port beam. The Chief Inspector of Shipping pointed out that while there appeared to be several contradictions in Captain Bartelds's account, they could see none in that of Captain Curtis, and for that reason they inclined to his version of events. The question of whether the radar was on, or whether the automatic steering gear was at fault, was of secondary importance. In their view the *Heron*'s compass had been showing a seriously wrong course for at least twenty minutes before she struck, and the person who had to take responsibility for this was the captain.

In giving its verdict, the Shipping Council stated that after passing Grosnez light the *Heron* had steered 'an incorrect, dangerous and irresponsible' course; that the captain's account of events was unpersuasive; and that they were not wholly convinced he had left the bridge. They commended the actions of Captain Curtis and of the master of the Port de Bouc, expressed condolences to the families of the three dead, and suspended Bartelds's master's certificate for two years.

On 19 September, three days after the sinking, an attempt had been made to locate the *Heron* with an echo sounder around and through the whole reef, the depth of water off the rocks being around 40 feet. Representatives of the ship's agents and an insurance assessor from the Netherlands were present on the search vessel. Nothing was found.

At the time of writing her position is still a complete mystery. The *Heron* was discovered in 2003 by local fisherman, Steve Maguire.

In July 1963 the master and crew of the *Cranborne* were presented with watches in Jersey for their part in the rescue.

MV Heron leaving St Helier harbour

MV *Radiant Med* (1984)

The great storm which devastated most of southern Britain and northern France in 1987 left the countryside altered for ever and has passed into folklore. The low pressure weather system that hit the Channel Islands three years previously in January 1984 was equally destructive along a narrower swathe. During the night of 23–24 January, gusts of Hurricane Force 12 were recorded in Guernsey and Jersey, and the wind did not drop below Force 9 (Severe Gale) between 6 p.m. and 10 a.m. the following morning. Hundreds of trees were blown down in the islands, and in Jersey a woman narrowly escaped by seconds when one crushed her car. Numerous phone lines were down, and in Guernsey a falling tree fractured a gas main and houses had to be evacuated. Roofs were blown off, a month's rain fell in twenty-four hours, and in St Helier a large plate glass window in the British Airways Office was shattered. All flights and sailings to the islands were cancelled, and a Poole to Cherbourg ferry which did sail had to turn back and shelter in Weymouth Bay overnight. A huge depression measuring 968 millibars stretched from Greenland down to the Eastern Mediterranean, bringing blizzards (and power cuts) to Scotland and northern England, gales and hail in the south, and hurricane force winds in the English Channel.

While islanders lay in bed listening to the howling gale and wondering how long their chimney pots would stay in place, a real nightmare was unfolding out in the churning white maelstrom and forty-foot waves to the west of the islands. The *Radiant Med*, a 2997 gross ton Greek freighter, with her holds full of grain, was thirty miles south-west of Guernsey. She was shipping heavy seas, and one of her hatch covers had gone, allowing water to pour into her Number Two hold. Originally headed from Belgium to the Congo via Las Palmas, she had turned around at 7 p.m. and was coming up towards Guernsey in the mountainous seas. At about 1.15 a.m. on the 24th, with one hold flooded, steering gone and her port side under, she broached, capsized and sank. Of the twenty-five crew on board only nine were saved and those rescued owed their lives to the initiative, skill and outstanding courage of the St Peter Port lifeboat crew

The *Radiant Med* was a steel, single-deck, singlescrew ship built in Japan in 1970 for use as a logger. She was 100.6 metres long, with two holds, and she carried four heavy-lift derricks, two for each hold. She was owned by Maritime Star Shipping of Greece, and she was registered in Liberia. She had all the necessary safety certificates, and her master, Captain A. D'Souza, held Indian and Liberian master's licences. The crew members were mostly Filipino, the officers Indians.

In the previous November, the *Radiant Med* had been at Piraeus for periodical survey and safety checks. Plating on the sides of her hatch combings was found to be corroded, so this was replaced with the permission of Bureau Veritas, her safety agency. Her hatch tops were secured with locking bars which hooked into the combing plates, and before she left Piraeus the bars were checked and found to fit satisfactorily. An inspector confirmed that the necessary twenty-eight locking bars were on board – thirteen for each hatch and two spares. The ship then sailed for Constanta on the Black Sea, and then to Brake, just downriver of Bremen in Germany.

On 20 January 1984, the *Radiant Med* arrived at Ghent to load loose maize and wheat for Pointe Noire in the Congo. Chief Officer Subhas Singh Tanwar was put in charge of the loading. His only previous experience of a grain cargo had been as an apprentice hand. On board the ship were three handbooks, a 'Stability' guide, a 'Loading' guide, and a 'Grain Loading' guide. The first two had been checked and approved by Bureau Veritas, but not the third. Using the first two guides, but not seeing the third, Chief Officer Tanwar prepared a stowage plan. When he showed this to the master, he was told that the loaders on the dock knew what they were doing, and just to ensure that he checked the ship's trim afterwards. The grain was loaded by chutes into the two holds and levelled – one had a 3385 tonne capacity, one 3508 tonnes – leaving about a metre clearance between the load top and the deckhead. The master then inspected, and was happy. No one from Ghent port made an inspection.

The two hatches, each approximately 28 by 9 metres, were intended to be closed in the following sequence: (a) thirteen heavy steel pontoons or slats, placed over each hatch entrance; these had narrow gaps between them and were not watertight (b) tarpaulins stretched over the pontoons, and held at the hatch edges by steel battens and wooden wedges (c) thirteen locking bars on each hatch, securing the whole (d) heavy netting over everything, securely roped down. At Ghent, with the master supervising the hatch sealing, no locking bars were put on. At the inquiry the chief officer told the assessors that there were only twelve locking bars on board, and they had not been used since Constanta. Unfamiliar with the loading procedure, he accepted the situation, assuming that the pontoons would stay in place by their own weight. Once the outer nets were rigged, the master ordered the derrick head blocks (the outer ends of the lifting arms) to be positioned over the centres of the hatches and secured to the netting (the derricks inclined downwards when not in use).

At 1600 on the 21st the *Radiant Med* left Ghent for Las Palmas in a moderate sea. By noon next day she was in mid-Channel, approximately between Portsmouth and Le Havre, and the wind had increased to gale force. At 0830 that morning Land's End Radio Station had issued a warning of W or SW winds, Force 6 to 8 in Portland, Plymouth and Biscay. That night the sea became very rough, and the *Radiant Med* was taking a lot of water over her deck. By noon on the 23rd, with the wind still increasing and with a forecast of Force 10 (Storm), the *Radiant Med* was pitching through huge waves at 4 knots about sixty miles west of Guernsey, screw racing on the wave crests.

At about 1700 she took a rapid succession of very heavy seas breaking over her, as a result of which the metal crutch post holding the arm of the derrick over Number Two hold broke. This allowed the derrick arm to swing from side to side as the ship rolled. The chief officer informed the master, and a work gang was formed to go out and secure the derrick. At the same time, the ship was turned NE to put her stern to the wind, and this eased her movement a little, but so much water was pouring over her it was considered too dangerous for anyone to go forward along the open deck. Shortly afterwards the swinging head of the derrick broke free from the netting to which it was attached, went into the space between two nets, and ripped the tarpaulin underneath. The steel pontoons and the gaps between them were now exposed to the hundreds of tons of water cascading at regular intervals over the ship.

The Radiant Med

At 1735 the master radioed his shipping office in Athens and requested permission to turn back and make for Le Havre. He then set a course of 70 degrees to take him back north-east towards the port. The wind was now Force 10, gusting 11. Shortly after 2100 the bosun reported water in the main deck starboard alleyway coming from Number Two hold's crew access hatch. The master ordered the hold bilges to be pumped, and at first the water was reduced, but by 2215 it was back in the alleyway and nearly a foot deep. Along the open deck most of the tarpaulin over Number Two hold's hatch had now been ripped away.

At 2150 the master drafted (the term is used in the report of the inquiry, and presumably means the message was not sent) a message for the harbourmasters at Le Havre and Cherbourg reporting that the Number Two hatch tarpaulins had been washed away, giving the *Radiant Med*'s position, and telling them he was making for one of their ports. The ship was now about 35 miles SW of Guernsey.

Between 2150 and 2230 the amount of water in Number Two hold, combined with the violent movement of the ship, forced some of the steel pontoons off the hatch, leaving the hatchway completely open to the sea. Despite this disastrous situation, things were not yet deemed to be bad enough to warrant a mayday call, and at 2230 the *Radiant Med* sent a w/t PAN alert; 'Position 4915.8N 03.26W. Hatch number two steel pontoon lifted. Hold number two taking water. All ships in the area please stand by.'

The call was heard at CROSSCO, the Brest-based French search and rescue centre, and CROSSCO relayed the message to all ships on w/t and r/t. Six minutes later, at 2236, the *Radiant Med* requested assistance on r/t channel 16 from any ship in the vicinity. This call was heard by the St Peter Port Signal Station, and by CROSSMA, CROSSCO's equivalent based at Beaumont on Cap de la Hague whose territorial responsibility began at a line running north-south to the west of Guernsey (at this point the *Radiant Med* was inside the CROSSCO zone). At 2239 a French frigate, the *Casabianca*, responded to the *Radiant Med*'s call, saying she was turning towards her. CROSSMA asked what assistance was needed, and at 2300 informed St Peter Port that CROSSCO was in control and the *Casabianca* was on her way. Just before this, at 2252, the *Radiant Med* had sent a mayday.

The crew access hatch to Number Two hold had been screwed down tighter, but it was not watertight, and on every pitch of the ship water was spurting up around the hatch edges into the alleyway. This water was now threatening the accommodation area. It also indicated that Number Two hold was so full of water that it was surging on top of the soaked grain. A later calculation estimated that the saturated grain could account for 1,000 tonnes, and the hold spaces for another 300 tonnes of water. This bulk, slopping around, was a serious threat to the vessel's stability, and she was struggling harder to lift her bow out of the sea on each drop.

Soon after the mayday was sent, the general alarm was sounded on board, and all crew put on lifejackets. The engineers were ordered to evacuate the engine room, leaving the ship at full speed ahead. The port and starboard lifeboats were prepared, and the starboard boat was swung out. At this point events took another bad turn with a report that the second engineer had collapsed in his cabin. The chief and second officers and the master went to the cabin, and finding no pulse or breathing after giving artificial resuscitation, assumed the man was dead. They laid him on a stretcher and put him outside the master's cabin. Nineteen crewmen then got into the starboard lifeboat, but it was being banged against the ship's side with such force that it was in danger of being smashed, and the master ordered the men out for their own safety.

At 2319 the *Casabianca* requested the *Radiant Med* to reduce speed so that she could reach her more quickly, and the chief and third engineers went down into the engine room to make the adjustment. At 2339 the *Casabianca* asked CROSSCO at Brest for a helicopter, and at 2348, after telling the *Radiant Med* to fire flares, she came up with the struggling vessel. Both ships now went into a slow-ahead holding mode, anticipating the arrival of the helicopter to lift the crew off.

At one minute after midnight the *Casabianca* asked the *Radiant Med* to reduce speed again, but got the reply that this was not possible because it would make her uncontrollable. The *Radiant Med* had been on manual steering for some hours, and the wheelman, AB S. Belarde, reported that she was yawing up to ten degrees either side of her course.

At 0009 on the 24th the *Casabianca* asked Brest for confirmation that the helicopter had taken off. The answer was 'not yet'. The *Casabianca* reported that the *Radiant Med* had less than an hour left, and at 0018 and 0024 the frigate again asked CROSSCO if the helicopter was on its way. At 0030 CROSSCO told her they were doing all they could, and at 0035 it was airborne.

On board the *Radiant Med* water overflowing from the hold was running freely into the accommodation section and the ship was beginning to list to port. At 0032 she asked the *Casabianca* for immediate assistance. The frigate replied that the helicopter was on its way, and that CROSSCO had also accepted the help of HMS *Orkney*, a Royal Navy Island-Class fisheries protection vessel which had picked up the distress calls via Plymouth (only a few hours prior to this the *Orkney* had gone to the aid of a yacht in trouble on its way from Falmouth to Gibraltar, reporting waves higher than her bridge). At 0037 the *Casabianca* outlined her strategy; she would remain astern of the *Radiant Med*, which should increase speed to ten knots on a heading for Cherbourg; if the situation worsened before the helicopter arrived, the *Radiant Med* should alter course to beach on one of the Channel Islands.

At 0052 CROSSCO informed the *Casabianca* that the helicopter had been struck by lightning and had been forced to turn back. Seven minutes later the *Radiant Med* reported that she had lost steering, was listing so badly that her port side deck was under, and that the crew was preparing to abandon. With her low freeboard it needed a list of only seven degrees to put the deck at water level, and she was rolling over on each wave to at least fifteen degrees. The *Casabianca* replied that she was putting scrambling nets over the side, apparently intending to go in close for anyone in the water, and it was also intended that she should put her boats over – an intention that was unrealistic in the view of the assessors at the inquiry.

With the *Radiant Med* turning out of control in a wide circle to starboard, beam on to the gale, the order to abandon ship was given and an attempt was made to launch her boats. At about this time, twenty miles away on Guernsey, gusts of Force 12 were being recorded. The inflatable life raft canister was thrown over the starboard side, and was immediately swept away. Efforts to launch the starboard boat failed when the boat refused to drop because of the list, and it was not possible to get at the port boat, now on the underside of the vessel. The *Radiant Med* then sent a desperate message to the *Casabianca*, asking her to send boats, and the frigate replied that 'she was coming'. At 0113 the *Radiant Med* sent her last message – the list was over twenty-five degrees and she was going under. It appears that the unsecured loose grain in the dry Number One hold had now shifted to tip the vessel further. The master ordered the crew to move aft and jump into the sea. The waves were thirty-five to forty feet high with the tops streaming off in the gale. Some of the men were immediately washed over the side, others jumped. The cook had the ship's deck and radio logs in a plastic bag around his neck, and these were later recovered when his body was found in the water. Chief Officer Tanwar said that no one was left on the bridge at this stage, the master being on the starboard side trying to launch a life raft. As they jumped or were swept into the sea the ship was going down underneath them.

After hearing the *Radiant Med*'s r/t Channel 16 message at 2236 and checking her position, the duty officer at St Peter Port Signal Station telephoned Captain John Petit, Guernsey harbourmaster, former lifeboat coxswain and secretary of the RNLI, at his home to inform him something serious might be developing, but telling him that at that point CROSSCO was in control. Captain Petit asked to be kept informed. St Peter Port continued to listen in to the worsening situation, and at 0102, with the *Radiant Med* in obvious trouble, asked CROSSMA at Cap de la Hague if they wanted the Guernsey lifeboat. No request had been made in the intervening critical two and a half hours. The reply was in the affirmative, and at 0105 Captain Petit ordered the boat out. St Peter Port then told the *Casabianca* that they were about to launch, and received the reply: 'No. I have some lifeboat inboard, do not require some lifeboat here'. This extraordinary response was ignored, and at 0125 – at about the time the *Radiant Med* was going under – the *Sir William Arnold*, coxswain Michael Scales, left her moorings and at 0132 passed through the pierhead. Thirteen minutes later they heard the *Casabianca* report that the *Radiant Med* was gone.

Peter Bisson, now retired after sixteen years on the Guernsey lifeboat, ex-coxswain, bronze and silver medal holder, and recipient of the MBE for services to the RNLI, was on the boat that night. When we talked to him in the summer of 2000 he conceded that the weather had been 'very dirty'. They went south around the island, and took a course of 260 degrees straight into the wind, going as fast as possible. It was gusting Force 12 and once past the Hanois conditions became extreme. He recalls how from the darkened wheelhouse they watched the approach of the mountainous white-tops coming down on them, throttling back as they were swept up the slopes. At one point the boat was lifted and swung around to face back the way it had come.

As the *Radiant Med* went down, the port boat had released itself. The chief officer and three or four men managed to swim to it and pull themselves in, but as the *Radiant Med* turned over her aft radio mast struck the boat, damaging and half swamping it. Others reached the boat until there were ten men in it, nine sitting up to their waists in water, one lying. They had two flashlights which they waved towards the *Casabianca*, whose lights could be seen, expecting her to come. After a while, AB Andal, lying in the bottom of the boat, was confirmed dead. Unfortunately the *Casabianca* was unable to get a boat out, and was unable to get close to the men because of the hazard created by the bow of the *Radiant Med*, sticking high up out of the sea (her stern was on the bottom in 60 metres of water). It is not clear whether the frigate expected the men to swim to her, an option that was out of the question because of their state of cold and exhaustion. Had they done so they would certainly not have survived, since medical evidence given at the inquiry estimated that the amount of water in the air up to a foot above the sea's surface was so great that they would have drowned even with their heads out.

The *Casabianca* directed the lifeboat in, and she arrived on the scene at 0305. The crew went on deck and rigged safety lines while the coxswain left the wheelhouse and went to the upper conning position. Using its searchlight the lifeboat located the survivors' boat in the driving rain and spray and moved towards it. There was danger from ropes trailing in the water, but the coxswain approached from windward and a line was thrown across. The *Radiant Med*'s crewmen had been pitching about in freezing conditions, soaked to the skin for nearly two hours and were too far gone to respond, and the lifeboat had the difficult task of getting right alongside. One of the trailing lines was grabbed and used to help pull the two boats together. With the lifeboat rolling down over the gunwale of the waterlogged boat, the lifeboat crew in pairs grabbed a man at a time on the downward roll, and hauled him inboard. As they did this the lifeboat's well deck was going three feet under each time. Mike Scales later told a *Times* reporter:

> Our boat was crashing down on theirs, and one man hanging over the side was hit by our hull. They were waist-deep in water, too stunned and cold to help themselves, and our men had to attach lines and go over to haul them out while their boat was breaking up.

The rescued were then dragged into the wheelhouse where they were safe from being washed over the side again. One of the rescued men grabbed a lifeboat crewman, refusing to release him, and had to be physically restrained for the safety of both. Mike Scales later said that in his view some of the men had only minutes left to live. The dead man lying in the boat was tangled in ropes, and it was decided to leave him behind. With nine survivors safely on board, the lifeboat backed off and began a search for any others who might be in the water. None were found. At one point the lifeboat came over the top of a huge wave and saw the *Radiant Med*'s bow projecting 'like a shark's fin' out of the trough ahead. Only rapid evasive action took them clear.

The dramatic rescue of the survivors from the Radiant Med by the Guernsey Lifeboat Sir William Arnold (painting by David Jory)

At 0244 the RN Auxiliary ship *Green Rover* had offered assistance, been accepted, and was making her way to the scene. At 0246 RN Culdrose was asked to send a Sea King helicopter, and this took off four minutes later at 0250. A second helicopter was requested from RAF Brawdy in West Wales and this was airborne at 0333. Lieutenant Robertson in one helicopter described conditions as being worse than those at Fastnet. At 0403 HMS *Orkney* under the command of Lt Commander David Childs arrived to take up the search, and the lifeboat turned back for St Peter Port, worried at the condition of some of the survivors. At 0418 the first helicopter arrived, followed by the second at 0447, and shortly after the *Green Rover* and a French tug, the *Abeille Languedoc*, came on the scene. The two Sea Kings picked eleven bodies out of the water, the *Orkney* two (with men going into the sea on lines), and the *Abeille Languedoc* one. A life raft was seen, but it was empty. Later that morning the body of AB Andal was found. The lifeboat arrived back in Guernsey at 0630, and the survivors were taken straight to hospital suffering from hypothermia, shock and extensive bruising. The dead were also taken to Guernsey and placed in a mortuary at the Oberlands. All of the *Radiant Med*'s crew was accounted for with the exception of the second engineer who was almost certainly dead before the ship went down.

The talk in Guernsey was of the lateness in requesting the lifeboat, and how an earlier call might have saved more lives, and the *Guernsey Evening Press* raised the issue on the 25th. On the same day the London *Times* quoted John Petit: 'the master of the *Casabianca* underestimated the situation in thinking he could pick the crew up…the weather was appalling, and when it sank he could not get at the survivors, and the British side was effectively called in too late.' The lifeboat had taken approximately one and a half hours to get to the scene. The *Radiant Med* had been in obvious major difficulties at 2230, and if the lifeboat had been requested at that point it would have arrived well before the ship went down. Even if no call had been made until soon after 2348 when the *Casabianca* got first sighting of her, the lifeboat would then have been on hand as the men went into the sea.

By the end of the 24th the *Radiant Med* had disappeared onto the seabed. On the 26th a large oil slick was seen moving north-west from her last position, and later in the week the broken, orange-painted bow of a boat was washed up on Jaonnet on Guernsey's south coast. The letters 'MV RADI' and 'MONROV' were visible. A heavy nylon cover also came ashore at Petit Bot, and a name plate from the ship was found on Herm. An inquest was held on the dead in Guernsey on Tuesday 31 January, with verdicts of death by misadventure. The medical officer estimated that the men would not have lasted more than twenty minutes in the water in the conditions that existed that night.

An inquiry into the loss of the ship was held in London between 5 and 9 March 1984 under Mr Richard Stone QC, sitting with Professor Tuan Wreh and Mr Neil Hunter. There was then an adjournment to check various matters of fact, including the load line regulations as they applied to the ship and the validity of the 'Grain Loading' guide on board, and the assessors' final report was published by the Liberian Government's Bureau of Maritime Affairs in May 1985. At the inquiry a great deal of evidence was taken and carefully evaluated, and the assessors pursued the issue of cargo loading and the hatch security with great rigour. Apart from the atrocious sea conditions, they identified a number of key factors combining to bring about disaster; securing the derrick head blocks to the netting over the hatch cover was a dangerous arrangement; nothing was done to secure the loose surface of the grain in the holds with bagging or strapping, and this was an infringement of regulations; regulations also required locking bars to be used on the hatch covers, and they had not been used – there had been an insufficient number of bars on board, and it was the responsibility of the owners to provide these and of the master to point out deficiencies if they were not provided. The accommodation area had been flooded because international regulations did not require crew access hatches to holds to be watertight. They were also of the view that the master had underestimated the weather situation when the first gale warnings had come in, and should have considered moving east of the Cherbourg Peninsula to find shelter.

Without attributing any blame, the assessors also noted that the lifeboat had had to take the initiative in volunteering to put to sea; that although the *Casabianca* had performed a valuable task in tracking the *Radiant Med* and guiding the lifeboat in, no backup had been prepared in the event of the Brest helicopter not being able to get to the ship, the contingency plan of beaching on one of the islands had little prospect of saving lives, and the plan to use scrambling nets underestimated how quickly men in the water in the conditions that prevailed could die. The *Casabianca*'s rejection of the lifeboat, although ignored, suggested that those on board were unfamiliar with RNLI craft and their function, and the difficulty of launching the *Casabianca*'s own boats in the sea condition was also underestimated. The assessors' six recommendations related principally to covering and securing hatches, derrick crutch posts, securing derricks, grain loading and the need for watertight access hatches.

The courage of the *Radiant Med*'s chief and third engineers in repeatedly going down into the partly flooded engine room to alter speed, with the possibility of the ship going down at any moment, was singled out for special mention, but it was the Guernsey lifeboat crew who received most praise, the report including the statement, 'The survival of nine members of the crew was ultimately due to the exemplary efforts of the crew of the St Peter Port lifeboat'. The Liberian Government reinforced this praise in its covering letter to the report; 'High praise and commendation must be given to the judgment and action of Captain John H. Petit, Harbourmaster of the States of Guernsey, and to the heroic rescue of nine crewmen from the sea by Coxswain Michael Scales and the crew of the Royal National Lifeboat Institution lifeboat *Sir William Arnold*. This is a dramatic example of the selfless service traditionally rendered to those in peril on the sea. More than courage was required to save those of the *Radiant Med* who were suffering from exposure in a waterlogged lifeboat. Coxswain Scales and his crew demonstrated a superlative degree of professional competence that is absolutely essential for a successful rescue in such demanding conditions...The entire world maritime community must applaud this superb and skilful performance.'

The Liberian Government recommended that certificates of commendation be awarded to Mike Scales and his crew, and a donation of £1,000 was made to the RNLI. The awards were made in November 1985 – to Michael Scales, Peter Bougourd, Alan Martel, Michael Guille, Robert Vowles, Peter Bisson and Richard Hamon.

Sources

Unpublished typescripts and documents

The Percy Boyle collection (papers relating to GWR vessels), Weymouth Reference Library (*Ibex, Roebuck*)

'The loss of His Majesty's Ships *Charybdis* and *Limbourne* 1943' nd. The Charybdis and Limbourne Association

R. G. Morgan '*Charybdis* August 1941–October 1943' 1946 (36-page typescript)

Michael A. Clapp 'The *Charybdis* and *Limbourne* story' 1974 (105-page typescript)

David Royle 'OHMS or All in a day's work' (*Charybdis*) nd. (22-page typescript)

John Eskdale, personal file on *Charybdis* and *Limbourne*

Sydney Leleux, personal handwritten diary and sketchbook for 1943 (*Charybdis*)

USS *Borum*, deck log for August 1944 (PT 509)

Action report by Lt H. Harris USNR on activities of PT Squadron 34, 31 Dec '43 – 31 October '44 (PT 509)

Action report by Ensign B. T. Heminway USNR, commanding officer PT 507, August 1944 (PT 509)

Log books of PT 500, PT 503, PT 507, PT 508, all for August 1944 (PT 509)

Summary of interview with John Leyden Page of the PT 509, Department of the US Navy, Washington (PT 509)

Action report for 8–9 August 1944 by H. J. Sherertz, to Commander Eleventh Amphibious Force, FC8-34/A12-1, 12 Sept 1944 (PT 509)

Correspondence between the Air Ministry and the Military Air Attache, American Embassy 6 February 1946; correspondence between the office of the Quartermaster General Washington and the CO American Graves Registration Command 4 December 1946

Personal diary of Frederick Brooks, formerly of USS *Borum* (PT 509)

Personal files of Shelton 'Bos' Bosley, formerly of PT 507 (PT 509)

Richard Keen, diving log 1969

Tony Titterington, diving logs for 1964, 1973, 1981 and 1984

Leigh Bishop diving log for 2001, 2002

Interviews

We were able to record extended interviews with the following:

Richard Keen, Tony Titterington, Fred Shaw

Rudolph Reuter (*Schokland*)

John Eskdale, Gerald Evans, Neil Wood, Roger Roberts, Jim Duckworth, Reg Moyes, Ernie Mosley, Eric Brookes (*Charybdis* and *Limbourne*)

Shelton Bosley, Hans Constabel, Christian Cremer (PT 509)

Peter Bisson MBE (*Radiant Med*)

Jean Rivoallan (*Caesarea*, PT509)

Other information provided in written correspondence or in telephone conversations: Martin Woodward (*Victory*); Bill Hustler, Alain Launay, Doris de Carteret (*Charybdis* and *Limbourne*); Peter Arnold (*Liverpool*); Royston Raymond, Dr Jason Monaghan (Alderney Elizabethan ship); Brigitte Meheust, Manonmani Filliozat (*Hilda*); Donald Fisher, Russ Schuster, Norman Hoyte, Al Duquette, Robert Hatmaker, James O'Leary, Vincent Ricci, Dean Wilkinson (PT 509)

Newspapers, gazettes and magazines

The Times, Evening News, The Globe, Daily Telegraph, Daily Mail, Lloyd's List, Shipping Gazette Weekly Summary, Naval Chronicle, Jersey Times, Jersey Evening Post, Guernsey Evening Press, Guernsey Star, Guernsey Comet, L'Union (St Malo and Dinard), *Le Salut* (St Malo and Dinard), *Le Rappel* (Paris), *Magnet Magazine, Stars and Stripes, PT Boater, Mariner's Mirror, Sea Breezes, Hampshire Magazine, Southern Daily Echo* (Southampton), *Southampton Observer, Southampton Times, Southern Times* (Weymouth), *Liverpool Echo*.

Reports

Papers relating to the court martial of the *Viper* crew 16 August 1901 PRO ADM1/7538

Alderney Maritime Trust; report for 1996–97

Report of the thirty-third ordinary general meeting of the Weymouth and Channel Islands Steam Packet Company 18 July 1889

Inquiry into the loss of the *Brighton*, Wreck Commissioner's Court, 8 March 1887

Inquiry into the stranding of the *Roebuck*, 14–15 September 1911

Board of Trade Inquiry, Accident to SS *Ibex* 1897 PRO RAIL 281/11, 253/148

Board of Trade Inquiry, Sinking of SS *Ibex* 1900 PRO RAIL 281/11

Reports of Inquiries into Wrecks, volumes for 1875–76, 1879–81, 1901–02, 1905–06 (all Board of Trade) SRL

Uitspraak van de Raad voor de Scheepvart inzake de stranding van het motorschip 'Heron' (Report of the Netherlands Shipping Council into the stranding and sinking of MV *Heron*) 1962

Report of the formal investigation into the causes of the flooding, capsizing and loss of life incident to the striking of the MV *Radiant Med*. Maritime Branch of the Liberian Government 1985.

(PRO Public Record Office; SRL Southampton Reference Library)

Books and key articles

Bonnard, Brian, *Wrecked around Alderney* (Alderney, 1993)

Bulkley, Robert J., *At Close Quarters – PT Boats in the US Navy* (US Government, 1962)

Cameron, N. A., 'The Wreck of the *Viper*', *An Alderney Scrapbook* (Alderney, 1972)

The Channel Pilot, 1999 edition

Coles, K. Adlard, *Channel Harbours and Anchorages* (7th edn, London, 1991)

Constabel, Hans, 'The Story of the PT 509', *Channel Islands Occupation Review* (1988)

Couling, David, *Wrecked on the Channel Islands* (London, 1982)

Coysh, Victor, and Toms, Carel, *Guernsey Through the Lens* (London, 1978)

Cruickshank, Charles, *The German Occupation of the Channel Islands* (London, 1975)

Davenport, Trevor, 'Alderney's Elizabethan Warship', *The Alderney Magazine* (Autumn 1992)

David, J. M., 'Wrecks in the Bailiwick of Guernsey', *Transactions of La Société Guernesiaise, 1961* (Guernsey, 1962)

Donavan, Robert J., *The War-Time Adventures of President John F. Kennedy* (USA, 1961)

Evans, Gerald, 'Operation Tunnel: A Survivor's Reminiscence', *Channel Islands Occupation Review* (1999)

Falla, Frank, *The Silent War* (London, 1967)

Firmin, Henri, *Les Bateaux Anglaises de Saint Malo et le Naufrage du Vapeur 'Hilda'* (Dinard, 1989)

Gilly, William O.S., *Narrative of Shipwrecks of the Royal Navy between 1793 and 1849* (London, 1850)

Ginns, Margaret, 'Preservation Progress', *Channel Islands Occupation Review* (1980)

Ginns, Margaret, 'The Missing Link – USS PC564', *Channel Islands Occupation Review* (1987)

Grocutt, Terence, *Shipwrecks of the Revolutionary and Napoleonic Eras* (London, 1977)

Hill, Roger, *Destroyer Captain* (London, 1975)

La Roncière, Charles, *Histoire de la Marine Francais* (Paris, 1899)

Le Scelleur, Kevin, *Channel Islands' Railway Steamers* (Wellingborough, 1985)

Lucas, A. H. S., 'The Casquets', *An Alderney Scrapbook* (Alderney, 1972)

Lyon, David, *The First Destroyers* (London, 1996)

Mayne, Richard, *Mail Ships of the Channel Islands* (Chippenham, 1971)

Mollet, Ralph, *Jersey Under the Swastika* (London, 1945)

Preston, Antony, *Strike Craft* (London, 1982)

de Rennefort, Souchu, *Histoire des Indes Orientales* (Paris, 1688)

Roskill, Stephen W. , *The War at Sea 1939–45* (London, 1954–61)

Rule, Margaret, and Monaghan, Jason, *A Gallo-Roman Trading Vessel from Guernsey* (Guernsey, 1993)

Saul, David, *Mutiny at Salerno* (London, 1995)

Sauvary, J. C., *Diary of the German Occupation of Guernsey 1940–45* (Guernsey, 1990)

Sciboz, Bertrand, *Epaves des Cotes de France* (Rennes, 2000)

Scott, Peter, *The Battle of the Narrow Seas* (London, 1945)

Sennett, Richard, and Oram, Henry, *The Marine Steam Engine* (London, 1908 edition)

Sharp, Eric, 'Wrecks in the Bailiwick of Guernsey: Addenda', *Transactions of La Société Guernesiaise, 1967* (Guernsey, 1968)

Sharp, Eric, 'The Guardians of the Channel: the Casquets', *Channel Islands Occupation Review* (1976)

Sharp, Eric, 'The Loss of the Liverpool', *Guernsey Evening Press,* 13 July 1978

Sharp, Eric, *Lighthouses of the Channel Islands* (Guernsey, 1979)

Sinel, L. P., *The German Occupation of Jersey* (Jersey, 1945)

Smith, Peter C., *Pedestal* (London, 1970, revised 1999)

Smith, Peter C., *Hold the Narrow Sea* (London, 1984)

Stevens Cox, Gregory, *Victor Hugo in the Channel Islands* (Guernsey, 1996)

Tetley, Eve (ed), *Alderney's Elizabethan Wreck* (Alderney, 1994)

Timewell, H. C., 'The Loss of HMS *Viper*', *Mariner's Mirror* Vol 60 No 3, 1974

Tupper, Henry, *History of Guernsey* (2nd edn, London, 1876)

Wallbridge, J. H., 'The sinking of HMS *Charybdis* and *Limbourne*' *Journal of the Channel Islands Occupation Society* (Guernsey, 1976)

Index

Abeille Languedoc 221, 222
Ada 104, 105, 107
Alberta 119, 120, 122
Albright, Elmer 195, 201
Alderney Elizabethan ship 14–18
Aldridge, John 192
Allix, Cpt. George 52, 54, 64, 66, 67, 68
Andal, AB 220, 222
Andrews, John 37, 39
Asterix, See Guernsey Roman ship
Ausley, William 188, 199, 202

Baines, Lt 169
Balchen, Admiral 23
Bartelds, Cpt. 207, 209, 210, 212, 213
Bates, Len 156
Baudins, Cpt. 68, 69, 70, 71, 72, 74
Bertha 129
Biele, Bob 192, 195
Bishop, Leigh 177, 180, 181
Bisson, Peter 219, 223
Brayes 58, 69, 70
Brighton 55–61
Brittany 44
Brookes, Eric 156, 162, 176
Brooks, Frederick 199
Bonne Nuit Bay 210
Boreas, HMS 27–32
Borum, USS 185, 199
Bosley, Shelton 191, 193, 195, 197, 199, 200, 201, 204, 206
Bougourd, Peter 223
Bound, Mensun 15, 18
Bowyer, Michael 15
Brettell, Robert 185
Bricker, Darril 196, 197, 199
Brumm, Boyd 192, 194, 195, 201
Buchholz, Hans 199
Burnand, First Officer 72
Burns, Bob 15

Caamano, Dominico 209, 211
Caesarea 118–126
Caledonia 51–54
Casabianca 217, 218, 219, 220, 222, 223
Casquets 8, 9, 21–26, 42, 43, 46, 50, 57, 61, 62, 69. 74, 75, 81, 86, 87, 88, 89, 94, 186

Charybdis, HMS 146–181
Chesnay, Truchot de la 19, 21
Constabel, Hans 188, 189, 201, 202
Corbière 9, 51, 64, 65, 66, 113, 130, 133, 186, 187, 195, 207, 211
Corblets 14, 94
Cosheril, Bertie 14
Courier 49, 50, 60, 95, 115
Cranborne 207, 209, 210, 212, 213
Cremer, Christian 186, 188, 189, 190
Crist, Harry 184, 185, 187, 188, 190, 199
CROSSCO 217, 218, 219
CROSSMA 217, 219
Curtis, Cpt. 207, 208, 209, 211, 212, 213

Dacam, J. 35
Daniel, J. J. 193
David, John 9, 10
De Carteret, William 173, 174
Dios, Francisco 207, 211, 212, 213
Doherty, James 185
D'Souza, Cpt. 214
Duckworth, Jim 155, 156, 162
Duke of Normandy 106, 115, 116, 124, 126, 130, 131, 134
Duquette, Al 192, 193, 195

Ecrehous, Les 141
Edwards, Lawrence 164, 165
Elizabeth Rippon 209, 210, 211
Ella 106
Elwood Mead 12
Eskdale, John 153, 166, 167, 168
Evans, Gerald 152, 163, 164, 172

Falla, Frank 172, 173
Fisher, Donald 192, 193, 195
Fontaine, Walter 106, 107
Fort Grey 32
Foulon cemetery 146, 171, 172, 174
Fours reef 113, 120, 125
Frederica 63, 64, 65, 66, 67, 68, 98, 119, 128

Gazelle 62, 65, 79, 111, 120
Glyn, Elinor 50
Godfray, John 94
Grande Amfroque 43, 44, 46, 47, 48, 50

Grande Grune 137
Grand Jardin light 99, 100, 104
Green Rover 221
Gregory, Cpt. 98, 100, 101, 106, 107, 108, 110
Grenville, HMS 149, 157, 167, 169
Grieve, Sub Lt 87, 88
Grinter, AB 101, 103, 104, 105, 107, 108, 109
Grosnez 9, 99, 207, 208, 210, 211, 212, 213
Grunes Vaudin 192
Guernsey Roman ship 11–13
Guille, Michael 223
Gundreda 123, 124
Gunman, Cpt. 20, 21

Hamon, Richard 223
Hanois lighthouse 9, 28
Hanois reef 27, 28, 31, 186, 219
Hanson, Arthur 201
Harvey, Cpt. 33, 34, 35, 36, 40, 41
Hatmaker, Bob 193, 195
Havre 46–50
Heminway, Buell 184, 185, 195
Heron, MV 207–213
Hilda 98–110
Hildebrandt, Heinz 199
Hill, Roger 157, 167, 169, 170
Holland 137, 138, 139, 140
Holley, Graham 206
Homeaux Florains 92, 93
Honfleur 48
Horsfall, Derek 125
Horsfield, Richard 196, 198, 199
Howard Davis Park 170, 196, 198, 202
Howe, Cpt. 104, 105, 107
Hoyt, Norman 192
Huffmeier, Admiral 187
Hugo, Victor 10, 40, 41
Hustler, Bill 162

Ibex 62–75
Isle of Sark 131

Jenkins, David 15

Kaines 112, 113, 114, 116, 119
Keeling, Steve 161, 162, 173, 175, 177, 181
Keen, Richard 11, 25, 30, 58, 60
Kellogg, Frederick 201
Kennedy, Douglas 185

Kennedy, J. F. 182, 183
Kilroy-Silk, R. 175
Kohlauf, Cpt. 152, 168, 170
Kornak, Charles 199
Krans, Henrik 208, 209, 211, 212

Lainson, Cpt. 51, 52, 54
Larbalestier, Ted 209, 211
Launay, Alain 175, 177
Le Feuvre, Cpt. 62, 64, 65, 66, 67, 68, 111, 112, 113, 115, 117
Leleux, Sydney 165
Lena 187, 192, 195
Le Riche, Silva 141, 142
Lewis, Cpt. Owen 92, 93, 94, 96
Lewis, Cpt. Percy 130, 131, 133
Limbourne, HMS 146–181
Line, Kenneth 199
Liverpool 92–97
Long, Cpt. 46, 47, 48, 49, 50
Longis Bay 60
Lossin, Marvin 199

Mabb, Cpt. 42, 43, 44, 45
Maloy, USS 184, 185, 186, 187, 191, 192, 195, 201
Marsham, Robert 67, 109, 117
Martel, Alan 223
Mary 33–41
Mathes, James 188, 199
M4626 186, 187, 188, 190, 195, 196
Miller, Engineer 130, 133
Minquiers 128, 129, 130, 133, 138
Mollet, Ralph 138, 183
Monaghan, Jason 11, 12, 17, 18
Morgan, Cpt. 84, 85
Morgan, R. G. 155, 158, 159, 160
Morris, Keith 177, 180
Mosely, Ernie 163, 164
Munsterland 149, 150, 151, 157, 168, 170

Nicholls, Dennis 148, 153, 161, 162
Nightingale, Bill 164
Noirmont 51, 54, 64, 65, 112, 113, 117, 118, 120, 122, 124, 137, 187
Noirmontaise Rock 64, 66
Normandy 33–41

Oddie, Commander 154

Orange, HMS 20, 21
Orion oil rig 12
Orkney, HMS 218, 221, 222
Oyster Rock 51, 52, 53, 122

Page, John 188, 189, 195, 199, 202, 205
Painter, Cpt. 57, 58, 59
Parsons, Sir Charles 76, 77
Passage Rock 144
Paternosters 9, 128, 207, 208, 209, 212
Paul, Ltn 152, 154
Pavlis, John 188, 199
Pearse, Arthur 161, 164
Pedestal, Operation 146, 148, 149, 164
Peppell, Paul 195
Petit, John 219, 222, 223
Phipps, Commander 156, 169
Pierres des Portes 101
Pillings, Bob 126
Platte Boue 43, 45, 46, 47, 49, 58, 69
Platte Fougere 9, 58, 59, 69, 70, 71
Pleinmont Point 27, 28
Port du Bouc 210
Princess Ena 127–135
PT 509, USS 182–206

Quesnard light 94

Radiant Med, MV 214–223
Randall, Francis 70, 72
Reindeer 111, 120
Reinhardt, Hermann 199
Rendell, Dave 14
Renonquet Rock 81, 83, 84, 87, 88, 89
Reuter, Rudolph 137, 139, 141, 145
Reynolds, Tony 199
Ricci, Alfred 199, 203
Ringwood 131, 132, 133
Rivoallan, Jean 126, 205
Robert Müller 8 185, 187, 195
Roberts, Owain 17
Roberts, Roger 156
Rocket, HMS 149, 157, 162, 167, 169
Roebuck 111–117
Rothery, H. C. 54
Royle, David 156, 167
Rozec, Louis 104, 105, 109
Rule, Margaret 11, 12

St Julien 131, 132
Saumarez, Admiral 27, 28, 29, 30
Sauvaray, J. C. 171
Scales, Michael 219, 220, 223
Schaffroth, Rudolph 196, 198, 199
Schokland, SS 136–145, 203
Schuster, Russell 183, 187, 191, 194, 195, 198
Schwen, Hermann 199
Scott, Cpt. Robert 27, 28, 29
Scott, Peter 184, 185, 186, 201
Shaw, Fred 12, 14, 15, 25, 90, 91
Sherertz, H. J. 186, 188, 192
Sinel, Leslie 137, 138, 183, 195, 196
Sir William Arnold 219, 221, 223
Smith, Cpt. E. T. 118, 119, 120, 122
South West Heads 145
Speke, Lt 81, 82, 83, 85, 86, 87, 88, 89, 90
Stevenstone, HMS 149, 152, 157, 161, 164, 167
Strannach, Cpt. 34, 37, 38
Sullivan, E. 193, 195

Talybont, HMS 149, 167, 169, 179, 181
Tanwar, S. S. 215, 219
Taylor, Ian 180
Thale, Edward 199
Titterington, Tony 124, 133, 142, 143, 203
Tunnel, Operation 149, 150, 168, 169

van der Zee, A. 207, 211
van der Zee, Elske 209, 211
Victory, HMS 21–26, 61, 86
Vierge de Bon Port 19–21
Viper, TBD 76–91
Voelcker, Cpt. 147, 149, 152, 164, 170, 174
Vowles, Robert 223

Waverley 42–45
Wensleydale, HMS 149, 151, 160, 162, 164, 166, 167
Westaway, John 41
Weymouth and CI Steam Packet Co. 55, 56, 58
Whorton, Calvin 185, 187
Wood, Neil 157, 181
Woodland, AB 69, 70, 71, 75
Woodward, Martin 14, 25
Wypick, Walter 197, 199

Zimmermann, Armin 187

About the authors

John Ovenden was born in Jersey. He began diving in 1989 and has extensive knowledge of the wrecks around the islands. A specialist in underwater videography, he formed his own company devoted to search and recovery and underwater film production. In 1995 he produced a video documentary, *The Wreck of the Stella*, which was broadcast on BBC, German and Discovery television channels. In 1999 he collaborated with David Shayer on the book *The Wreck of the Stella*, and this was followed in 2001 by a 60-minute video, *PT 509: the Last Patrol*. John is also a passionate and talented photographer. Visit his website at: www.johnovenden.com

David Shayer passed away in April 2010. He was born in Guernsey. He was a graduate of the Universities of Wales and Oxford, and published books and articles on literary criticism, education and Channel Island history. An interest in the *Stella* led him to publish a paper in 1982 on the ship's loss, and collaboration with John Ovenden followed on the full-length book, *The Wreck of the Stella*, in 1999. Following retirement as a university teacher, he lived in Caerleon in South Wales.